October 14, 201_

Dear Marie Louise,

Please be inspired!

Now: From our table to yours...

"Bon Appétit! "

Warmest Regards,

Margaret

MARGARET'S TABLE

EASY COOKING & INSPIRING ENTERTAINING

Margaret H. Dickenson

Margaret H. Dickenson

Margaret's Table

Easy Cooking & Inspiring Entertaining

Food Stylist: Margaret Dickenson
Photographer: Larry Dickenson

MARGARET'S TABLE

EASY COOKING & INSPIRING ENTERTAINING

Published by **Margaret's Sense of Occasion**
2 Seneca Street
Ottawa, Ontario, Canada K1S 4W5

Copyright © 2006

Cover photo of Margaret Dickenson © Rogers Television
All other photos © Larry Dickenson
Executive Editor: Margaret H. Dickenson

This cookbook is a collection of unique and enticing recipes
created personally by Margaret H. Dickenson.

ISBN: 0-9739874-0-5

Designed and Manufactured by
Favorite Recipes® Press
An imprint of

FRP

P. O. Box 305142
Nashville, Tennessee, USA 37230
800-358-0560

Art Director: Steve Newman
Editorial Director: Mary Cummings
Project Editor: Linda Bennie

Manufactured in China
First Printing: 2006

ACKNOWLEDGMENTS

I dedicate this book to my very supportive family: husband, Larry; daughters, Tonya and Christa; their husbands, Max Tessier and Peter Camp; and our four adorable grandchildren, Catherine, Nicolas, Sophie and Hugo.

Indeed, my special thanks goes to Tonya who took as her thesis project for her Executive MBA, Queen's University, the next steps in my career — or as we fondly say "marketing Mom"! She invested hundreds of hours in her thesis and continues to contribute with helpful suggestions.

As for my husband, Larry, I don't know where to begin. Meeting on the first day of university, we have had a wonderful and adventurous life together. We have always worked as a strong unique team. Although the girls and I supported him in his foreign service career, since his retirement in particular, Larry has devoted much of his time to assisting me. He is my official taster, computer assistant, accounts manager, proofreader and now photographer! Congratulations, Larry! (Your photos are stunning.) Thank you for your endless loving interest and participation.

A warm appreciation is extended to those at Favorite Recipes Press who approached Larry, me and the project with kind, sensitive and personalized professionalism. Thank you to Sheila Thomas, Dave Kempf, Mary Cummings, Linda Bennie and Steve Newman.

Also, the interest and support of Sandra MacInnis, Julie Henson and Diane Dufour have indeed touched us.

My final recognition must include four amazing women who have been extremely generous mentors during different stages of my adult life. They believed in me, trusted me and presented me with opportunities to evolve from one career and stage of life to the next. Given our international lifestyle, they come from various corners of the globe — Muriel Cobb (Ottawa, Canada), Sawsan Dajani (then Kuwait, now Cairo), Shirley Hew (Singapore) and Colette Watson (Ottawa). To them I owe much.

CONTENTS

RECIPE LIST

ICON LEGEND:

 No Time, No Talent ✦

 Barbecue/Grill (optional) ✦

INTRODUCTION

Whether you are an accomplished culinary professional or a "home" or "weekend" cook, if you have the desire to add creativity, pizzazz and certainly good "tastes" to your culinary repertoire, then this book is for you!

Insisting that both food and entertaining should offer a delightfully memorable experience, I find myself persistently developing a wide variety of flavourful, innovative recipes with universal appeal — and where presentation plays a key role! My insatiable appetite to be original, to get what I want out of what I have, to make the ordinary extraordinary and to dazzle both family and guests is constantly stimulating and inspiring me. I thrive on "coming up with" unique flavour combinations (simple or complex), terrific ideas for themes & menus, strategies to make virtually everything convenient and easy, to be and remain relaxed! My culinary philosophy is driven by the reassurance of having at least some recipes prepared in advance. **Margaret's Table: Easy Cooking & Inspiring Entertaining** is designed to share my passion and secrets with others — and to have fun!

FLASH: *Margaret's Table: Easy Cooking & Inspiring Entertaining is filled with a wealth of helpful tips:* time saving, shopping, "do ahead", "make ahead", "on hand", "No Time, No Talent", quantity, storage, "saving" remaining ingredients/recipes, handling, wine/bar/beverages, alternative ingredients/ cooking techniques/uses, vegetarian options, "children's favourites", presentation, serving, planning events, menu planning, preparing "themed" occasions, setting the table, seating plans, table etiquette as well as general information, detailed instructions for recipes and more!

FOR YOUR INFORMATION: Taken in our home or our garden, all photos are of real food (i.e., no additives for "cosmetic" effects). Many recipes were made with supplies "on hand" (i.e., in the refrigerator, freezer or dry storage). And, my husband and I devoured the food after each shot!

SECRETS TO RELAXED COOKING AND SUCCESSFUL ENTERTAINING

IN A NUTSHELL:

✦ Develop a repertoire of (or choose) doable impressive recipes and menus.

✦ Focus on clever presentations, a well-set table and at least a touch of decor. These offer welcome **bonus points**! "People eat with their eyes!"

✦ Learn to limit the time required for final cooking/preparation.

✦ Add your own personal touch and warm hospitality.

✦ Be as organized as possible. (This definitely avoids "last minute" panic and allows you to enjoy the event!)

✦ Remember to taste everything before it is served.

EXPANDING ON THE SECRETS:

Remember this phrase: "If you know where you are going and how to get there, you will succeed!"

A well-developed repertoire of recipes (from hors d'oeuvres, appetizers, soups — right through to desserts and finishing touches) is invaluable. Start with those recipes which you love/can do and which guests adore. You'll be cooking in your comfort zone. Confidence is important. Let these recipes be the basis for your own **personal "Signature" Recipes**. Be proud of them, present them in a *style unique to you* and don't hesitate to repeat them particularly with different guests.

Training oneself to be able to prepare recipes in stages is wise. What can be prepared in advance and kept on hand (even for an extended period of

time), what can be done closer to the time required and what needs to be done just before serving? This skill/art can be acquired with only a limited amount of practice. You will be amazed at how many recipes will end up virtually requiring ***nothing more than assembly or a minimum amount of "last minute" cooking/preparation***. You will also notice that an element prepared for one recipe may very well be a component for others.

As for myself, having a ready supply of "Basic Recipes" (homemade or commercial) on hand is essential. There is no need to start daily meal preparation or entertaining from scratch! Without them, I would never be able to "WOW" my family or guests in a relaxed manner.

"WOW" TIP: If **you take a few hours** to prepare some **Basic Recipes** (e.g., crêpe batter, flavoured mayonnaises, sauces, pesto, etc.; pages 204 to 216), you will be excited to see how much easier recipe preparation, daily meals and entertaining can be. Or **spend a day or a weekend** making many of them, plus several simple but versatile **"Signature" Recipes** (e.g., soups, chutney, ice creams, chocolates, honeys), then experience an entirely new and relaxed approach to your culinary endeavors.

Now "WOW" Your Guest! With the help of "Basic Recipes" and "Signature Recipes", you are ready to put together events, particularly "finger food" occasions, with remarkable ease and pizzazz!

MENUS

A Creative Holiday Table (page 26)

Not every event needs to be a dinner party!
*Learn the secret formula to mesmerizing guests
with a **Drinks, Cocktail** or **Garden Party**
as well as a **Cocktail Reception!***

"WOW" TIP: Try my "Finger Food Event Formula".
Serve what would appear to be "a parade" of finger food
(simple or elaborate, homemade and/or commercial).
Use this formula and in the order outlined:

1   Hors d'Oeuvres (The number will vary with the type of
    event. Try to have at least 1 hot.)

2   A Canapé Soup* (on hand in freezer)

3   A Taster Dessert (small portions of something on hand
    such as ice cream, squares, pastry)

4   Chocolates

    * A Canapé Soup is a puréed soup served in tiny glasses
    (e.g., shot or liqueur glasses) or cups (e.g., sake), along with
    canapés/hors d'oeuvres, at finger food events.

ADVANTAGES
    ✦ There is one basic formula for several types of events.
    ✦ You only have to prepare the hors d'oeuvres and
       arrange the food.
    ✦ You are giving people what they love (i.e., different
       tastes, a "little sweet" and definitely a chocolate!)
    ✦ The items can be homemade and/or commercial.
    ✦ Menus are flexible.
    ✦ Results are predictable.

Ginger Strawberry Canapé Soup (page 102)

iWOW GUESTS
WITH FINGER FOOD OPTIONS

Tarragon Scallops on Oriental Porcelain Spoons (page 82)

A DRINKS PARTY

One of the easiest ways to entertain (and to spend time with guests) is by inviting a few friends in for drinks. Some tasty "bites", a touch of pizzazz and warm hospitality will make the simple gathering memorable.

ADVANTAGES

- Versatile formula for entertaining a *few guests (from 1 to 10)*.
- *Flexible* timing from mid-afternoon to late evening, any day of the week or on weekends.
- *Limited resources are required*, including the time of the host/hostess and guests.

- *Not required* are a lot of food, a set table, a table centrepiece, lengthy preparations or cleanup, a late night, extra help.
- *Simplify beverage service* (and reduce costs) by offering sparkling wine in Champagne glasses. (Of course, guests may have something else if they prefer.)

Note: The **same menu** would also be suitable for serving to a *few guests coming for "coffee" or "tea"*.

"WOW" TIMING TIP: The "Cinq à Sept" or 5 to 7 PM "Cocktail Hour" is the perfect modern formula of "getting together" for busy working people who want to spend the evening with children/family, continue on to other activities or just cocoon at home for the night.

SAMPLE MENU

Serve 2 or all 3 of the following hors d'oeuvres:
(Allow 2 or 3 pieces of each type per person)

Pancake Coins with Goat's Cheese and Sun-Dried Tomato *(page 73)*
Tarragon Scallops on Oriental Porcelain Spoons *(page 82)*
Heart of Palm Prosciutto Wraps *(page 68)*

FOLLOWED BY SWEETER TASTES (OPTIONAL)

Ginger Strawberry Canapé Soup* *(page 102)*
Mini Flowerpots** of Chocolate Mint Ice Cream* *(page 183)*
Assortment of Chocolates (homemade, pages 192 to 198, or commercial)

*Allow one each per person (**Note:** Be creative in what you use as small containers.
These need not be expensive. A visit to a dollar store may inspire you!)
**Option: For convenience, particularly if guests are standing, use mini ice cream cones.

Chopsticks of Oriental Marinated Lamb (page 81)

COCKTAIL PARTY/COCKTAIL RECEPTION/GARDEN PARTY

I f you have had a few friends in for drinks, then inviting a dozen or even several dozen guests for a cocktail party will "be a breeze"! Just extend your drinks party menu to include additional hors d'oeuvre recipes. This is my "well-tested" formula, which has won us hundreds of dear friends over the years. Expanding on that same formula, for a cocktail party to become a cocktail reception, increase the number of nibbles calculated per person. Hold the event in your garden to make it a garden party! It's all so logical!

COCKTAIL PARTY/COCKTAIL RECEPTION/GARDEN PARTY MENU TIP: Simply extend your Drinks Party menu (page 17) to include more hors d'oeuvre recipes. Allow a total of 8 to 12 savoury "pieces" (of hors d'oeuvres) per person (depending on the event) as well as the 3 sweet "plus" items.

SAMPLE MENU

Select additional and/or optional hors d'oeuvres (as desired) from the following suggestions:

Asian-Glazed Chicken Morsels/Skewers (page 80)
Spicy Shrimp with Zesty Ginger Mayonnaise (page 83)
Chopsticks of Oriental Marinated Lamb (page 81)

Sweet-and-Sour Salmon in Zucchini Cups (page 77)
Minted Fresh Figs with Feta (page 72)

If desired, choose alternative sweet "plus" items (3 total) from the following:

Macadamia Mango Soup* (page 105)
The Ultimate Coffee Spoons* (page 188)
Blackberry Butterscotch Cocktail Fondue (page 174)
Saucy Chocolate Blueberry Spoons* (page 196)

Chocolate-Dipped Cherries (page 197)
Minted or Toffee Chocolate-Dipped
Strawberries (page 198)
Pecan Chocolate-Dipped Pears (page 198)

*Allow one per person. (**Note:** For the others, allow 2 or more per person.)

WINE TIP: The amount required will vary with the length of the party, the guest list and the options of other beverages such as whisky, gin and beer. In general, allow 1/2 bottle of wine per person plus a few extra bottles. The portion of red to white wine depends on local culture (e.g., in some, women consume more white, men more red). During hot weather, white wine and beer consumption tends to increase.

EXTRA-ASSISTANCE TIP: If you need an extra pair of hands (particularly with more than a dozen guests), someone is certain to offer to help — so accept! As a quick rule of thumb, for every dozen to 15 guests, you would welcome the assistance of one person. In general, guests are truly delighted to assist in passing food and looking after drinks. (**Note:** For larger parties, you might consider getting someone to manage the kitchen thus allowing you to spend more time serving and mingling with guests.)

Cocktail Reception with "Grazing" Table(s) or Food Stations

Choose 4 or more of the following stations:

SOUP STATION
Macadamia Mango Soup (page 105)

SEAFOOD STATION
Seductive Sushi Rolls* (e.g., page 87)
Salmon Gravlax** on Pumpernickel Bread (page 74)

MAIN COURSE STATION
Quick Chinese Spiced Wings/Drumsticks (page 132)
and/or
Korean Bulgogi*** with Marinated Water Chestnuts (page 135)
Oriental Mango Rice (page 165)
and/or
Korean Mixed Vegetables and Noodles (page 164)

CHEESE AND FRUIT STATION
Assortment of Cheeses and Pâté
Anise-Walnut Raisin Chutney (page 79)
Seedless Green Grapes
Fresh Cherries and Ground Cherries

DESSERT STATION
Blackberry Butterscotch Cocktail Fondue (page 174)
Chocolates* (e.g., pages 192 to 198)

COFFEE/TEA STATION
Regular and Decaffeinated Coffee
Tea

***Option:** Homemade or commercial
** **Option:** If desired, substitute smoked salmon for the gravlax in the recipe.
*** This recipe may be barbecued/grilled.

Quick Chinese Spiced Wings/Drumsticks (page 132)

FINGER FOOD OPTIONS

Zen's the Word (page 29); Herb and Spice Sorbet (page 125)

iWOW GUESTS
WITH MENUS & THEMES

Themes, without doubt, make an event memorable.

"WOW" TIP: *Themes instill an easy "Sense of Occasion".*
With a theme, entertaining is perceived to be more exotic but often entails little extra effort. Themes actually can *assist* in deciding on a menu, tableware, table decoration as well as general decor, music, lighting and even the dress code. Simple or extravagant, themes *set a particular mood* and frequently establish a "total look". Take advantage of past travel, collectibles, special occasions or events to design your own themes. Be inspired! Be experimental! (**Note:** At least one hors d'oeuvre and a "finishing touch" would be added to the sample menus that follow.)

Caramel Mango Tarts with Sugar Stencil Art (page 182)

ALFRESCO LUNCH

For a relaxed summertime mood, capture the panache of outdoor dining. (**Note:** Of course, this menu could also be used for an evening meal.)

Mood: Relaxed, casual, embracing an "outdoor" spirit

> **DECORATING TIP:** *Tall houseplants* can be temporarily *moved outdoors* and placed around the table to create a more effective "outdoor" mood. Flower baskets also generate ambiance. Place (or hang) them on decks, side tables, the lawn and/or fences.

Total Look: Casual, with remarkable "fresh-air" appeal; colourful, with a certain degree of pizzazz

Menu and Presentation: Light, refreshing, fresh, reflecting nature, featuring seasonal produce and herbs, enticing recipes and flavours, inviting food styling (simple but artistic) and, if possible, playful

Table: Inviting, arranged with flair, refreshing, colourful with exuberant flowers, charming table linens/place mats

Chinaware/Tableware: Casual, colourful, pottery, baskets, shells

Stemware: Preferably coloured glass or "good" plastic (The latter is essential around a swimming pool.)

Music: Jazz or soft popular

Lighting (for evening dining): Lanterns, floating candles, torches, gas lamps

SAMPLE MENU

Heart of Palm Cucumber Soup Eclipse (page 104)

Aromatic Asian Seafood Noodles (page 153)
(or Chili-Crusted Salmon* with Macadamia Aïoli Shrimp Topping, page 146)

Caramel Mango Tarts with Sugar Stencil Art (page 182)

*Barbecue/Grill Option

A CREATIVE HOLIDAY TABLE

As the holiday season draws near, life becomes even more hectic — and the feasting begins! To ensure that the holiday dinner is a doable feast, I conveniently design a menu where most of the work can be done in advance. The soup, sauces, sweet potatoes and ice cream may be prepared/procured weeks ahead of time. Even the elements for my extravagantly filled main course chicken breasts may be done a couple of days in advance, with actual assembly the day before. Last-minute preparations and cooking for our sumptuous and scrumptious feast are fast, easy and efficient. (**FLASH:** As a "No Time, No Talent" alternative to the stuffed chicken breasts, try my "Amazing Cajun Roasted Chicken", page 133.) When it comes to decor, a non-traditional colour theme never ceases to amaze and impress. Be adventurous! Our choices have included blue and silver, copper, purple, ivory, Victorian pink and burgundy.

Mood: Holiday/Christmas; jubilant, festive, merry

Table and Total Look: Wintry and/or "Christmasy"; Christmas trees, poinsettias, balls, ribbons/bows, lights, boughs, holly, mistletoe, candles, garlands and wreaths

Menu: Designed to create a "once a year" special dinner; usually long and sumptuous; including at least 1 or 2 traditional foods or foods found on the market specifically at that time of year

Chinaware: Your best or, if possible/suitable, with a holiday motif

Stemware: Your best or, if possible/suitable, red or green

SAMPLE MENU

Cranberry Melon Salad (page 113)

Savoury Soup of Choice

Cinnamon-Scented Pomegranate Seeds (page 127)

Portobello Deluxe Stuffed Chicken Breasts* (page 130)
Roasted Red Pepper Cream Sauce (page 214)
Asparagus
Spinach Tortellini

Ice Cream Meringue Nests with Honey Mustard Dessert Vinaigrette (page 181)
or "Bouquet" of Assorted Ice Cream Balls (e.g., pages 173, 179, 186)

*Barbecue/Grill Option

Herb and Spice Sorbet (page 125)

Zen's The Word

Minimalism, serenity, strong clean lines and contrasts are the essential elements in creating an enchanting Zen experience. One interpretation of "Zen" could be "less is more" but with an Asian mood.

Mood: Strong, serene, calm, self absorbing and semi-detached, in quiet harmony with those present at the table

Total Look: Simple, uncluttered, with clean straight lines artistically brought together in an appealing minimalist statement
+ An Asian version of "less is more"

Menu and Presentation: Not necessarily Japanese food, but should include some oriental ingredients
+ Preferably one course requiring the use of chopsticks
+ Choose some recipes that consist of single units (e.g., large scallops or shrimp, slices of meat) that lend themselves to being arranged in an isolated manner on plates with clean-cut precision and lots of space around them.

Chinaware: Monochromatic, geometric, flat, with a domination of black (or white)

Stemware: Simple clear crystal/glass

Table: Crisp, powerful, simple sophistication, dark principal elements (e.g., vases, candle holders and place mats), dominance of straight lines (e.g., candle holders, place mats, stemware, chopstick bars, chopsticks, napkins), stark contrasts (e.g., tall and low, black and white, metal and fabric)

Music: Hypnotic Japanese pieces, played very softly

Lighting: Low; subtle tea candles could be arranged artistically in sand or river stones

"BEWARE" TIP: A traditional "table centre" flower arrangement, cut crystal glasses or elaborate candle sticks would *shatter the calm and serenity of a "Zen" theme.*

Sample Menu

Prosciutto-Wrapped Wasabi Pears (page 89)

Herb and Spice Sorbet (page 125)

Twin Sesame Seed-Crusted Pork Tenderloin with Lemon Mustard Sour Cream Sauce (page 138)
Perfect Rice with Toasted Slivered Almonds (page 168)
Cumin Date Chickpea Salad (page 116)

Prunes in Port with Chestnut Mousse (page 185)

CELEBRATING SPRING/EASTER

To celebrate Easter and/or to pay tribute to the arrival of spring, plan a relaxed dinner (or lunch) for family or friends. Your menu should include foods which reflect spring. Even for the "more serious" types, this is an occasion to playfully dress your table in "spring colours" and decor. Have fun! (**Note:** If Easter arrives late enough so that both wild garlic and fiddleheads are available on the market, the filet mignon recipe is definitely my first choice for main course. Served with wild rice, could there possibly be a better or more original Canadian spring combination?)

Mood: Fresh, spring like

Table and Total Look: Fresh and playful colours, reflecting the rebirth of nature (green, purple, yellow, perhaps light blue and pink), eggs, nests, grass

Menu and Presentation: Springtime foods (e.g., salmon, spring lamb, fresh herbs, asparagus, berries); creative refreshing presentations, announcing the arrival of spring

Chinaware and Stemware: Of choice

Music: Lively, "sparky", orchestral

Lighting: Tapered candles, preferably pale green or a stunning combination of pale green, yellow, pink or blue

SAMPLE MENU

Smoked Salmon Crispy Stacks
with Avocado and Mango (page 90)
Petit "Plate" Bouquets of Fresh Herbs (page 202)

Springtime Filets Mignons*
with Fiddleheads and Wild Garlic (page 136)
Mushroom Wild Rice (page 167)
or
Seed-Crusted Rack of Lamb (page 144)
Mustard Mint Sauce (page 213)
Asparagus Spears
Deluxe Sweet Potato Cream (page 160)

Mini Flowerpots of Chocolate Mint Ice Cream (page 183)
with Dark Chocolate Toffee Butterflies (page 194)
Fresh Strawberries

*Barbecue/Grill Option

MENUS & THEMES

A "SMART CHIC" DINNER

I t's fun to get dressed up (even if it is not in your nature) and celebrate a special event or to just have a bit of "New Year's" or "upscale" amusement! You may want to get "really dressed up" and make it a black-tie dinner; however, it must not be a dry stuffy affair! Think "smart chic" when deciding on your menu, presentations, table and general decor. During the party, check out the noise level. It's a sure sign of success!

Mood: "Smart chic" or elegant (but not "starchy"), modified formality, relaxed

Total Look: Warm, appealing pizzazz; impressive attention to detail; more of "this and that" (e.g., food, wine, candles, etc.); at least a notch or two above that of regular entertaining (try to add a light or playful touch)

> **TIP:** Choose a doable menu. Select recipes which can be broken down into tasks, most of which could be done in advance.

Music: Soft classical (e.g., piano or strings)

Lighting: Candles, candles and more candles!

Chinaware/Tableware: Fine china or rather elegant "affordable" dinnerware

  ✦ Use chargers if available (or oversized dinner plates) and liners as much as possible

Stemware: Crystal/glass, with several glasses designated for each person

Menu and Presentation: Rather elaborate menu, tantalizing, strategically designed with visually appealing and thoughtfully plated recipes

  ✦ Mesmerize the palate; each course offers a unique taste experience and is beautifully, (sometimes) intriguingly presented

  ✦ Some ingredients are perceived as gourmet or exotic

  ✦ Excellent wines/Champagne

  ✦ Chocolates and liqueurs served with coffee

Table: Chic but naturally inviting

  ✦ Rather breathtaking or intriguing fresh floral arrangement, tapered candles in elegant candlesticks, impeccable linens (tablecloth or place mats and napkins), a parade of stemware and silver, shiny chargers, several sets of petit salt and pepper shakers; perhaps place cards, menu cards and couteau (i.e., knife) bars (**Note:** Chopstick bars may be used as couteau bars.)

SAMPLE MENU

Irresistible Teased Catfish Oriental Salad (page 98)

Sorrel Cappuccino (page 107)

Apple Brandy Trou Normand with Dried Apple Wafer (page 124)

Decadent Lamb Medallions* with Seared Pâté (page 142)
Fruit and Nut Buckwheat/Quinoa Pilaf (page 162)
Miniature Vegetables

Caramel Mousse Chocolate Cups (page 178)
Chocolate Curl Sticks (page 200)

*Barbecue/Grill Option

Extraordinary Sun-Dried Tomato Shrimp on Squid Ink Pasta (page 152)

MORE INSPIRING
MENUS & THEMES

NOTE: At least one hors d'oeuvre (in most cases) and a "finishing touch" would be added to these menus.

SUPER GAME/AWARDS NIGHT

Join the hype of a super game or an awards night (i.e., film, television, music) by hosting your own party where you and your guests can together watch (or catch glimpses of) the "real thing" on TV! To set the mood for the occasion, ask guests to arrive "appropriately" dressed (e.g., NHL shirts, tennis whites, Hollywood "chic"). Capture the essence and mood of the event through your table decorations and general decor — perhaps even the lighting and food (e.g., "Referee's" Beef Carpaccio, "Half-Time" Sushi, "People's Choice Shrimp" or "Celebrity Style Berries").

SAMPLE MENU

Asian Beef Carpaccio Spoons (page 67)

Seductive Sushi Rolls (e.g., page 87)

Extraordinary Sun-Dried Tomato Shrimp on Squid Ink Pasta (page 152)
Mesclun Salad and Fresh Herbs

Fresh Berries (Misted with Orange-Flavoured Liqueur)
Whisky Whipped Cream (page 210)

"WOW" TIP: Serve this menu on a convenient "grazing buffet table" or in courses at a table in such a way that everyone can "catch the show"!

A "TOP NOTCH" BREAKFAST

Particularly with visiting family or friends (or for a special occasion), serve up a bit of fun with a snappy breakfast menu! You'll enjoy it too!

SAMPLE MENU

Blueberry Watermelon Tower (page 56)

Smoked Salmon-Portobello Eggs Benedict (page 58)

Toasted English Muffins
Whisky Ginger Marmalade (page 63)
Rosemary Honey (page 63)

Minted or Toffee Chocolate-Dipped Strawberries (page 198)

EAST MEETS WEST

Liven up your dinner party! Surprise and impress guests by offering them Asian inspired dishes but with a well-defined Western "spin". Your china, decor, music, overall style and mood should effectively reflect this unique encounter of "East" and "West"!

SAMPLE MENU

Ginger Squash Soup with Almond Liqueur (page 106)

Oriental Grilled Quail* (page 134)
Sesame Balsamic Vinegar Sauce (page 154)
Double Sesame Quinoa/Buckwheat (page 161)

Tiramisu-Wasabi Ice Cream Parfaits (page 189)

*Barbecue/Grill Option

FAMILY DINNER — A "SURE-HIT" WITH CHILDREN

In our home everyone is a VIP — children included! When children visit, one menu is prepared for everyone and is offered with the same amount of pizzazz that all our guests receive! The recipes are intriguingly presented and the table smartly set. There are definitely name cards as children are "seriously" impressed to see their names in writing at the table. Service is like that of a dinner party. Sounds strange? — Not at all! Children love ceremony! They want to be part of it; they also want to help. So select a menu where children can assist in the plating of food and invite them to the kitchen to "help"! By the way, you can bet that children will **absolutely** adore this "fun" menu! Everyone will!

SAMPLE MENU

Chopsticks of Oriental Marinated Lamb (page 81)
Mustard Mint Sauce (page 213)

Ginger Strawberry Soup (page 102)

Quick Chinese Spiced Wings/Drumsticks (page 132)
Oriental Mango Rice* (page 165)
Grape Tomatoes and Corn on the Cob

Taster Dessert Plates (page 187)
(e.g., Dark Chocolate Toffee Coins, page 194, Mini Cup of Ice Cream, Fresh Cherries)

* Offer simple "Perfect Rice" as an option.

Oriental Grilled Quail (page 134)

MORE MENUS & THEMES

Macadamia Mango Soup (page 105)

A "STATION STOP" BUFFET

I have come up with a foolproof way of having a good-sized group for dinner without extra help or overtaxing oneself! My formula includes using different spaces in your home for each course, enjoying your guests and leaving the cleanup behind for later as you move to the next location/part of the menu! (The formula also "nourishes" your guests' curiosity regarding your home!) This concept works particularly well when a theme is chosen. Decorating the different areas to suit the theme not only automatically "pulls" the entire evening logically together, but everyone also has fun. Select a theme that is personal to you (e.g., book club, Mardi Gras, golfing, Valentine's, New Years, a birthday). Here's an example of what we do.

Our years spent in Indonesia have inspired my Indonesian "Station Stop" Buffet. As torches blaze, guests arrive wearing Indonesian shirts (frequently borrowed from my husband) and sarongs. After drinks and hors d'oeuvres in the garden, with gamlan music setting the perfect mood, we then move inside to fetch our soup from a station set up in a corner of the living room. Placing the empty soup cups on a tray, guests are invited to the dining room where the table is appropriately decorated with exotic batik and ikat fabrics, wooden carvings, shells and pearls. Picking up a plate and cutlery/chopsticks (conveniently rolled in napkins), guests then proceed to select Indonesian/Asian-inspired appetizers, main course dishes, salads and breads — all intriguingly presented on handmade Indonesian pottery as well as in rice bowls, dimsung and wicker baskets. While exiting the dining room to find free seating (on the patio, in the living room or garden), guests help themselves to a glass of wine (their choice of red or white) or water. When the main course is completed, used plates and cutlery are left in a designated area before we continue on to other stations. Usually it's up to the second floor hall to collect dessert, then my study to pick up coffee and on to our final destination, the loft. Ultimately, as the last treats (chocolates and liqueurs) are savoured, the exciting evening draws to a close. After the departure of guests, Larry and I reluctantly return to reality but only to focus on that part of the cleanup deemed "essential". Why disturb the gratifying mood of the evening — a definite "sense of occasion". The rest of the tasks will be there for us to do in the morning!

SAMPLE MENU

HORS D'OEUVRE STATION
Zippy Smoked Oysters on Oriental Spoons (page 78)
Asian-Glazed Chicken Morsels/Skewers (page 80)

SOUP STATION
Macadamia Mango Soup (page 105)

APPETIZER STATION
Individual Avocado Crab Pies (page 86)

MAIN COURSE STATION
Coconut Cream Kaffir Lime Shrimp (page 150)
Twin Sesame Seed-Crusted Pork Tenderloin (page 138)
with Lemon Mustard Sour Cream Sauce (page 92)
Perfect Rice (page 168)
Mixed Salad

DESSERT STATION
Orange-Infused Chocolate Lava Cakes (page 184)
Decadent White Chocolate Sauce (page 215)
Lychees Stuffed with Fresh Raspberries

COFFEE AND CHOCOLATES STATION
Java Coffee, Jasmine Tea
Chocolates (e.g., pages 192 to 198)

Mini Flowerpots of Chocolate Mint Ice Cream (page 183)

COME FOR COFFEE

Preparing a short written menu when guests are coming for coffee saves me from uselessly investing in a myriad of cancelled decisions! You know: "I'll serve this. No, this might be better, etc."! We have all been there!! Remember, I have a basic formula established for "Finger Food" events (page 14). With it in mind, I proceed and enjoy the company of friends with little effort.

SAMPLE MENU

Avocado Crêpe Rolls (page 66)
Date Nut Cocktail Sandwiches (page 70) and Fresh Cherries
Ginger Strawberry Soup (page 102)
Mini Flowerpots of Chocolate Mint Ice Cream (page 183)
Coffee

A NEW TWIST TO SUNDAY BRUNCH/LUNCH

Entertaining family and/or friends for a Sunday brunch/lunch is a great idea, in that the remainder of the day is free to pursue other activities or commitments. Serve breakfast, lunch or even dinner items — or anything your mood inspires you to create! Frankly, I enjoy serving some of my more exotic fare. You may want to consider this option as you try to conveniently fit a little entertaining into everyone's busy life! (**Note:** As an alternative to the seared tuna for the main course, serve sliced "Portobello Deluxe Stuffed Chicken Breasts", page 130, either warm or cold.)

SAMPLE MENU

Persimmon Endive Salad (page 120)

Seared Tuna* with Sesame Balsamic Vinegar Sauce (page 154)
Sushi Rice (page 207)
Wasabi and Pickled Ginger
Sesame Zucchini "Noodles" (page 169)

Goat's Cheese-Stuffed Fresh Figs
with Anise-Infused Lemon Syrup (page 180)

*Barbecue/Grill Option

WINTER CHALET WEEKEND

When you are off for a weekend at a chalet, it's critical to keep the food preparations to a minimum. If others are joining you, divide the food responsibilities between different parties according to individual meals or entire days. In this suggested menu, virtually all the items may be prepared in advance and easily transported. "On-site" last minute cooking is necessary only for the shrimp, the regular crêpes (not the lace crêpes) and for the assembly of the pasta. Don't forget candles, linens, wine glasses and something for the centre of the table! You are certain to experience "snazzy" dining at its "country" best!

SAMPLE MENU

LUNCH
Tarragon Roasted Red Pepper Soup (page 109)

Gourmet Kasha Salad (page 119)
(or Salmon Gravlax, page 74/Smoked Salmon on Pumpernickel Bread)
Mixed Salad with Mustard Herb Vinaigrette (e.g., page 211)

Cheese and Anise-Walnut Raisin Chutney (page 79)

Fresh Fruit

DINNER
Spicy Shrimp with Zesty Ginger Mayonnaise (page 83)

Parmesan Sorrel Oil Dip (page 124)
Whole Wheat Bread
Roasted Tomato and Goat's Cheese Fusilli (page 158)
(or Fragrantly Poached Mussels, page 155, and Perfect Rice, page 168)
Mâche with Mustard Herb Vinaigrette (e.g., page 211)

Blackberry Butterscotch (and Banana)
Cocktail Fondue (page 174)

Chocolates (e.g., pages 192 to 198)

BREAKFAST
Orange Juice

Fruit-Filled Lace Crêpes (page 57)

Toasted Bagels
Walnut Honey (page 62)

A CHIC LIGHT LUNCH

I adore the opportunity of preparing a light lunch where exquisite but light recipes make up the entire meal. This is the perfect occasion to serve an appetizer or a salad as a main course. In our home, my Chic Light Lunches appear particularly when houseguests are staying for a few days (or during the holiday season) and when "dining/eating" becomes a major activity! "Cutting back" on lunch allows us to exhibit at least some degree of discipline and to be ready for the next culinary adventure!

SAMPLE MENU

Heart of Palm Cucumber Soup Eclipse (page 104)

Smoked Salmon Kasha/Wild Rice Martinis (page 92)
Multigrain or Pumpernickel Rolls

Caramel Mousse Chocolate Cups (page 178)

AN INTIMATE DINNER FOR TWO

Several times a year, my husband and I have a particularly unique "Intimate Dinner for Two". Here's our technique. Search for a romantic nook somewhere in your home (e.g., in front of the fireplace or a window), garden or on the patio. After installing a small table, temporarily transform the area into a cozy dining spot for two! A long tablecloth, soft lighting (don't forget the candles) and mood music instantaneously create the perfect ambiance for an intimate dinner. I suggest a chic but relatively "simple to execute" menu; however, do what suits you (and, of course, your partner). You are certain to have a special evening.

SAMPLE MENU

Chopsticks of Oriental Marinated Lamb (page 81)

Balsamic-Glazed Seared Pâté on Lentils (page 97)

Extraordinary Sun-Dried Tomato Shrimp on Squid Ink Pasta (page 152)

Seductive Chocolate Ice Cream Parfaits (page 179)

A FIVE-STAR "POTLUCK" BARBECUE

Have you ever joined a few couples or families and held a Five-Star "Potluck" Barbecue? It's easy! Coordinate your efforts by together deciding on a menu in advance and delegating tasks. One person prepares the hors d'oeuvres, another the appetizer salad, 2 look after the main course (fish/meat), someone else the vegetables and side salad. It's best if everyone brings "beverages". The host and hostess might be in charge of dessert as well as the set-up (including the barbecue and associated equipment, tables, napkins, china, glassware, lighting, music) — and definitely a bit of decor! Will there be a theme or a dress code? Be strategic and generate as much fun as possible! (**Note:** Use your own personal recipes for the barbecued steaks and/or burgers and if desired, serve them with garlic butter sautéed mushrooms and Armagnac Creamy Steak Sauce, page 212.)

SAMPLE MENU

Heart of Palm Prosciutto Wraps (page 68)
Sweet-and-Sour Salmon in Zucchini Cups (page 77)

Breaded Scallop Salad with Sesame Balsamic Vinegar Sauce (page 94)

Quick Grilled Salmon Steaks/Fillets*
with Nutty Mango Salsa (page 148)
(and/or Steaks*/Burgers*)
Garlic Butter-Sautéed Mushrooms
Armagnac Creamy Steak Sauce (page 212)

Baked Potatoes*
Corn on the Cob*

Garden (or Mâche) Salad
Mustard Herb Vinaigrette (e.g., page 211)

An Ice Cream Cone Fix (page 173)

Saucy Chocolate Blueberry Spoons (page 196)

*Barbecue/Grill Option

Quick Grilled Salmon Steaks/Fillets with Nutty Mango Salsa (page 148)

HARVEST SPLENDOR

There is nothing like a trip to a farmers' market to instill the spirit of Thanks Giving in us. Enjoy seeking out and choosing locally harvested products to prepare a special menu, decorate the table and your home.

SAMPLE MENU

Bocconcini Tomato Salad with Fresh Herbs (page 115)
(or Tarragon Roasted Red Pepper Soup, page 109)

Seed-Crusted Rack of Lamb (page 144)
Mustard Mint Sauce (page 213)
Asparagus Spears
Deluxe Sweet Potato Cream (page 160)

Berries and Cream Exotic Straw Sandwiches (page 172)

A WEEKEND BREAKFAST THAT PAMPERS

Is it someone's birthday, do you have overnight guests or do you just want to spoil yourself and family/partner with a leisurely breakfast?

SAMPLE MENU

Irresistible Meringue Porridge Pies (page 60)

Assortment of Hams and/or Cheeses (optional)

Croissants with Almond Honey (page 62)

Berries and Cream Exotic Straw Sandwiches (page 172)

MORE MENUS & THEMES

Blueberry/Pomegranate and Almond Rice Salad (page 112)

PICNICKING WITH PIZZAZZ

When it comes to picnicking, with a dash of creativity, I spontaneously pack lunch or dinner (from appetizer to dessert) into handy oriental steaming baskets as well as attractive boxes and a couple of well sealed jars. The trick is to line the steaming baskets with plastic wrap and then fit a plate securely into the bottom, allowing the food to sit comfortably and naturally in the baskets; cover the food loosely with plastic wrap before adding another steaming basket or its lid. (If possible, refrigerate the filled baskets overnight or until you are ready to leave.) Place the steaming baskets in a cooler and pack the other items around them. To introduce some extra fun, I often plan a menu where chopsticks can be used. Yes, our picnics are always packed with good food, playfulness and lighthearted pizzazz.

SAMPLE MENU

Pâté and Cheese
Whole Wheat Baguette
Anise-Walnut Raisin Chutney (page 79)

Sorrel Soup on Ice (page 107)

Asian-Glazed Chicken Morsels/Skewers (page 80)
(and/or Spicy Shrimp with Zesty Ginger Mayonnaise, page 83)

Blueberry/Pomegranate and Almond Rice Salad (page 112)
Fresh Sprigs of Garden Herbs and Salad Leaves (e.g., coriander,
regular and lemon basil, thyme, arugula, endive)
Mustard Herb Vinaigrette (e.g., page 211)

Fresh Cherries and Blackberries
Creamy Butterscotch Dessert (Dipping) Sauce (page 214)

A CHIC SHEIK'S OUTDOOR BUFFET

Let your fantasy run wild in recreating a previous (or a desired) experience/trip! Our happy years spent in Egypt and the Arabian Gulf frequently inspire us to transform our deck and garden into an Arabian paradise. Guests are mesmerized by a "Thousand and One Nights" atmosphere — incense, antique copper/brass vessels, carpets, kilims, blazing torches, lanterns, belly-dance music and a very personal twist to my Arabic menu. Be inspired to recreate your own fantastic theme. Live "vicariously"!

SAMPLE MENU

Seductive Shrimp Tabbouleh Sandwiches (page 75) and/or
Minted Fresh Figs with Feta (page 72)
Pine Nut Tabbouleh* (page 121)
Irresistible Sun-Dried Tomato Hummus (page 71)
Cumin Date Chickpea Salad (page 116)
Pita Bread

Pesto Butterflied Leg of Lamb** (page 140)

Mustard Mint Sauce (page 213)
Middle East Rice Pilaf (page 166)
Garlicky Feta and Pecan Spinach Salad (page 118)
Corn on the Cob**

Lemon Phyllo Napoleons (page 177)

Mint Tea and Arabic Coffee

* Homemade or commercial

**Barbecue/Grill Option

MAKE IT BLACK AND WHITE
(Lunch/Light Dinner)

Setting a table and devising a menu, both according to a particular colour scheme, is an intriguing challenge which you might want to consider. Of course, guests must come dressed in "suitably coloured" attire!

SAMPLE MENU

Currant and Celery Root Salad (page 117)

Escargots and Orzo in Portobello Dish
with Instant Goat's Cheese Sauce (page 156)
Mesclun with Mustard Herb Vinaigrette (e.g., page 211)

Tiramisu-Wasabi Ice Cream Parfaits (page 189)

Dark Chocolate Toffee Dominoes (page 194)

LAST MINUTE ENTERTAINING

With last minute guests coming for dinner, my advice is to keep your cool and immediately decide on an easily "put together" menu. Of course, you will want to impress your guests, but make certain that the menu is "risk free"! As far as decorating the table, open a few cupboard doors and find something suitable for a centrepiece. Remember the candles and music. Guests will think that you have spent days preparing!

SAMPLE MENU

Individual Avocado Crab Pies (page 86)

Quick Grilled Salmon Steaks/Fillets*
with Nutty Mango Salsa (page 148)
Cognac White Wine Cream Sauce (page 213)

Ice Cream Meringue Nests
with Honey Mustard Dessert Vinaigrette (page 181)

*Barbecue/Grill Option

Tiramisu-Wasabi Ice Cream Parfaits (page 189)

MORE MENUS & THEMES

Orange-Infused Chocolate Lava Cakes (page 184)

RECIPES

The joy of lingering over a wonderful breakfast seems to have fallen victim to busy schedules and a preoccupation of "cutting back" on our food consumption! However, on special occasions (particularly during the holiday season) or with the overnight visit of family or friends, this is the opportunity to slow down, to enjoy the company and conversation of others and to spoil everyone (ourselves included) with a leisurely and rather exceptional breakfast. For those times, I take simple enough ingredients and artistically design a scrumptiously impressive breakfast where fun and pizzazz are definitely on the menu!

Note: 🐇 designates a "No Time, No Talent" recipe.

CONVENIENCE TIP: *Facilitate "Easy Cooking & Inspiring Entertaining" by making "BASIC RECIPES" in advance and/or having them on hand*. *Or use your own substitutes, including commercial products (e.g., for this section:* **Double Ginger Sour Cream Sauce, Zesty Ginger Mayonnaise** *and* **Crêpe Batter**). *You will find yourself using these "Basic Recipes" repeatedly in your kitchen!*

Walnut Honey and Almond Honey (page 62)

BREAKFAST

BLUEBERRY WATERMELON TOWER

Makes 4 servings

When family or guests come down for breakfast, I want to have something that looks like "fun" on the breakfast table. My use of watermelon is deliberate. Yes, it presents a stunning contrast to the blueberries in terms of colour, shape, flavour and texture; but, more sensitively, how many of us use this childhood favourite in any type of imaginative way beyond eating it off the rind? Let's raise the bar!

1¹/₂ cups (375 mL) matchstick pieces* of seedless watermelon flesh
³/₄ tsp (4 mL) superfine sugar
¹/₃ tsp (2 mL) ground ginger
¹/₄ cup (60 mL) Double Ginger Sour Cream Sauce**, divided
1 cup (250 mL) fresh blueberries
1 tsp (5 mL) orange-flavoured liqueur (optional)

GARNISH (optional)
small edible flowers or sprigs of fresh mint

1 Sprinkle watermelon with sugar and ground ginger; toss gently.

2 Divide watermelon equally between 4 glasses (e.g., parfait*** or martini). Add about 2 tsp (10 mL) of Double Ginger Sour Cream Sauce to each glass.

3 If desired, toss blueberries with orange-flavoured liqueur or basic sugar syrup and add to glasses. If not serving immediately, refrigerate.

4 Just before serving, if desired, garnish fruit in each glass with drizzles of sauce and an edible flower or a sprig of fresh mint.

* Length: 1 inch or 2.5 cm
** To make the Double Ginger Sour Cream Sauce, stir together ¹/₃ cup (80 mL) of sour cream, 1¹/₂ tbsp (23 mL) of icing sugar, 2 tsp (10 mL) of chopped ginger in syrup, ¹/₃ tsp (2 mL) of ground ginger and if desired, ¹/₃ tsp (2 mL) of Armagnac liqueur or cognac. (Makes ¹/₃ cup or 80 mL of sauce.) Store the sauce refrigerated for up to 10 days. (**Note:** Ginger in syrup is different from candied ginger. Both are available in health food stores.)
*** Volume of parfait glasses: ²/₃ cup (170 mL)

"WOW" PRESENTATION TIP: This Blueberry Watermelon Tower is definitely "fun" when I use parfait glasses and balance a parfait spoon in a horizontal position across the top of the glass!

SIMPLE-ALTERNATIVE TIP: Cut the watermelon into cubes, sprinkle with ground ginger and sugar, then toss. Arrange the cubes of melon in bowls or on dessert plates and drizzle with sauce. Scatter the blueberries over the melon and garnish as desired. (**Note:** More watermelon will probably be required. Adjust the recipe to suit you.)

ALTERNATIVE-USE TIP: For those not normally tempted by ***dessert***, this recipe could be an ideal option.

Fruit-Filled Lace Crêpes

Makes 4 servings

The inspiration for my "lace crêpes" came from the military's camouflage nets which we encountered during the first Gulf War. A transfer from Kuwait to south-east Asia soon revealed that my "new" creation had existed for generations in Malaysia as "Roti Jala", very large lacy pancakes. Rolled individually into tight parcels, these pancakes are eaten with Malay food. In contrast, my crêpes are smaller and placed over a delightful combination of ingredients where flavours, textures, colours and shapes make breakfast an exciting affair! (**Note:** *Feel free to adjust the "filling" ingredients to suit your own taste and/or resources on hand.*)

1³/₄ cups (430 mL) crêpe batter (e.g., page 205), divided
2 cups (500 mL) fresh strawberries (stems removed and sliced) or other berries/diced mango
3 cups (750 mL) banana, sliced
1 tbsp (15 mL) orange-flavoured liqueur, optional
3 tbsp (45 mL) strawberry jam
¹/₄ cup (60 mL) Double Ginger Sour Cream Sauce (page 56) or crème fraîche (e.g., page 204) or yogurt
3 tbsp (45 mL) creamy butterscotch dessert sauce* or maple syrup
2 tbsp (30 mL) toasted slivered almonds or chopped pecans, optional
1 tbsp (15 mL) chopped chocolate, optional

GARNISH (optional)
As desired whole fresh strawberries and/or sprigs of fresh mint
¹/₂ cup (125 mL) maple syrup (for passing)

1 In a large nonstick skillet over medium-low heat, prepare 4 large crêpes (diameter: 7 inch or 17 cm) using ¹/₄ cup (60 mL) of batter per crêpe. Arrange each on individual dinner plates.

2 With remaining batter, make 4 "Lace Crêpes". Using about 3 tbsp (45 mL) of batter for each crêpe, first quickly drizzle a ring about the same diameter as the prepared crêpes and then continue to drizzle in a haphazard manner within ring to form a thin "lace" crêpe. Cook until top surface is set. (Note: **To simplify the drizzling process, place the batter in a clean plastic squeeze bottle fitted with a medium-size nozzle.**)

3 Using a pancake flipper, carefully peel lace crêpe away from skillet and turn; cook second side briefly. Remove from skillet and stack on a plate, separating each crêpe with a layer of wax paper; set aside.**

4 Place sliced bananas and strawberries in separate bowls; bathe with liqueur.

5 Using about ¹/₄ of total amount for each crêpe, spread strawberry jam evenly over each plated crêpe (i.e., regular crêpe), add bananas and dabs of Double Ginger Sour Cream Sauce. Drizzle with butterscotch sauce, top with sliced strawberries, toasted nuts and chopped chocolate.

6 Top with lace crêpe enclosing fruit mixture between crêpes.

7 Drizzle crêpes with a touch of maple syrup; garnish with whole fresh strawberries and/or sprigs of fresh mint. Pass maple syrup at table.

* Commercial or homemade (e.g., page 214)
** Crêpes are best used the day that they are prepared. (However, if the crêpes have been prepared in advance, **warm** them briefly in their plastic storage bag in a microwave oven to restore much of their original quality.)

TIME-SAVING TIP: Using an **"assembly line" technique**, these Fruit-Filled Lace Crêpes are simple and quick to prepare.

FLAVOUR TIP: To enhance the flavour of berries and peeled fruit, I frequently bathe/toss/spray them with an **orange-flavoured liqueur**. As an **"alcohol free"** option, use Basic Sugar Syrup (e.g., page 208).

SMOKED SALMON-PORTOBELLO EGGS BENEDICT

Makes 4 servings

If you only need one "Special Occasion Breakfast" recipe (e.g., for Mother's Day, Christmas breakfast, house guests), here it is! Melting Swiss cheese and drizzles of Zesty Ginger Mayonnaise amplify the robust flavour of grilled portobello mushroom caps. But the real drama lies in the assembly. Poached eggs are nestled comfortably into the mushroom caps, then temptingly bathed in a mesmerizing Tarragon Hollandaise Mayonnaise Sauce, crowned with extravagant folds of luscious smoked salmon and set on an inviting bed of seasoned wilted spinach. It is the ultimate breakfast or brunch treat!

4 large Portobello mushroom caps*
1/4 cup (60 mL) olive oil (preferably garlic-infused), divided
To taste salt and crushed black peppercorns
3 oz (85 g) Swiss cheese, thinly sliced
4 oz (115 g) fresh spinach leaves, no stems
2 tbsp (30 mL) Zesty Ginger Mayonnaise (page 212) or mayonnaise**
4 large eggs
3 tbsp (45 mL) Tarragon Hollandaise Mayonnaise***
6 oz (175 g) smoked salmon, thinly sliced

GARNISH (optional or as desired)
fresh chive stems
capers, well drained

1 Rub mushroom caps with olive oil (about 1 1/2 tbsp or 23 mL); season with salt and crushed black peppercorns to taste.

2 Heat about 1 1/2 tbsp (23 mL) of olive oil in 2 very large skillets (or on a griddle) over medium-high heat and add mushroom caps ("top side" down). Cook mushrooms until just barely tender, turning once. (**Note:** Hot mushrooms continue to cook when removed from heat.)

3 Transfer mushroom caps immediately to a baking tray with underside of caps facing "up". Cover exposed "gill" surfaces with Swiss cheese and place in a warm oven (i.e., 150°F or 73°C).

4 Heat remaining oil in skillets (or on a griddle) over medium-high heat. Add spinach and quickly season with salt and crushed black peppercorns. Turn leaves constantly until they barely begin to wilt; transfer immediately to a plate.

5 For individual servings, place equal portions of sautéed spinach in centre of 4 oversized plates and arrange in a circular bed (larger in diameter than that of Portobello mushroom caps). Drizzle each circular portion of spinach with Zesty Ginger Mayonnaise (1 tsp or 5 mL), top with a Swiss cheese-garnished mushroom cap and drizzle remaining Zesty Ginger Mayonnaise over melted cheese.

6 Meanwhile, poach eggs to desired degree of doneness.

7 Carefully place one poached egg into each mushroom cap, top with Tarragon Hollandaise Mayonnaise (2 tsp or 10 mL) and crown artistically and gently with smoked salmon (e.g., twisted into a rose formation).

8 Garnish plates with fresh chive stems and capers. Serve immediately.

* Weight of each cap (no stem): about 2 oz or 60 g
** The "Zesty Ginger Mayonnaise" is definitely the better choice!
*** To make the Tarragon Hollandaise Mayonnaise, combine 1/4 cup (60 mL) of mayonnaise, 1/2 tsp (3 mL) of prepared mustard (sandwich type) and a pinch of crushed dried tarragon leaves. (Makes 1/4 cup or 60 mL.) Store refrigerated in a well-sealed jar. (Do not heat.)

HOW-TO TIP: To make **poached eggs**, pour about 3/4 inch (2 cm) of water into a large skillet. Add 1 tsp (5 mL) of white vinegar (to assist in setting the egg white) and a bit of salt; bring the water to a simmer. Working with one egg at a time, break it into a small bowl and slip the egg into the simmering water. Repeat this process for the remainder of the eggs. Allow the eggs to cook uncovered until the whites are almost set. Bathe the top of the yolks with spoonfuls of simmering water until a film forms over the yolks. If necessary, continue to cook the eggs only until the whites are firm but the yolks are still soft. (**Note:** Some people do not like their yolks "runny". In that case, cover the skillet and allow the yolks to cook to the desired degree of doneness.) Carefully lift out the eggs with a slotted pancake flipper, drain and transfer to a plate. If desired/necessary, trim edges with a small sharp knife to form neat, circular, poached eggs. Serve.

ALTERNATIVE-USE TIP: Smoked Salmon-Portobello Eggs Benedict are fantastic for a **brunch** or **light family dinner** particularly when served with a small portion of pasta and/or corn on the cob as accompaniments.

IRRESISTIBLE MERINGUE PORRIDGE PIES/PIE
(Cream of Buckwheat/Cream of Wheat)

Makes almost 3 cups (750 mL) of porridge or about 6 ramekin dish servings (about 1/2 cup or 125 mL each) or one pie* (e.g., diameter: 10 inches or 25 cm) suitable for 4 to 6 servings

"WOW" FACTOR: This creative porridge recipe **placed second** in the cream of buckwheat category in The Birkett Mills International Association of Culinary Professionals' buckwheat competition.

I dedicated this international award winning recipe to my dear mother who always insisted that porridge was as delicious as ice cream! Nutmeg and ginger-scented cream of buckwheat, exotically laced with chopped macadamia nuts, rests suspended on a layer of sweet peach slices. Crowned with an enticing cloud-like meringue, the recipe is equally attractive when prepared in individual ramekin dishes or as one large pie. Although I serve it hot for a "special" or weekend breakfast, this "porridge" pie could be the ultimate "cold weather" dessert for the appropriate casual occasion, particularly after chilly outdoor activities. Actually, my husband finds it irresistible all year round whether it is served hot, at room temperature or directly from the refrigerator!

1 1/2 tsp (8 mL) **unsalted butter**
1 cup (250 mL)** **thinly sliced peaches (peeled and
    stones removed)**
1 1/2 tbsp (23 mL) **brown sugar**
1 1/2 tbsp (23 mL) **maple syrup**
3 cups (750 mL) **milk**
1 1/2 tbsp (23 mL) **granulated sugar (first addition)**
1/2 tsp (3 mL) **ground ginger**
1/4 tsp (1 mL) **salt**
1/8 tsp (Pinch) **ground nutmeg**
1/2 cup (125 mL) **cream of buckwheat*****
    (or 6 1/2 tbsp/100 mL cream of wheat)
2 tbsp (30 mL) **coarsely chopped macadamia nuts**
2 tbsp (30 mL) **chopped ginger in syrup (drained)**
3 **egg whites (room temperature)**
6 tbsp (90 mL) **granulated sugar (second addition)**

1 Melt butter in a medium-size skillet over medium heat; add peach slices and brown sugar; sauté for a couple of minutes to soften peaches slightly and to glaze. Immediately, transfer to a plate to avoid overcooking; set aside. (**Note: Peaches may be cooked hours in advance.** Refrigerate if not using within a couple of hours.)

2 To prepare individual servings*, use 6 ramekin dishes (1/2 cup or 125 mL size). Arrange glazed peach slices in bottom of dishes and drizzle with maple syrup.

3 Place milk, granulated sugar (first addition), ground ginger, salt and nutmeg in a medium saucepan over medium to medium-high heat; bring to a boil, stirring occasionally.

4 Whisk in cream of buckwheat and continue to whisk constantly until mixture returns to a boil. Reduce heat to medium-low and let mixture boil gently (uncovered), stirring frequently, until cream of buckwheat is tender and porridge is thick (about 9 to 11 minutes). Remove from heat.

5 Stir in macadamia nuts and chopped ginger in syrup. (If desired, add a touch of extra milk or heavy cream to keep mixture light and fluffy.) Cover and set porridge aside.

6 About 25 minutes before serving, beat egg whites in a medium bowl at medium speed until soft peaks form; gradually sprinkle in granulated sugar (second addition), one spoonful at a time, and continue beating until shiny, very stiff peaks form.

7 Fill ramekin dishes almost to rim with hot porridge. (Reheat porridge if necessary.) Cover each dish with beaten egg white to form a meringue cap.

8 Place meringue-capped dishes on 2 baking trays for convenience in handling; separate dishes well. Bake in middle of a preheated oven at 375 °F (190 °C) until meringue is golden (about 6 to 8 minutes).

9 Serve as soon as possible (but not necessarily immediately as one might need to serve a soufflé).

* **Simpler "WOW" Option: One large pie** may be made in a glass pie plate with a 4 cup (1 litre) capacity. Place the pie plate with the meringue pie on a baking tray and bake the pie for 8 to 9 minutes. To serve, cut the pie into wedges and place individual wedges in oversized bowls; garnish with sprinkled nutmeg and sprigs of fresh mint.

** This is about 3 medium or 2 large size peaches. (**Note:** Sliced, unpeeled nectarines may be used; however, the red tint in the skin will probably "bleed" and discolour the slices.)

*** Cream of buckwheat is available in health food stores as well as in some supermarkets and specialty food stores.

OPTION TIP: Feel free to use either **cream of buckwheat or cream of wheat.**

MAKE-AHEAD TIP (STEPS 3, 4 & 5):
The **porridge** may be prepared up to 2 days in advance; store refrigerated.

WALNUT HONEY

Makes 1¹/3 cups (325 mL)

I relish the surprise and the few moments of pleasure which pure simplicity can achieve. To quietly "blast" breakfast to an unexpected "WOW" level, take 3 and 3. That is 3 minutes to stir only 3 simple ingredients together. With its addictive crunch and exceptional flavour, my Walnut Honey is absolutely divine! Definitely it's a **No Time, No Talent** *recipe. (***Note:*** A photo appears on page 55.)*

"WOW" TIP: Feel free to **gradually add more chopped walnuts** as the honey is consumed. (**Note:** Adding extra walnuts when preparing the recipe makes stirring the "jarred" honey very difficult.)

1 cup (250 mL) liquid honey
¹/4 tsp (1 mL) maple extract
¹/2 cup (125 mL) **coarsely chopped walnuts**

1 Pour honey into a medium bowl. First, stir in extract thoroughly, and then carefully stir in walnuts.

2 Store in a well-sealed jar at room temperature for up to several weeks. Stir before using.

SERVING TIP: Because the walnut pieces tend to rise to the top of the jar, it is best to serve the honey **in a shallow dish or already spread** on toasted and buttered English muffins/bagels/bread (or on buttered scones/tea biscuits).

ALMOND HONEY

Makes 1¹/3 cups (325 mL)

Studded with crisp whole almonds, this amazing honey is truly unique and delicious! Almond fans are certain to go nuts! This simplest of recipes can turn an ordinary breakfast into a culinary experience — no exaggeration! (A photo appears on page 55.)

1 cup (250 mL) liquid honey
¹/4 tsp (1 mL) almond extract
¹/2 cup (125 mL) **whole almonds (with skins)**

1 Pour honey into a medium bowl. First, stir extract in thoroughly, and then carefully stir in almonds.

2 Store in a well-sealed jar at room temperature for up to several weeks.

3 Stir well before using. Serve in a shallow dish or spread directly on buttered toast/English muffins or bagels.

ROSEMARY HONEY

Makes 1 cup (250 mL)

I was not certain that honey required any enhancement until I added chopped fresh rosemary. The combination is remarkable! Of course, it is great for breakfast, but also try it with scones or tea biscuits (savoury or sweet, with or without cream).

1 cup (250 mL) creamed honey (room temperature)
1¹/₂ tbsp (23 mL) finely chopped fresh* rosemary

1   Combine ingredients thoroughly.

2   Store refrigerated in a well-sealed jar or in an airtight plastic container for up to several months.

3   Remove from refrigerator about 15 minutes before serving and if necessary stir well.

* **Option:** 1¹/₂ tbsp (23 mL) dried crushed rosemary; however, it is best to use fresh rosemary.

WHISKY GINGER MARMALADE

Makes 1 cup (250 mL)

One of my passions is coming up with appealing quick "tricks" to make breakfasts more exciting. Imagine traditional orange marmalade fragrantly spiked with a splash of whisky and a dash of ginger. This recipe converts even those who are not fond of marmalade! — "WOW"!

1 cup (250 mL) orange marmalade (commercial)
2 tsp (10 mL) whisky*
¹/₂ tsp (3 mL) ground ginger

1   Stir ingredients together.

2   Place marmalade in a well-sealed jar and store refrigerated for up to several months.

* A high-quality whisky works best.

ALTERNATIVE-USE TIP: Whisky Ginger Marmalade is also superb with *tea biscuits* or *scones* (served with or without whipped/clotted cream).

Hors d'oeuvres are critical to my repertoire of recipes, constituting the first element of my "bookends" philosophy on entertaining (i.e., an "Hors d'Oeuvre" at the beginning of an event and a "Finishing Touch" at the end). As an immediate indication of a personal and warm welcome, every occasion in our home begins with an hors d'oeuvre. Recognizing that first impressions count, I want these hors d'oeuvres to be something superb, something relatively unique in terms of ingredients and presentation!

My hors d'oeuvres are both substantive and versatile. Many have become "Signature Recipes", conveniently and successfully making up the principle part of our drinks, tea, coffee, cocktail, garden party and reception menus. Guests leave such events convinced that they have not only had a "cutting edge" experience but also a **light meal!**

I adore passing hors d'oeuvres. That offers me an intimate and warm opportunity to interact with all our guests, which otherwise might be difficult to achieve.

Note: 🐇 designates a "No Time, No Talent" recipe.

*For this section, the suggested "**BASIC RECIPES**" (or commercial substitutes) to have on hand include **Mustard Herb Vinaigrette, Honey Mustard Mayonnaise, Herb Cream Cheese, Herb Garlic Butter, Sweet-and-Sour Hot Sauce, Mustard Mint Sauce** and **Crêpe Batter**. These "Basic Recipes"/ingredients will be used repeatedly throughout the book.*

HORS D'OEUVRES

Avocado Crêpe Rolls

Makes 12 rolls (6 hors d'oeuvre servings)

*This is a "**NO-FAIL**" recipe regardless of one's culinary skill. — Just follow the instructions. Whether prepared with buckwheat or regular crêpes, the recipe's complexity of mesmerizing flavours never goes unnoticed. Normally, I serve the rolls as an hors d'oeuvre or appetizer, particularly for a vegetarian option. However, served with a simple salad, they make a tempting main course choice for a brunch, casual lunch or light family dinner. (In that case, allow 4 or 5 rolls per serving.)*

1 avocado, ripe (about 9 oz or 250 g)
1 to 1¹/2 tsp (5 to 8 mL) lemon juice
12 prepared crêpes* (diameter: 4¹/2 inches or 11 cm)
¹/4 cup (60 mL) sour cream
2 tbsp (30 mL) Zesty Ginger Mayonnaise (page 212)
    or mayonnaise
1 tbsp (15 mL) black or red caviar (e.g., well-drained
    lumpfish roe), optional
³/4 tsp (4 mL) maple syrup**

1 Cut avocado in half, remove stone and peel carefully. Cut avocado lengthwise into 12 thin wedges; bathe lightly in lemon juice and set aside.

2 Immediately, lay out crêpes on a clean flat surface. Spread central and bottom areas of each crêpe with sour cream (1 tsp or 5 mL) and drizzle with a touch of Zesty Ginger Mayonnaise (¹/2 tsp or 3 mL). Place one wedge of avocado in a horizontal position near bottom edge of crêpe; sprinkle central area of avocado with caviar (¹/4 tsp or 1 mL) and drizzle with a few drops (i.e., ¹/16 tsp or 0.3 mL) of maple syrup.**

3 Starting from bottom edge, roll crêpe securely around avocado wedge to form a roll. Arrange avocado rolls with seam side down.

4 If not serving immediately, arrange rolls in a single layer in an airtight plastic container and store refrigerated.

* Both buckwheat (e.g., page 204) and regular crêpes (e.g., page 205) work well in this recipe, with the latter offering a milder flavour. For the more adventurous palate, choose the buckwheat option!
** The few drops of maple syrup add the necessary balance, particularly when the avocados are not perfectly ripened.

MAKE-AHEAD TIP: The **crêpes** can be prepared earlier in the day (i.e., hours in advance). However, if using black lumpfish caviar, make the **crêpe rolls** only an hour or so before serving because the caviar tends to "weep" black ink. The red caviar allows the rolls to be prepared several hours in advance, but it has a more distinct "fish oil" flavour.

"WOW" PRESENTATION TIP: I like to **wrap and knot a fresh chive stem around the centre** of the individual rolls. Just before serving, I **insert a small edible flower** (e.g., a Johnny Jump-Up) at the knot.

Asian Beef Carpaccio Spoons

Makes 24 spoons (8 to 12 hors d'oeuvre servings)

*Upon discovery that my innovative Sesame Honey Mustard Cognac Sauce was a superb match for both sushi rice and raw beef, I concocted this intriguing Asian version of beef carpaccio. With simple additions of fresh basil leaves and crunchy roasted sesame seeds the combination is addictive! (**Note:** Oriental porcelain spoons or larger teaspoons are required on which to arrange the hors d'oeuvre.)*

24 spoons (preferably oriental porcelain)
3 oz (85 g) beef tenderloin
³/4 cup (180 mL) cooked sushi rice (e.g., page 207),
    room temperature
³/4 tsp (4 mL) sesame oil
1 tbsp (15 mL) Honey Mustard Mayonnaise (page 211)
24 small* fresh basil leaves

Sesame Honey Mustard Cognac Sauce
1 tbsp (15 mL) each of Dijon mustard, sesame oil
    and honey
1 tsp (5 mL) cognac
Pinch crushed black peppercorns

Garnish
1¹/4 tsp (6 mL) roasted white sesame seeds

1   Freeze beef tenderloin. Transfer to refrigerator to soften slightly (i.e., frozen but not "frozen solid").

2   To make the Sesame Honey Mustard Cognac Sauce, whisk sauce ingredients together and set aside.

3   With a very sharp straight-edged knife, shave tenderloin into paper thin (translucent) slices. Spread on a platter in a single layer; bathe generously with Sesame Honey Mustard Cognac Sauce. Tear slices into smaller pieces. (**Note: This may be done several hours in advance; cover beef closely with plastic wrap and refrigerate.**)

4   Just before preparing hors d'oeuvres, toss rice lightly with sesame oil.

5   Add only a touch (i.e., ¹/8 tsp or a pinch) of Honey Mustard Mayonnaise to centre of bowl of individual spoons; top with about 1 tsp (5 mL) rice.

6   Lay one small basil leaf across each portion of rice; top with about 1 tsp (5 mL) of sauce-bathed beef. (Note: **Spoons may be prepared to this stage up to 1¹/2 to 2 hours before serving.** Cover the filled bowls of the spoons with wax paper and refrigerate.)

7   Just before serving, sprinkle surface of beef generously with toasted sesame seeds.

*Option: Larger leaves torn artistically into smaller pieces

MAKE-AHEAD TIP: I keep a couple of cups of **cooked sushi rice** on hand in the freezer particularly for the preparation of hors d'oeuvres like these. **Note:** If using previously stored (refrigerated or frozen) sushi rice, to restore its original quality, place it in a small microwave proof bowl, cover loosely and reheat briefly (i.e., until just hot) in a microwave oven.

MAKE-AHEAD TIP (STEP 2): The **Sesame Honey Mustard Cognac Sauce** may be prepared up to several weeks in advance and stored refrigerated. (**Note:** I generally make it in larger quantities; see page 214.)

Hors d'Oeuvres

HEART OF PALM PROSCIUTTO WRAPS
(with Vegetarian Option)
Makes about 20 pieces (7 to 8 hors d'oeuvre servings)

My heart of palm wrapped in prosciutto ham is a simple, but amazingly enticing recipe. Many people have never tasted heart of palm. Few have introduced it into their culinary repertoire. As I say, that is all the more reason why you must try this recipe which will soon become a favorite! What makes these Heart of Palm Prosciutto Wraps exceptional is first the fresh dill rolled up into the wraps along with Herb Cream Cheese. But the crowning glory is definitely the macadamia nut topping!

4 slices prosciutto ham* (very thinly sliced)
¹/₂ to ²/₃ cup (125 to 170 mL) herb cream cheese
    (e.g., page 205 or commercial), divided
3 tbsp (45 mL) chopped fresh dill weed
    (i.e., feathery leaves)
4 whole stems of heart of palm**, rinsed and
    well drained

GARNISH
¹/₄ cup (60 mL) coarsely chopped macadamia nuts

1   Lay out individual slices of ham (side by side and well separated) on a clean dry surface with short edges in a horizontal position. Spread each slice entirely and evenly with about 1¹/₃ tbsp (20 mL) of herb cream cheese.

2   Sprinkle 2 tsp (10 mL) of chopped fresh dill over cream cheese covering bottom half of each prosciutto ham slice.

3   At lower edge, arrange one entire "log-like" stem of heart of palm horizontally across dill and cream cheese garnished slice of prosciutto.

4   Tightly roll ham around heart of palm stem, gently spreading/stretching ham along length of heart of palm and expelling trapped air. Trim off any protruding heart of palm.

5   Wrap rolls (seam side down) in plastic wrap and refrigerate. (**Note: The rolls may be prepared to this point up to 24 hours before serving.**)

6   Before serving, remove rolls from refrigerator and remove plastic wrap. Arrange rolls with seam side down; add a line of herb cream cheese (about 2 tsp or 10 mL) along top of each roll; press chopped macadamia nuts into cream cheese garnish.

7   With a sharp knife, cut each roll crosswise into 5 equal slices/pieces. **Note: *Steps 6 and 7 may also be done hours in advance;*** store the hors d'oeuvres (reassembled in rows and closely covered with plastic wrap) in an airtight plastic container and refrigerate.

8   To serve, artistically arrange slices in a standing position (macadamia nuts up).

* Proscuitto Ham is rectangular in shape (usually about 7 × 3 inches or 17 × 8 cm). **Note:** Other varieties of paper-thin sliced ham, air-dried beef, or corned beef may be used.
** Heart of Palm comes from the small cabbage palm. The hearts are peeled, then processed and packed into cans with a light salt brine. Heart of Palm comes principally from Central and South America. The diameter of the stems may vary; avoid using stems that are thicker than 1 inch (2.5 cm) in diameter.

FLASH: This hors d'oeuvre can be **quickly prepared by the dozens (and easily stored)** for large parties!

CAUTION TIP (STEP 7): Avoid cutting slices wider than ¹/₂ inch or 1.25 cm thick as this hors d'oeuvre should definitely be "one-bite" in size.

"WOW" VEGETARIAN OPTION: Dab a little (about ¹/₄ tsp or 1 mL) herb cream cheese in bottom of oriental porcelain spoons. Add a single basil leaf (top side facing up), more herb cream cheese (about ¹/₂ tsp or 3 mL), one slice of heart of palm (thickness: ¹/₄ inch or 0.6 cm), another dab of herb cream cheese and crown with chopped macadamia nuts (about ¹/₂ tsp or 3 mL). **Note:** If oriental spoons are not available, simply assemble the ingredients on larger basil leaves. The hors d'oeuvres, however, will be "trickier" to handle.

HORS D'OEUVRES

DATE NUT COCKTAIL SANDWICHES

Makes about 24 petit cocktail sandwiches (8 to 12 hors d'oeuvre servings)

To alleviate the potential stress of "not having" something on hand to serve unexpected guests, I developed this versatile (and indeed original) cocktail sandwich filling. It can be stored refrigerated for a couple weeks or frozen for months. To do this and to give the recipe universal appeal, I deliberately manipulated the sweetness of dates with careful additions of mustard, mayonnaise, cheddar cheese and nuts. The resulting filling is a delightfully mellow, "sweet and savoury" combination with dynamic flavours and textures. With this filling, my Date Nut Cocktail Sandwiches have become a unique and easy addition to a reception of any kind including garden, tea, coffee or drinks parties. They marry well with non-alcoholic and alcoholic beverages.

1 cup (250 mL) chopped dates*
1/3 cup (80 mL) mayonnaise, divided
1 tsp (5 mL) mustard (sandwich type)
1/2 cup (125 mL) finely grated cheddar cheese (old)
1/4 cup (60 mL) coarsely chopped walnuts
6 to 8 slices** oatmeal (whole wheat or bran) bread
3 tbsp (45 mL) butter, unsalted and soft

GARNISH (optional)
sprigs of fresh herbs (e.g., lavender, mint or parsley)
fresh cherries or seedless grapes
edible flowers

1 To make filling, on a dinner plate (i.e., versus in a bowl, for ease of "mashing"), cream together dates, 3 tbsp (45 mL) mayonnaise, and mustard. Lightly fold in cheese and then walnuts. (Makes about 1 1/3 cups or 325 mL of filling.)

2 Arrange bread in sandwich pairs on a clean flat surface; butter generously. Spread remaining mayonnaise (as required) over all buttered surfaces. Add filling to one prepared slice of each sandwich pair creating a rather thick even layer (similar to thickness of bread slice). Close sandwiches.

3 To serve, trim away all crusts and cut sandwiches into "petit" artistic shapes (e.g., small triangles).

4 If desired, serve in a doily-lined basket or box; garnish with sprigs of fresh herbs, cherries/seedless grapes and/or edible flowers.

* I use the "block" dates. This is about 6 1/2 oz (190 g).
** Use 6 large slices or 8 regular slices, or as required depending on the thickness of filling desired. I definitely prefer using oatmeal bread. (**Note:** There is usually a loaf of oatmeal or whole wheat bread in our freezer, ready to make into sandwiches.)

> **MAKE-AHEAD TIP (STEP 1):** The **filling** can be prepared in advance, placed in an airtight plastic container and stored refrigerated for up to a few weeks or frozen for months.

> **MAKE-AHEAD TIP (STEP 2):** Wrap the **prepared sandwiches** securely in plastic wrap, place in an airtight plastic bag and refrigerate (for up to 2 days or freeze for up to a couple of weeks) until ready to serve. (**Note:** When storing prepared sandwiches for longer than a matter of hours, I include an extra slice of bread at each end of the pile of sandwiches to ensure freshness.)

IRRESISTIBLE SUN-DRIED TOMATO HUMMUS

Makes more than 1 cup or 250 mL (6 to 8 servings)

So easy, so tasty! Sun-dried tomatoes and mayonnaise make this toothsome recipe a deluxe cross between hummus and a spread. As a dip, part of a meze or tapas table, the recipe is outstanding!

1 cup (250 mL) cooked* chickpeas
3 tbsp (45 mL) mayonnaise, regular or low calorie
3 tbsp (45 mL) chopped sun-dried tomatoes in
    seasoned oil (drained, but reserve oil)
1¹/2 tsp (8 mL) sesame oil
1 tsp (5 mL) ground cumin
¹/2 to ³/4 tsp (3 to 4 mL) (Indonesian)** hot chili paste
¹/4 to ¹/3 tsp (1 to 2 mL) finely chopped fresh garlic
2 to 3 tbsp (30 to 45 mL) water
48 Parmesan Toasted Pita Wedges (e.g., page 72) or
    3 pita breads (diameter: 6 inches or 15 cm)

GARNISH (optional)
1 to 2 tsp (5 to 10 mL) light olive oil (preferably
    garlic-infused)
1 tbsp (15 mL) roasted pine nuts
As desired fresh basil leaves or sprigs of fresh
    herbs, optional

1 Place chickpeas, mayonnaise, sun-dried tomatoes, sesame oil, cumin, chili paste and garlic in food processor. Purée until smooth, adding, as required, a little seasoned oil from the drained sun-dried tomato (e.g., 1 tbsp/15 mL) and water to form a rather smooth but thick mixture.

2 If possible, place hummus in an airtight container and store refrigerated overnight (or for at least several hours) to allow flavours to blend and develop.

3 To serve as a dip, place hummus in a dish or shallow bowl. Drizzle with olive oil, sprinkle with roasted pine nuts and garnish with fresh basil leaves. Serve along with wedges of pita toast or pita bread.

* Drained canned chickpeas may be used successfully.
** The Indonesian hot chili paste which I use is called "Sambal Oelek". It is available in oriental food stores as well as specialty food stores and some supermarkets.

MAKE-AHEAD TIP: This hummus retains its quality for up to a week when refrigerated or for a couple of months when frozen.

ALTERNATIVE-USE TIP: Slather the hummus **in sandwiches** (including vegetarian types) or let it be a principle component **in creative appetizers or vegetarian stacks**. It never goes undetected!

STORAGE CONTAINER TIP: At a wholesale grocery supply outlet, I purchase "sleeves" (long plastic bags) filled with **inexpensive, clear plastic, airtight containers and lids** (i.e., the type used at deli counters). (**Note:** If there is not such an outlet in your area, ask at the deli counter of your local supermarket where the containers might be purchased.) Most of my products from flavoured mayonnaises and sauces to ice creams and chopped nuts are stored in this type of container. It is easy to see at a glance what I have on hand. The 1 cup (250 mL), 1¹/2 cup (375 mL) and 2 cup (500 mL) containers are my favourite sizes. On multi-use labels (available at business supply stores), I write the product name and date before applying the labels to the lids.

Parmesan Toasted Pita Wedges

Makes 48 thin wedges (8 to 12 servings)

These are addictively delicious — and require no time, no energy to prepare! Serve the toasted pita wedges with dips, hors d'oeuvres, soups, salads, as part of a meze or tapas table — or as a simple snack. They are always a treat!

3 pita breads (diameter: 6 inches or 15 cm)
2 tbsp (30 mL) melted butter
2 tbsp (30 mL) garlic-infused olive oil
3 tbsp (45 mL) pregrated Parmesan cheese
To taste salt (optional)

1 Using scissors, cut each pita bread into 8 wedges. Separate each wedge into 2 triangles (using a knife if necessary). Place wedges in a single layer, rough (inner) side up, on parchment paper-lined baking sheets.

2 Combine melted butter and garlic-infused oil. Brush surfaces of pita wedges with butter-oil mixture; sprinkle with Parmesan cheese and sprinkle lightly with salt.

3 Bake in a preheated (375 °F or 190 °C) oven until golden brown (about 5 to 6 minutes).

4 Serve toasted pita wedges directly from oven or allow to cool thoroughly before storing in a cool dry place for up to a couple of weeks.

> **OPTION TIP:** To make plain Toasted Pita Wedges, use 1/4 cup (60 mL) of butter and eliminate the garlic-infused oil and Parmesan cheese.

Minted Fresh Figs with Feta

Makes 12 pieces (6 servings)

In this quick recipe, the fresh flavour of mint, the saltiness of feta cheese and tartness of herb vinaigrette are carefully and strategically balanced to bring out the delicate flavour of the figs. Tiny edible flowers make this treat irresistible! (A photo appears on page 64.)

6 fresh whole figs, ripe (each: 1¼ oz or 35 g)
2 to 3 tsp (10 to 15 mL) vinaigrette (a mustard herb type), divided
12 tiny cubes (1/3 inch or 0.8 cm) feta cheese
12 fresh mint leaves, rather large

GARNISH (optional)
12 tiny edible flowers or fresh mint leaves

1 Wipe figs clean; cut each in half vertically through stem, leaving stem attached.

2 Arrange fig halves cut side up. Using a finger, press an indentation into centre of each fig half to create a deep depression. (Avoid cracking edges of figs.)

3 Carefully drizzle cut surfaces of fig halves with a few drops of vinaigrette, cautiously cutting it into flesh with tip of a spoon. (**Avoid "soaking" the figs with vinaigrette**. The hors d'oeuvres must not drip.)

4 Add one large mint leaf to surface of each fig half, pressing down at centre to retain indentation.

5 Bathe cubes of feta lightly with vinaigrette. Place one bathed feta cube into mint-lined depression of each fig half and garnish with a tiny edible flower. Store in an airtight container in refrigerator for up to several hours.

PANCAKE COINS WITH GOAT'S CHEESE AND SUN-DRIED TOMATO

Makes 24 pieces (8 to 12 hors d'oeuvre servings)

I believe that it is essential to include at least a few vegetarian choices in your repertoire of recipes. The undisputed, flavour-rich pairing of goat's cheese and sun-dried tomatoes is featured in this quick and easy hors d'oeuvre. Temptingly perched on tiny dark buckwheat pancakes and garnished with pieces of black olive and dainty sprigs of tender young thyme, the tomato and cheese duet offers an exciting complexity of subtle tastes. Although we much prefer this recipe with buckwheat pancakes, regular pancakes may also be used.

2 tsp (10 mL) all-purpose flour
1/2 cup (125 mL) Buckwheat Crêpe Batter (page 204)
  or crêpe batter (e.g., page 205)
1/3 cup (80 mL) soft goat's cheese (unripened)
To taste crushed black peppercorns
1/4 cup (60 mL) julienne-cut sun-dried tomatoes in
  seasoned oil (drained)
4 black olives

GARNISH
24 young tender sprigs of fresh thyme

1 To create a pancake batter, whisk flour into crêpe batter to form a smooth mixture.

2 Working in batches, slowly and carefully drop 1 tsp (5 mL) portions of pancake batter onto a perfectly level nonstick skillet over medium-low heat to form tiny coin pancakes (diameter: about 1 1/4 inch or 3 cm). When batter sets on surface of pancakes, turn pancakes over and cook second side briefly.

3 Transfer pancakes to a plate and stack carefully in piles. If not using immediately, cover stacks with wax paper and store refrigerated in an airtight plastic bag.

4 Cut each olive into 6 vertical pieces. (Discard pits.)

5 To prepare hors d'oeuvres, lay out coin pancakes on a clean surface (with first side cooked "up"). Add a small mound (i.e., 1/2 tsp or 3 mL) of goat's cheese to centre of each pancake; sprinkle lightly with crushed black peppercorns; top with a bit of sun-dried tomato (i.e., 1/3 tsp or 2 mL) and one piece of olive; garnish delicately with a single sprig of thyme.

6 Serve Pancake Coins with Goat's Cheese and Sun-Dried Tomato in a single layer on a large flat plate.

MAKE-AHEAD TIP (STEPS 1,2 & 3):
Tiny pancake coins may be prepared and successfully frozen for up to several weeks. However, to restore their original quality, it is best to reheat them briefly (in their plastic storage bag) in a microwave oven until they are **just warm.**

MAKE-AHEAD TIP: These hors d'oeuvres may be prepared up to several hours in advance, arranged on a plate in a single layer, covered closely but carefully with plastic wrap, slipped into an airtight plastic bag and refrigerated until ready to serve. (**Note:** Verify that the oil from the sun-dried tomatoes has not seeped through or around the pancakes. If necessary, transfer the hors d'oeuvres to another plate before serving.)

SERVING TIP: I like **to include a small cocktail knife on the serving tray to assist guests,** if necessary, in picking up the bite-size pancakes. (**Note:** When personally serving this hors d'oeuvre, I balance the plate in one hand and slip the cocktail knife under the crêpe with the other.)

SALMON GRAVLAX

Sufficient for about 30 hors d'oeuvre sandwiches (10 to 15 hors d'oeuvre servings)

Salmon Gravlax is one of those recipes which is consistently well-received. Everyone would be making it if they only realized how simple it was — you can do it too! House guests feel very spoilt when they are served it for breakfast as an "extra" after a main egg dish.

1 lb (450 g) fresh salmon fillet (deboned),
   with skin attached
2 tbsp (30 mL) granulated sugar
2 tbsp (30 mL) chopped fresh dill weed
2 tbsp (30 mL) vodka
1¹/₂ tsp (8 mL) anise seed
1¹/₂ tsp (8 mL) crushed black peppercorns
1 tsp (5 mL) crushed dried tarragon leaves
1 tsp (5 mL) salt
As required pumpernickel bread or bagels

GARNISH (as desired/required)
smoked salmon cream cheese (commercial)
thin slices of red onion
capers, drained
sprigs of fresh dill
Zesty Ginger Mayonnaise (page 212), optional

1 Place salmon fillet in a flat glass baking dish (slightly larger than fillet) with skin side down. In a small bowl, mix together sugar, chopped dill weed, vodka, anise seed, crushed peppercorns, tarragon and salt; rub mixture into flesh of salmon (upper/flesh side and edges). Cover surface of salmon with plastic wrap and place dish of salmon into a loose plastic bag.

2 Locate a weight (e.g., bricks or flat stone) of suitable size to cover entire surface of salmon; place weight on salmon. (**Note:** Weight is placed on exterior surface of plastic bag that encloses salmon.)

3 Refrigerate for at least 12 hours or up to a couple of days, turning salmon fillet over in dish from time to time.

4 Before serving, remove marinated fillet from dish and drain. (It is not necessary to remove herbs and spices that stick to flesh.) Carefully cut skin* and any dark central fatty areas away from flesh, and discard. Cut marinated fillet into thin vertical slices (thickness: ¹/₅ inch or 0.5 cm).

5 Serve gravlax with pumpernickel bread/bagels, smoked salmon cream cheese, thin slices of red onion, capers, fresh dill and if desired, Zesty Ginger Mayonnaise.

* If desired, reserve the skin and reassemble the sliced Salmon Gravlax on its skin for a dramatic presentation when serving the salmon on its own (i.e., not as sandwiches).

> **"WOW" SERVING TIP (STEP 5):** We adore slices of Salmon Gravlax arranged on pumpernickel bread (or pumpernickel bagels sliced vertically into oblong shapes) already spread with smoked salmon-flavoured cream cheese. The Salmon Gravlax is then garnished with a drizzle of Zesty Ginger Mayonnaise, a small thin ring of red onion, several capers, a sprig of fresh dill and perhaps a few grains of black caviar (e.g., well-drained lumpfish). It's great! (About 5 or 6 bagels cut vertically into ¹/₅ inch or 0.5 cm thick slices and 1¹/₄ cups or 300 mL of smoked salmon cream cheese are required.)

SEDUCTIVE SHRIMP TABBOULEH SANDWICHES

Makes 24 mini pita sandwiches (8 to 12 hors d'oeuvre servings)

Our Middle East exposure has inspired me to assemble these outrageously seductive mini pita halves! Packed with a superb tabbouleh and sautéed peppercorn shrimp, the hors d'oeuvre elevates simple Arabic food to a gourmet level. The combination is guaranteed to be an immediate "crowd pleaser"! (*Note:* **This recipe may be modified to use mini pastry cups or oriental porcelain spoons instead of the mini pita breads.**)

12 mini pita breads (diameter: 2¹/₂ inches or 6 cm)
¹/₄ cup (60 mL) butter, soft
1 cup (250 mL) Pine Nut Tabbouleh (page 121, omit heart of palm) or commercial variety*
1 tbsp (15 mL) Zesty Ginger Mayonnaise (page 212) or mayonnaise
1 tbsp (15 mL) herb garlic butter (e.g., page 205) or butter
12 large shrimp**, peeled and cleaned
To taste salt and crushed black peppercorns

1 Using scissors, cut mini pita breads in half. Butter interior of each pita half (i.e., pocket); add about 1¹/₂ to 2 tsp (8 to 10 mL) of tabbouleh to one side of pita "pocket" (filling pita only ¹/₃ full to avoid drips) and top with ¹/₈ tsp (pinch) of Zesty Ginger Mayonnaise. Set aside; cover with plastic wrap and then a clean damp tea towel.

2 In a preheated medium-size skillet, over medium heat, melt garlic butter and sauté shrimp, seasoning with salt and crushed black peppercorns. Remove shrimp from skillet when barely cooked. (Avoid overcooking.)

3 Cut shrimp in half lengthwise and tuck one half shrimp into each filled pita half on top of mayonnaise. Serve warm or at room temperature.

* Tabbouleh is available fresh at many deli counters, health food stores, Arabic or specialty food stores. **Note:** With a commercial variety (i.e., not the recipe in this book), just before using, place the tabbouleh in a sieve and drain well, gently pressing out excess liquid. Stir in ¹/₄ cup (60 mL) crumbled feta cheese and 1²/₃ tbsp (25 mL) of roasted pine nuts.
** Total weight (after peeling and cleaning): about 4 oz or 115 g.

TIME-SAVING TIP: The ingredient list includes 3 of my Basic Recipes; however, **commercial tabbouleh** may be purchased at many deli counters. The use of butter instead of garlic butter to sauté the shrimp and ordinary mayonnaise offer "compromised" short cuts!

MAKE-AHEAD TIP: If not serving these hors d'oeuvres warm, they may be prepared up to a day in advance. Arrange the filled pockets between damp paper towels in an airtight plastic container and store them refrigerated until 20 minutes before serving. (**Note:** To keep the "pockets" moist, leave them in the container until serving time.)

TIP (ALTERNATIVE TO SHRIMP): Instead of grilled shrimp, use seasoned flaked crabmeat (see: Individual Avocado Crab Pies, page 86), pieces of smoked ham/turkey, cheese/etc. Let your creativity and palate be your guide!

SWEET-AND-SOUR SALMON IN ZUCCHINI CUPS

Makes 12 filled zucchini cups (4 to 6 hors d'oeuvre servings)

For family evenings, I enjoy assembling this quick, inexpensive and tasty hors d'oeuvre. Canned red sockeye salmon drizzled with a sweet-and-sour hot sauce becomes even more delightful when combined with Aïoli Mayonnaise! Served in petit fresh zucchini cups and invitingly crowned with fried vermicelli noodles, the hors d'oeuvre is certain to become a favorite.

½ can* red sockeye salmon (can size: 7½ oz
    or 213 g)
1 to 1½ medium zucchini, fresh and whole (length:
    about 7 inches or 17 cm; diameter: 1½ inches
    or 3.5 cm)
2 tsp (10 mL) sweet-and-sour hot sauce
    (e.g., page 214) or sweet chili sauce**

AÏOLI MAYONNAISE
¼ cup (60 mL) mayonnaise
½ tsp (3 mL) finely chopped fresh garlic

GARNISH (optional)
¼ cup (60 mL) Fried Vermicelli Noodle Straw
    (page 201)

1 Drain salmon; remove bones, skin and dark areas and discard. Break salmon into largish flakes and set aside. (**This may be done up to a day in advance**.)

2 Cut off and discard ends of zucchini. Cut zucchini into ½ inch (1.25 cm) thick slices. With a small spoon (e.g., a ½ tsp or 3 mL round measuring spoon), scoop out centre of 12 zucchini circles to form petit cups. (Avoid cracking edges or piercing bottoms.) Set aside. (**This may be done hours in advance, placed in an airtight container and refrigerated.**)

3 Sprinkle salmon flakes with sweet-and-sour hot sauce and toss. (**Note**: Avoid "soaking" the salmon with sauce. The hors d'oeuvres must not drip.)

4 To make Aïoli Mayonnaise, stir together mayonnaise and garlic.

5 Place a dab (e.g., ⅓ tsp or 2 mL) of Aïoli Mayonnaise in bottom of each zucchini cup; add seasoned salmon (e.g., 1½ tsp or 8 mL) and top with another touch of Aïoli Mayonnaise (¼ tsp or 1 mL).

6 If desired, just before serving, crown each filled zucchini cup with a few threads of Fried Vermicelli Noodle Straw.

* Option: Cooked and cooled fresh salmon.
** This product is available at oriental food stores and some supermarkets.

TIP: Only use canned "red" sockeye salmon.
(**Note**: The subtle flavour and colour of "pink" salmon make the hors d'oeuvres less appealing.)

MAKE-AHEAD TIP (STEP 4): The **Aïoli Mayonnaise** may be prepared weeks in advance and stored refrigerated in an airtight plastic container. (You may want to make it in larger quantities.)

MAKE-AHEAD TIP (UP TO STEP 6): The zucchini cups may be filled hours in advance, covered loosely and refrigerated.

ZIPPY SMOKED OYSTERS ON ORIENTAL SPOONS
(with Zucchini "Noodles")
Makes about 15 spoons (5 to 7 hors d'oeuvre servings)

This unusual hors d'oeuvre features smoked oysters superbly lacquered with a hot mustard glaze and elegantly perched on sesame scented zucchini "noodles". Soya Wasabi Mayonnaise reinforces a definitely Asian touch.

15 oriental porcelain spoons
1 can smoked oysters (can size: 3 oz or 85 g)
1 tbsp (15 mL) **Fiery Hot Mustard Sauce***
1 small zucchini, whole
1 tsp (5 mL) sesame oil
1/2 tsp (3 mL) (total) black and toasted white sesame
    seeds
2 tbsp (30 mL) **Soya Wasabi Mayonnaise****

GARNISH
**Small tender sprigs of fresh dill weed or fresh red bell
    pepper (cut into small chips or threads)**

1 Drain oysters well and rest briefly on paper towels. If necessary, cut larger oysters in half to obtain 15 pieces (i.e., whole and halved oysters). Rub each oyster/piece with a "spot" of Fiery Hot Mustard Sauce (1/16 tsp or 0.3 mL).

2 Grate zucchini (on coarse side of grater) into long "noodle-like" strings. (Makes about 1/2 cup or 125 mL.) Toss with sesame oil and seeds; set aside. **(This may be done hours in advance.)**

3 Place a "drop" of Fiery Hot Mustard Sauce in bottom of individual oriental porcelain spoons. Add about 1 1/2 tsp (8 mL) of sesame zucchini strings to each spoon; top with a dab (1/3 tsp or 2 mL) of Soya Wasabi Mayonnaise and one smoked oyster (or half oyster piece).

4 Garnish each oyster/piece with small tender sprigs of dill weed or bits of red bell pepper.

5 Arrange oyster-filled spoons on a serving tray accompanied by an empty container (e.g., oversized cognac glass) to catch empty spoons.

* To make the Fiery Hot Mustard Sauce, mix together 2 tbsp (30 mL) each of powdered mustard and granulated sugar. Stir in 1 tbsp (15 mL) of hot water and 1 tsp (5 mL) of lemon juice to form a smooth mixture. (Makes almost 3 tbsp or 45 mL of sauce.)
** To make the Soya Wasabi Mayonnaise, mix together 1/4 cup (60 mL) of mayonnaise, 2 tsp (10 mL) of soya sauce and 1/4 tsp (1 mL) of wasabi paste. (Makes about 1/4 cup or 60 mL.)

> **MAKE-AHEAD TIP:** The **Fiery Hot Mustard Sauce*** and **Soya Wasabi Mayonnaise**** may be prepared in advance (e.g., weeks) and kept on hand refrigerated. (**Note:** The **Zippy Smoked Oysters** would then be a "No Time, No Talent" recipe.)

> **"WOW" SERVING TIP FOR SPOONS:** Use circular plates with a small dish at the centre. To stabilize the filled spoons, arrange them around the dish which serves as a necessary hub. Or arrange the spoons in a narrow boat-like tray (e.g., something wider and shallower than an olive tray).

ANISE-WALNUT RAISIN CHUTNEY

Makes almost 2 cups or 500 mL (10 to 16 servings)

Asian sauces and spices bring a unique and alluring flavour to this walnut raisin chutney. Small amounts astonishingly transform any type (or priced) cheese and paté as well as simply grilled and roasted meat or poultry into a gourmet treat. Serve the chutney warm, chilled or at room temperature.

2 tbsp (30 mL) each of hoisin sauce and water (first addition)
1¹/₃ tbsp (20 mL) each of tomato paste and honey
2 tsp (10 mL) each of soya sauce, raspberry vinegar and finely chopped fresh garlic
¹/₄ to ¹/₂ tsp (1 to 3 mL) (Indonesian) hot chili paste
¹/₂ tsp (3 mL) crushed star anise
Pinch ground cinnamon
1¹/₂ cups (375 mL) Sultana raisins
3 tbsp (45 mL) water (second addition)
¹/₂ cup (125 mL) coarsely chopped walnuts
Up to 2 tbsp (30 mL) water (third addition)

1 In a medium-size microwave ovenproof bowl*, stir together all ingredients except raisins, walnuts and second and third additions of water.

2 Cover loosely and place in microwave oven at half heat (i.e., "defrost" mode), stirring occasionally until mixture is hot.

3 Stir in raisins; cover loosely, return to microwave oven and cook at half heat until mixture is hot.

4 Remove from oven, stir in second addition of water and let mixture cool (covered) allowing flavours to develop and blend. Stir in walnuts.

5 Cover and refrigerate at least overnight, stirring occasionally and, if desired, adding up to 2 tbsp (30 mL) of water (third addition). (**Note:** The raisins should be plump, the mixture moist and flavours balanced.)

6 Transfer chutney to well-sealed jars or airtight plastic containers and store refrigerated for up to a couple of months.

* The chutney could be prepared on a stove in a medium-size covered saucepan over low heat.

> **TIP:** As a chutney, the flavours are forceful. It should be consumed in small quantities to enhance certain dishes and foods as mentioned in the introduction/"header".

HORS D'OEUVRES

Asian-Glazed Chicken Morsels/Skewers

Makes about 28 cocktail skewers (8 to 12 hors d'oeuvre servings)

Everyone is certain to enjoy this fast and enticing Asian treat. It is the sesame Balsamic Red Wine Drizzle/Sauce combined with the caramelized hoisin glaze that makes these chicken morsels particularly unique; however, the sauce is not absolutely necessary.

**28 wooden skewers or cocktail sticks
    (length: 4 inches or 10 cm)
1 lb (450 g) chicken fillets*, sinew removed
To taste crushed black peppercorns**

Marinade/Glaze
**1/3 cup (80 mL) hoisin sauce
11/2 tbsp (23 mL) sweet soya sauce/paste
11/2 tbsp (23 mL) unsalted butter, very soft
1/4 tsp (1 mL) (Indonesian) hot chili paste
3/4 tsp (4 mL) finely chopped fresh garlic**

Sauce (optional)
**2 tbsp (30 mL) sesame oil
2 tbsp (30 mL) Balsamic Red Wine Drizzle/Sauce
    (page 213)**

Garnish (optional)
**sprigs of fresh coriander
whole cashew nuts, salted**

1 Soak skewers in water overnight.

2 Cut chicken fillets into 11/2 inch (3.5 cm) pieces.

3 To make the marinade/glaze, stir together hoisin and soya sauces, butter, chili paste and garlic. (Makes 1/2 cup or 125 mL.)

4 Toss chicken with half of marinade/glaze (i.e., 1/4 cup or 60 mL); season with crushed black peppercorns.

5 Thread 2 pieces of chicken onto individual skewers. (***This may be done up to several hours in advance** and stored refrigerated in an airtight plastic container.*)

6 Spray an oven grill pan/tray with oil. Just before serving, arrange skewers (separated and in a single layer) on grill pan.

7 Place chicken 4 inches (10 cm) below a preheated broiler and cook for about 3 minutes until glaze begins to caramelize.

8 Remove tray from oven, turn chicken over and brush remaining marinade/glaze over surface of chicken. Return to oven (under broiler) and cook until chicken is done and glaze begins to caramelize (about another 2 minutes).

9 Meanwhile, whisk sesame oil into Balsamic Red Wine Drizzle/Sauce.

10 Dab top side of chicken very lightly with sauce.

11 If desired, arrange chicken on a bed of fresh coriander and sprinkle with cashew nuts. Serve. (Include on the serving tray a container to catch used skewers.)

* Chicken fillets are the thin tender pieces which tend to fall away from the boneside of the chicken breasts. They may be purchased; however, I simply remove the fillets when deboning chicken breasts, freeze them and make this recipe from my "accumulated" supply. (**Note:** If chicken fillets/"tenders" are not available, thin chicken breasts could be used.)

Make-Ahead Tip (Step 3): The **marinade/glaze** may be prepared weeks in advance and stored refrigerated in a well-sealed jar. (**Note:** I also make this marinade/glaze in larger quantities to have on hand as a time-saving trick.)

"Wow" Tips:
1 For convenience, sometimes I cook the chicken fillets just before guests arrive and serve them at room temperature.
2 Or, serve the chicken morsels cold. (Often, I remove them from the skewers; wrap individual morsels in a leaf of lemon basil and thread them onto toothpicks.)
3 The chicken is also great on its own without the sesame Balsamic Red Wine Drizzle/Sauce.

CHOPSTICKS OF ORIENTAL MARINATED LAMB

Makes about 20 pieces (6 to 8 hors d'oeuvre servings)

"Presentation, presentation, presentation" is a familiar expression and can claim some credit for the amazing popularity of this recipe. The enchanting marinade with a honey, teriyaki and oyster sauce base, plus cooking the lamb to perfection, make the hors d'oeuvre truly memorable. These morsels are quick, easy, certainly tasty and loads of fun! It is rather amusing to see both exuberant children and more restrained adults lust after the lamb-garnished chopsticks with extraordinary zeal! (**Note:** *A photo appears on page 18.*)

6 oz (175 g) lamb tenderloin, sliced (thickness of
    slices: about 1/2 inch or 1.25 cm)*
4 tbsp (60 mL) Oriental Marinade**, divided
20 chopsticks (or skewers)***
3 tbsp (45 mL) Mustard Mint Sauce (page 213) or
    commercial mint sauce

1 Arrange lamb slices in a single layer in a plastic container (or on a plate). Drizzle with only 3 tbsp (45 mL) of Oriental Marinade and allow to rest refrigerated for a couple of hours, turning occasionally.

2 Just before serving, sear slices briefly (both sides) on a preheated well-oiled grill pan or skillet over medium heat. (Total cooking time: about 1 minute. Lamb should definitely be pink in centre.) Immediately transfer to a cutting board.

3 Quickly cut slices into bite-size pieces (i.e., 3/4 inch or 2 cm squares) and toss with remaining 1 tablespoon (15 mL) of unused marinade.

4 Pierce centre of each piece with tip of a chopstick, allowing lamb to rest near tip. Serve promptly along with a small shallow dish of Mustard Mint Sauce and a container to catch the used chopsticks. (Do not heat Mustard Mint Sauce.)

* **Option:** If available, I prefer to use very small lamb tenderloins weighing about 2 oz (60 g) each. Three are sufficient for the recipe. They are particularly convenient as I only need to cut the seared tenderloins crosswise into bite-size pieces (i.e., about 7 per tenderloin).

** To make 1/2 cup (125 mL) of Oriental Marinade, whisk together 3 tbsp (45 mL) of both teriyaki and oyster sauce, 2 tbsp (30 mL) of honey, 1 1/2 tsp (8 mL) of both olive oil and red wine vinegar, 1 tsp (5 mL) of grated fresh gingerroot (peeled) and 1/2 tsp (3 mL) each of grated lemon zest, finely chopped fresh garlic and dried crushed mint. Store the marinade refrigerated in a well-sealed jar for up to several months. (**Note:** I prepare jars of Oriental Marinade in "5 minute" pockets of time to keep on hand for this and other recipes.)
*** The skewers definitely make for a less interesting presentation!

ON-HAND TIP: I use grated fresh gingerroot almost as frequently as chopped fresh garlic. There is always **peeled and grated fresh gingerroot** (e.g., 1/3 cup or 80 mL) on hand in a small plastic container in the freezer. (By the way, I also store grated lemon and orange zest in this manner.)

"WOW" PRESENTATION TIP: To present this hors d'oeuvre, I use a rather tall (e.g., 6 inch or 15 cm) box-like, metal container **half filled with uncooked rice.** The "handle" ends of the chopsticks are poked into the rice to secure them in position with the meat-garnished tips projecting vertically like incense sticks above the container. A second rather tall (i.e., 4 inch or 10 cm), empty, heavy bottom container accompanies the presentation in order to catch the used chopsticks.

Tarragon Scallops on Oriental Porcelain Spoons
(with Orange Zest Mayonnaise and Wild Rice)
Makes 18 spoons (6 to 9 hors d'oeuvre servings)

Are you looking for **one of the best simple hors d'oeuvre recipes** *that can possibly be assembled? For seafood fans, this recipe is a "must"! The orange- and ginger-infused mayonnaise performs the real magic, with a taste of fresh tarragon offering a final burst of "nippy" freshness to delight the palate. Let me assure you that no one will have tasted the combination. It's a "winner"!* (**Note:** *A photo appears on page 16.*)

18 spoons (preferably oriental porcelain)*
9 thick medium-size sea scallops (total weight: 6 oz
    or 175 g)
1/4 cup (60 mL) Orange Zest Mayonnaise (page 211)
1/2 cup (125 mL) cooked tasty wild rice (e.g., page
    207), room temperature
1 tbsp (15 mL) herb garlic butter (e.g., page 205)
    or butter
To taste salt and crushed black peppercorns
1/3 tsp (2 mL) crushed dried tarragon leaves

GARNISH
36 fresh tarragon leaves

1 Drain scallops well; cut each scallop in half horizontally (to create 2 flat round "scallops"); refrigerate if not using immediately. (**This may be done up to a day in advance.**)

2 Before cooking scallops, arrange 18 spoons individually on a tray. In centre of each spoon, add a touch of Orange Zest Mayonnaise (1/8 tsp or a pinch); sprinkle mayonnaise with tasty wild rice (1 tsp or 5 mL); add another touch of Orange Zest Mayonnaise and set aside. (Note: **The spoons may be prepared to this stage up to several hours in advance, covered and refrigerated.** In that case, allow the spoons to rest at room temperature for 10 minutes before adding the seared scallops and serving.)

3 Just before serving, add herb garlic butter to a preheated medium-size nonstick skillet over medium to medium-high heat and immediately add scallops. (Be quick so that scallops sear and butter does not burn. If necessary, remove skillet temporarily from heat.)

Season scallops with salt and crushed black peppercorns and sear (shaking skillet) until first side is slightly caramelized (about 1 minute).

4 Turn scallops, sprinkle with dried crushed tarragon leaves and cook for a few more seconds, shaking skillet. Immediately remove skillet from heat.

(**FLASH:** For a **"vegetarian option"**, replace seasoned and seared, hot scallops with **slices of bocconcini cheese** similar in size and shape to scallops but at room temperature. Continue the recipe exactly as outlined below.)

5 Transfer one seared scallop to each wild rice-garnished spoon, pushing scallop down gently to secure on wild rice. Top each scallop with a drop of Orange Zest Mayonnaise and garnish with 2 fresh tarragon leaves arranged in a "X" formation over scallop.

6 Serve immediately along with an empty container (e.g., oversized cognac glass) to catch empty spoons.**

* If oriental porcelain spoons are not available, use large teaspoons. Oriental porcelain spoons are available in Asian markets/shops (and often Asian supermarkets) as well as many general home interior stores. If you do not have access to these sources, perhaps a local Chinese restaurant would order some for you.
** **Note:** The scallops and the wild rice are eaten directly off the spoons in one mouthful.

> **SHOPPING TIP:** Purchase **medium-size "thick" sea scallops** so that when cut in half horizontally they are luscious and when arranged on spoons, they are not too high to fit comfortably into one's mouth.

Spicy Shrimp with Zesty Ginger Mayonnaise

Makes 18 spicy jumbo shrimp (6 to 9 hors d'oeuvre servings)

*If you are only going to have a limited number of hor d'oeuvres in your culinary repertoire, include this one! Plump shrimp sautéed in herb garlic butter and spiced to perfection are even more devastatingly delicious when dipped into my Zesty Ginger Mayonnaise. You will want to serve this recipe on a regular basis. No one ever tires of it! As a matter of fact, previous guests will probably relish the idea of having them again! The recipe is quick and easy to prepare. (**Note**: Served with rice, it makes a fabulous "no-fuss" main course.)*

18 jumbo shrimp (about 1 lb or 450 g), deveined but unpeeled* (no heads)
2 tbsp (30 mL) herb garlic butter (e.g., page 205)
To taste salt and crushed black peppercorns
²/3 cup (170 mL) Zesty Ginger Mayonnaise (page 212)

1 Peel shrimp, **leaving tails attached**; refrigerate.

2 Just before serving, drain shrimp well.

3 Sauté shrimp in melted garlic butter in a large skillet over medium heat; season according to taste with salt and crushed black peppercorns. As under-side of shrimp becomes pink, turn shrimp. Cook only until barely done. (Avoid overcooking.)

4 Serve immediately with Zesty Ginger Mayonnaise as a dipping sauce. Place a small dish on serving tray to catch discarded tails.

* Note: Starting with unpeeled shrimp allows you to retain the tails during the peeling process. The tails will later serve as "handles" for picking up and dipping the shrimp.

> **Make-Ahead TIP (Step 1): Peel the shrimp**, place them in an airtight plastic container and store them refrigerated for up to a day or frozen for weeks. (I tend to keep several containers of prepared shrimp on hand ready in my freezer.)

> **"WOW" Presentation TIP:** I often serve the shrimp perched on a bed of **deep fried squid ink fettuccine** arranged in a basket, large sea shell or some sort of interesting container. The presentation is fabulous and most appropriate!

In our home, appetizers are usually the first course which is served at the table. Again, strategically, "first impressions count"! I believe it is critical to capture everyone's attention with a clever presentation as well as a particularly tempting recipe and ingredients. Thus, in general, guests "perceive" my appetizers to be "haute cuisine" or "gourmet", which in reality may not necessarily be the case! Many of my appetizers have a refreshing salad dimension; all offer a myriad of delightful experiences, mesmerizing both the eye and palate! Appetizers can be a good indicator of what's to come. "Ça s'announce" as one would say in French!

Note: 🐇   designates a "No Time, No Talent" recipe.

*For this section, the recommended **"BASIC RECIPES" (or commercial substitutes)** to make ahead/have on hand (not mentioned in previous sections) include: **Balsamic Vinegar Syrup, Balsamic Red Wine Drizzle/Sauce, Tasty Wild Rice, Savoury Kasha** and a few **Kataifi Straw Disks**. Trust me, any and all of these rather easy "Basic Recipes" will seriously impress family and guests (even if some are professional chefs)! You will be "raising the bar"!*

APPETIZERS

Individual Avocado Crab Pies

Makes 4 small ¹/3 cup (80 mL) appetizer servings or 2 large ¹/2 cup (125 mL) servings

*Presented in **small ramekin dishes** or **small oriental tea cups**, this recipe makes a wonderfully simple appetizer particularly when served with ice cold vodka! (**FLASH**: I have discovered that a pinch of chili powder and a splash of herb vinaigrette can remarkably enhance the flavour of crabmeat — even the "processed fish" variety! You will find numerous uses for this amazingly tasty mixture.)*

Avocado Cream

1 very large avocado*, ripe
1¹/2 tsp (8 mL) lemon juice
Pinch (to taste) hot chili powder (first addition)
Pinch crushed black peppercorns
To taste salt and granulated sugar
¹/4 cup (60 mL) sour cream

Crab Topping

2 oz or ¹/3 cup (60 g/80 mL) crabmeat, cooked
and flaked
Pinch (to taste) hot chili powder (second addition)
1¹/2 tsp (8 mL) vinaigrette, a mustard herb type
(e.g., page 211 or commercial)

Garnish (optional)

4 sprigs fresh herbs (e.g., tarragon, dill weed)

1 Peel avocado, remove stone and mash flesh.
To make an Avocado Cream, add lemon juice, chili powder (first addition), crushed black peppercorns, salt and sugar; blend thoroughly.

2 Divide Avocado Cream between four small ramekin dishes** (size: ¹/3 cup or 80 mL). Top each dish with 1 tbsp (15 mL) of sour cream, completely sealing in Avocado Cream.

3 Toss crabmeat and chili powder (second addition) together.

4 Just before serving, drizzle seasoned crabmeat with vinaigrette and toss. Divide into 4 portions and arrange one portion in a pile on top of sour cream in each ramekin dish.

5 If desired, garnish each serving with a sprig of fresh herbs.

* About ³/4 cup (180 mL) avocado flesh
** Option: **Small** bowls, glasses or cups of choice

Portion-Size TIP (Step 2): For heartier
appetites, use two ¹/2 cup (125 mL) size
ramekin dishes and adjust the recipe
accordingly.

Make-Ahead TIP: Steps 1, 2 and 3 can
be done hours (even a day) in advance and
refrigerated. (**Note:** Store the crab mixture in
a small airtight plastic container and cover the
individual ramekin dishes with plastic wrap.)

"WOW" Ice Cold Vodka TIP: In our
home, there is always a bottle of ice cold vodka
in the freezer. We serve/enjoy a little "shot"
with caviar (i.e., any type), crab and smoked
fish. This Dickenson tradition was inspired by
our stay in Moscow decades ago.

SEDUCTIVE SUSHI ROLLS

Makes about 24 to 30 pieces

My Seductive Sushi Rolls include all those tastes for which I crave in every piece of sushi! Crabmeat, avocado, carrot, cucumber, wasabi and sesame seeds. The myriad of textures, colours and flavours is outrageously appealing! Of course, soya sauce is a must for dipping, with plenty of pickled ginger and extra wasabi also being critical accompaniments. To be honest, if you can afford "genuine" red caviar, sprinkle some over the arrangement of ingredients before you roll the sushi.

1 bamboo sushi rolling mat*
2 sheets toasted nori (seaweed), each: 8 x 7 inches or
    20 x 17 cm
1¹/2 cups (375 mL) cooked sushi rice (e.g., page 207),
    room temperature
¹/2 tsp (3 mL) wasabi paste, divided
2 oz or ¹/3 cup (60 g/80 mL) crabmeat, separated into
    long flakes
¹/2 medium avocado (peeled with pit removed), cut
    into ¹/3 inch (0.8 cm) wide wedges
²/3 oz or ¹/4 cup (20 g/60 mL) julienne-cut carrots
    (peeled)
²/3 oz or ¹/4 cup (20 g/60 mL) julienne-cut English
    cucumber (i.e., only unpeeled exterior edges)
2 tsp (10 mL) toasted white sesame seeds
drops of egg white

GARNISH
3 to 4 tbsp (45 to 60 mL) soya sauce
3 tbsp (45 mL) pickled ginger
2 tsp (10 mL) wasabi paste (extra to above)
sprigs of fresh herbs (e.g., lemon basil), optional

1 Place bamboo mat on counter with bamboo sticks parallel to edge of counter. Arrange one nori sheet on mat with shiny side down and long edges in a horizontal position.

2 Using wet fingers and a small damp metal spatula, press ³/4 cup (180 mL) of cooked sushi rice evenly over nori to within 1 inch (2.5 cm) of top edge.

3 One-third inch (0.8 cm) from bottom edge, spread a thin horizontal line of wasabi paste (¹/8 tsp or a pinch) over rice.

4 Using half the ingredients, arrange crabmeat in a straight line over wasabi and top with avocado. Add a row of carrot and finally a row of cucumber.

5 Rub a thin layer of wasabi (¹/8 tsp or a pinch) over ingredients. Sprinkle ingredients and exposed rice with sesame seeds (1 tsp or 5 mL).

6 With wet fingers, hold filling ingredients in place while rolling mat (from bottom edge) tightly over them. Using mat to assist, continue to roll and squeeze, compressing ingredients securely together within roll. (Peel mat away as roll forms.) Brush exposed edge of nori with egg white to seal roll.

7 When completed, use mat to press and verify roll is evenly shaped. Push any ingredients that might have escaped at ends back into roll.

8 Repeat procedure with remaining ingredients to make another roll. If not serving immediately, store sushi rolls refrigerated and covered loosely with wax paper for up to 10 hours.

9 When ready to serve, trim ends with a wet sharp knife. Cut rolls into slices (thickness: ¹/2 inch or 1.25 cm), wetting knife blade between slices.

10 Serve sushi slices well separated in a single layer. Arrange a small bowl of soya sauce along with some pickled ginger and a little wasabi paste to accompany sushi. Garnish with sprigs of fresh herbs if desired. (**Note:** Serve within several hours or at least the day of preparation.)

* Bamboo sushi rolling mats are available at most kitchen supply stores and oriental markets.

> **TIP:** *Sushi* is easy to prepare. Perhaps the biggest challenge is to make the rolls tight. However, that will come with practice.

PROSCIUTTO-WRAPPED WASABI PEARS

Makes 4 servings

Whenever possible, I delight in adding a bit of easy pizzazz to a meal. The textures, colours and flavours orchestrated into this appetizer are dramatic and irresistible! **Basically an "assembly" recipe, it is ideal when hosting a few last minute guests**.

4 whole ripe pears (e.g., Bosc, each: 4 oz or 115 g), peeled and cored with stems attached
2 tsp (10 mL) wasabi paste*, divided
4 tbsp (60 mL) soft unripened goat's cheese (first addition)
4 slices (thin) prosciutto ham (total weight: 3 oz or 85 g)
8 fresh young sprigs of coriander

GARNISH
2 tbsp (30 mL) soft unripened goat's cheese** (second addition)
2 tbsp (30 mL) sieved blackberry jam

1 Just before serving, rub all interior and exterior surfaces of each pear with wasabi paste (about 1/4 tsp or 1 mL per pear).

2 Fill cavity of individual pears with 1 tbsp (15 mL) of goat's cheese.

3 Place each stuffed pear in centre of an oversized dinner plate; wrap pear elegantly with one slice of prosciutto ham.

4 Tuck sprigs of young coriander dramatically into folds of ham at pear stem.

5 To complete each presentation, garnish plates artistically with a small scoop of goat's cheese (1 1/2 tsp or 8 mL) and drizzles of sieved blackberry jam (1 1/2 tsp or 8 mL).

6 At (or near) top of plate, add an individual drop of wasabi to be consumed as (or if) desired.

* Available in oriental food stores, many specialty food stores and supermarkets

** **Note:** Frequently I pop the "remaining" portions of a package of soft unripened goat's cheese into an airtight plastic bag and freeze it for future use.

MAKE-AHEAD TIP: Peel the pears, keeping the stems intact. Working carefully from the base of each pear, remove the blossom end and the core to create a central cavity. Trim the bottoms so that the pears stand securely in an upright position. This can be done hours in advance. Wrap the prepared pears individually and closely with plastic wrap.

TIP: Wasabi loses its "spark" if it is applied to the pears more than 10 minutes or so before serving. Adding an extra drop of wasabi paste to each plate before it is served assists in compensating for any reduction in the strength of the wasabi applied to the pears.

ALTERNATIVE-USE TIP: Add young salad leaves, more ham and cheese, and serve the recipe as a creative **main course for a brunch or very light casual lunch**.

SMOKED SALMON CRISPY STACKS
(with Avocado and Mango)
Makes 4 servings

Wait until you taste this! Smoked salmon stacked colourfully together with ripe avocado and mango is a curious but beautifully delicate marriage of flavours and textures. Unquestionably, the drops of "highly charged" lemon oil and the puzzling Kataifi Straw Disks contribute unusually clever touches to this recipe. **Note:** *Our many years of Middle East postings and my fascination with the Arabic "thread-like" pastry (i.e., kataifi) have inspired me to "come up with" my very versatile "Kataifi Straw Disks"!*

8 oz (225 g) smoked salmon, sliced
1 large avocado, ripe
1 fresh mango, ripe
4 Kataifi Straw Disks* (page 209)
1/3 cup (80 mL) vinaigrette, a mustard herb type
   (e.g., page 211 or commercial)

GARNISH (optional)
4 Petit "Plate" Bouquets of Fresh Herbs (e.g., chervil,
   coriander, dill) or Shoots** (page 202)
1/4 tsp (1 mL) lemon oil

1 Divide smoked salmon slices into 8 equal portions; set aside.

2 Cut avocado vertically in half and remove pit. Keeping entire half of avocado intact, carefully remove peel. Cut each avocado half vertically into large oval slices (thickness: 1/3 inch or 0.8 cm). Choose 4 of the largest slices and set others aside for another purpose.

3 Peel mango. Similarly cut mango vertically into large thick oval slices on either side of pit. Choose 4 attractive slices. Leaving top of slice attached, cut each of the 4 mango slices in a fan-like manner.

4 Use 4 dinner plates to make 4 individual servings. For each serving, place one portion of smoked salmon in a circular fashion (diameter: 4 inches or 10 cm) in centre of each plate.

5 Add 1 Kataifi Straw Disk; drizzle with 2 tsp (10 mL) of vinaigrette; add another portion of smoked salmon.

6 Top with a slice of avocado and then a slice of mango.

7 Drizzle stack with more vinaigrette (about 2 1/2 tsp or 13 mL).

8 If desired, garnish stacks with Petit "Plate" Bouquets of Fresh Herbs or Shoots.

9 Cautiously and sparingly add only 3 drops of lemon oil discreetly to each plate.

10 Serve immediately (ensuring that Kataifi Straw Disks retain their crispness).

* Option: Use 1 cup (250 mL) of mâche rosettes (or similar salad leaves) per serving, which makes this a "No Time, No Talent" recipe.
** e.g., young snow peas, sunflower, asparagus, corn

MAKE-AHEAD TIP: The ingredients for the recipe may be assembled and portioned out as required in advance, ready for quick last minute assembly.

MAKE-AHEAD TIP: The **Katifi Straw Disks** are very simple to make and are definitely included in my "Basic Recipes". When I have a free half hour, I prepare them by the dozen. They retain their quality for weeks.

SHOPPING TIP: When **avocados** and/or **mangoes** are required for a recipe, I try to purchase them about 5 days in advance. If they are not perfectly ripened, I place them in a dark cupboard and refrigerate them when they have done so. My second trick is to always buy at least 50% more than what is required of both because the quality may not be satisfactory once I remove the skins.

Smoked Salmon Kasha/Wild Rice Martinis

Makes 4 servings

"WOW" Factor: This most original and tasty recipe **placed first** in the kasha category in The Birkett Mills International Association of Culinary Professionals' buckwheat competition.

Served in martini glasses*, these martinis (pictured on page 84) undoubtedly capture everyone's attention! Just think what a universally accepted treat the combination of smoked salmon, cream cheese and pumpernickel bread is. Actually, there is a certain likeness between pumpernickel bread and kasha. And, my Lemon Mustard Sour Cream Sauce is an extravagant evolution of the cream cheese or crème fraîche which is frequently served with smoked salmon. Although our family may prefer the kasha component, wild rice offers a truly "Canadian" experience!
Note: Once the kasha (or wild rice) is prepared, this is basically an "assembly" recipe. No stress!!

5 oz (150 g) smoked salmon (sliced), divided
1 cup (250 mL) Savoury Kasha (page 206) or Tasty
    Wild Rice (page 207), room temperature or chilled
1¹/2 tsp (8 mL) grated lemon zest
1 tbsp (15 mL) lemon juice
1 tbsp (15 mL) small capers

Lemon Mustard Sour Cream Sauce
¹/2 cup (125 mL) sour cream
1¹/2 tbsp (23 mL) Dijon mustard
2 tsp (10 mL) grated lemon zest
1 drop yellow food colouring, optional

1 To make Lemon Mustard Sour Cream Sauce, stir together sour cream, mustard, lemon zest and food colouring until well blended. (Makes about ¹/2 cup or 125 mL.)

2 Cut slices of smoked salmon into bite-size pieces; divide into 4 portions. (Makes about 1 cup/250 mL.)

3 Place 1 tbsp (15 mL) of Savoury Kasha (room temperature or chilled) in bottom of each of 4 martini glasses*; level surface of kasha. Carefully spread 1 tsp (5 mL) of Lemon Mustard Sour Cream Sauce over kasha in each glass and add about ¹/3 of one portion of smoked salmon.

4 To each glass, add 2 tbsp (30 mL) of kasha and then 2 tsp (10 mL) of sauce, creating a "pile" effect.

Continue "layering" with another 1 tbsp (15 mL) of kasha and 1 tsp (5 mL) of sauce before crowning with remaining portion of smoked salmon.

5 Garnish salmon artistically with lemon zest. If not serving until later, hood individual glasses with plastic wrap and refrigerate until 15 minutes before serving. (Note: **The glasses may be filled up to several hours before serving.**)

6 Just before serving, drizzle each Smoked Salmon Kasha Martini with a touch of lemon juice and garnish with capers.

* **Option:** Other types of stemmed glasses or dishes

Make-Ahead Tip (Step 1): The **Lemon Mustard Sour Cream Sauce** may be stored refrigerated for up to 2 weeks.

"WOW" Trick (Steps 3 and 4): If desired, for convenience in layering, place a 1 inch (2.5 cm) tall cylinder (diameter: 2¹/2 inch or 6 cm) over salmon. (**Note:** A cookie cutter without a handle or a ring cut carefully from a small soft plastic yogurt container will do.) Remove the ring before adding the garnish.

Handling Tip (Step 5): If refrigerating the Smoked Salmon Kasha Martinis and the original box holding the martini glasses is available, arrange the filled glasses in it.

Tuna Carpaccio
(with Wasabi Crème Fraîche and Caviar)

Makes 4 servings

Exquisitely delicate with flashes of hot and creamy plus the "tender" crunch of caviar, this tuna carpaccio turns every host and hostess into a star chef!

1¹/₂ tsp (8 mL) wasabi paste, divided
3 tbsp (45 mL) crème fraîche (commercial or
    page 204)
8 oz (225 g)* fresh tuna steak(s), skin removed and
    frozen (thickness: at least 1 inch or 2.5 cm)
3 tbsp (45 mL) vinaigrette, a mustard herb type
    (e.g., page 211 or commercial)
1¹/₂ tbsp (23 mL) black caviar
    (e.g., well-drained lumpfish)

Garnish
fresh dill weed
fresh chive stems/blooms, optional

1 Carefully fold ¹/₂ tsp (3 mL) of wasabi paste into crème fraîche. Place wasabi crème fraîche in a very small (i.e., tiny) plastic bag; close bag with an elastic and snip off just a small portion of one bottom corner to create a "piping bag"; set aside.

2 On a large cutting board and using a very sharp straight-edged knife, "shave" frozen tuna steak(s) into paper-thin (i.e., virtually transparent) slices. (Try to keep slices whole.) Transfer slices (as they are shaved) directly to 4 individual oversized dinner plates, arranging slices in a slightly overlapping manner to form a skin-like layer on plates.

3 Drizzle each portion of tuna with 2 tsp (10 mL) of vinaigrette; spread vinaigrette to evenly coat entire surface of tuna. (**Note: *This may be done up to several hours in advance of serving.* **Cover the surface of the tuna closely with plastic wrap and refrigerate.)

4 Just before serving, drizzle surface of tuna on each plate in a "zig-zag" manner with 1¹/₂ to 2 tsp (8 to 10 mL) of wasabi crème fraîche.

5 Randomly add dots (e.g., 5) of caviar (total: about 1 tsp or 5 mL per serving) to crème fraîche.

6 Garnish surface of tuna with dainty plumes of fresh dill weed. If desired, add chive stems/blooms.

7 Decorate rim of plates with a few minuscule dots of wasabi paste. Serve promptly.

* 6 oz (175 g) is sufficient for 4 servings; however, a slightly larger quantity makes the "shaving" process easier and less dangerous.

BREADED SCALLOP SALAD
(with Sesame Balsamic Vinegar Sauce)
Makes 4 servings

Although usually reserved for entertaining, I frequently make this appetizer salad as a "treat" for my husband and myself. We adore it! But, so do we adore anything drizzled with my sesame balsamic vinegar sauce! Crusty breaded bay scallops scattered on an array of crisp young salad leaves are definitely on that list. **With the sauce on hand, the recipe takes only a matter of minutes to prepare.**

1/2 cup (125 mL) dry bread crumbs
1/4 to 1/3 tsp (1 to 2 mL) ground nutmeg
To taste salt and crushed black peppercorns
1/3 cup (80 mL) lightly spiced flour (e.g., page 206)
1 to 2 eggs, lightly beaten
7 oz (200 g) bay scallops, very well drained
5 cups (1.25 litres) fresh mesclun leaves or young
    salad leaves
1 1/3 tbsp (20 mL) vegetable oil
1 1/3 tbsp (20 mL) butter

SAUCE
3 tbsp (45 mL) Balsamic Vinegar Syrup (page 204)
3 tbsp (45 mL) sesame oil

GARNISH (optional)
**fresh small edible flowers (e.g., purple Johnny
    Jump-Ups)**

1 In a flat bowl, season bread crumbs to taste with nutmeg, and lightly with salt and crushed black peppercorns. Arrange spiced flour and lightly beaten egg separately in 2 other flat bowls.

2 Working in batches, toss well-drained scallops with spiced flour, bathe in beaten egg and then toss with seasoned bread crumbs. Arrange breaded scallops on a parchment paper-lined tray; cover loosely with wax paper and refrigerate for at least 30 minutes to assist coating to stick more securely to scallops.

3 Just before serving, arrange mesclun on 4 individual dinner plates or a platter.

4 Heat oil and butter in a large skillet over medium-high heat. Add breaded scallops; fry until coating is golden brown and scallops are done (about 3 minutes). Drain on paper towels.

5 Artistically and gently drop scallops over mesclun leaves.

6 Whisk together Balsamic Vinegar Syrup and sesame oil; drizzle over salad according to taste.

7 If desired, sprinkle salad lightly with salt and crushed black peppercorns before garnishing with edible flowers. Decorate plates/platter with drops of remaining sauce.

8 Serve immediately.

> **MAKE-AHEAD TIP (STEPS 1 & 2):** The **scallops** may be "breaded" up to a day in advance.

BALSAMIC-GLAZED SEARED PÂTÉ ON LENTILS

Makes 4 servings

To confirm how "the ordinary" can become "extraordinary", I suggest you check out this recipe! It is quick, tasty and definitely impressive. Petit mounds of flavourful cooked lentils are crowned with crisply crusted squares of seared pâté and seductively drizzled with a thick "fruity" Balsamic Red Wine Sauce. **All the components for the recipe may be prepared in advance** *and kept on hand in the refrigerator or freezer.* **This appetizer then becomes one of my favourite "N/N" (No Time, No Talent) recipes,** *be it for family meals or elegant entertaining.*

½ cup (125 mL) dried lentils (black or brown)
1½ to 2 tsp (8 to 10 mL) herb garlic butter
 (e.g., page 205) or butter
To taste salt and crushed black peppercorns
5 oz (150 g) pâté (of choice)*, cut into 12 squares
 (1¼ inch or 3 cm; thickness: ⅓ inch or 0.8 cm)
2 tbsp (30 mL) all-purpose flour
¼ cup (60 mL) Balsamic Red Wine Drizzle/Sauce
 (page 213)

GARNISH
½ cup (125 mL) fresh "baby" basil or watercress
 leaves**, optional

1 Rinse lentils, removing any foreign material. Place in a small saucepan; add enough water to cover lentils by a least 2 inches or 5 cm. Bring water to a boil; immediately reduce heat to low, cover and simmer gently until tender (about 10 to 12 minutes). **Note:** Avoid adding salt to lentils before they are completely cooked. (Salt tends to toughen cooking lentils.)

2 Remove saucepan from heat. Drain lentils well; toss with herb garlic butter, salt and crushed black peppercorns. (Makes about 1¼ cups or 300 mL.)

3 Coat all exterior surfaces of pâté lightly with flour; place on a wax paper-lined tray and refrigerate for at least 30 minutes (so that flour clings more effectively to pâté).

4 For individual servings, shortly before serving, artistically arrange 3 mounds (1 tbsp or 15 mL each) of cooked lentils on each of 4 dinner (or oversized) plates.

5 Immediately before serving, in a preheated nonstick medium skillet over medium-high heat, quickly sear flour-coated pâté squares (for a matter of seconds per side) until exterior is golden brown and slightly crisp. Promptly place one square of seared pâté directly on top of each mound of lentils.

6 Drizzle individual squares of pâté with Balsamic Red Wine Sauce (i.e., ½ tsp or 3 mL) and top with small basil or watercress leaves.

7 Drizzle vacant spaces of each plate with touches of extra sauce (i.e., total 1½ tsp or 8 mL per plate).

* **Options:** chicken, duck, turkey, pork. I prefer a cognac peppercorn type.
** **Option:** touches of fresh herbs (e.g., chervil, dill weed, parsley) or delicate curly endive

---

MAKE-AHEAD TIP (STEPS 1 & 2): Cook the lentils, place them in an airtight plastic container and store them refrigerated for up to a few days or frozen for months.

TIME-SAVING TIP (STEP 3): Pâté squares may be **coated with flour** and refrigerated up to a day in advance. (**Note:** I actually prepare several "batches" of floured pâté squares and store them in the freezer for up to several weeks. The squares are thawed in the refrigerator before searing.)

IRRESISTIBLE TEASED CATFISH ORIENTAL SALAD

Makes 4 servings

We are all excited by unusual and delectable appetizers which will have guests raving. You can count on this warm appetizer salad to meet that criteria! First of all, guests are absolutely intrigued by the word "teased" and playfully inquire how I tease a catfish. Secondly, the unparalleled multi-dimensional harmony achieved in the salad makes it irresistible — spicy and mellow flavours with soft, crisp and chewy textures, as well as appealing colours! **Although the recipe requires only limited culinary talent, it generates accolades normally reserved for "accomplished" executive chefs!**

12 oz (340 g) Cajun* spiced catfish fillets
1 tbsp (15 mL) vegetable oil
2 cups (500 mL) shredded Romaine lettuce
3 tbsp (45 mL) Honey Mustard Mayonnaise (page 211)
2 tbsp (30 mL) sweet-and-sour hot sauce
   (e.g., page 214)
1 cup (250 mL) julienne-cut mango flesh
   (well ripened)

GARNISH
4 sprigs of coriander
clusters fresh basil leaves (e.g., purple or purple
   bush), optional

1 Using tines of a fork, tear flesh off fish fillet in a "teased" fashion. (Discard any remaining sinew-like material.) Refrigerate until ready to use.

2 Heat oil in a large skillet over medium-high heat. Add "teased" catfish; stir constantly, separating flesh into small pieces (resembling large crumbs); fry until just cooked.

3 Just before serving, for individual portions, arrange 1/2 cup (125 mL) of shredded lettuce on each plate; toss with Honey Mustard Mayonnaise (about 1 tsp or 5 mL) and drizzle with only a touch (about 1/3 to 1/2 tsp or 2 to 3 mL) of sweet-and-sour hot sauce.

4 Divide warm(ed) catfish into four portions. Scatter one portion on top of lettuce on each plate; drizzle carefully with sweet-and-sour hot sauce (about 1/2 tsp or 3 mL); crown attractively with mango and drizzle with another touch (about 1/4 tsp or 1 mL) of sweet-and-sour hot sauce.

5 Garnish each salad with sprigs of fresh coriander and, if desired, with a cluster of fresh basil leaves.

6 Drizzle plates artistically with Honey Mustard Mayonnaise.

* If Cajun spiced catfish is not available, use Cajun spice to season (fairly generously) regular catfish. (**Note:** To reduce the "zip" when using already seasoned catfish, scrape away a portion of the spice mixture sprinkled on the fillets to suit your taste and discard it.)

> **MAKE-AHEAD TIP (STEP 1):** I always **"tease"** my **catfish** in advance and store it refrigerated in an airtight container for up to a day.

> **MAKE-AHEAD TIP (STEP 2):** The teased catfish may be fried shortly before guests arrive and set aside.

ALTERNATIVE-USE TIP: The recipe can also be served in small portions on oriental spoons as **an hors d'oeuvre**, or in larger quantities as a **main course for a brunch/lunch**. (**Note:** I freeze any excess cooked teased catfish to have on hand to make last minute hors d'oeuvres.)

I find making soup therapeutic! From time to time, on a quiet Saturday or Sunday morning, I prepare quantities of it and put it in the freezer. Virtually all the soups featured in this book freeze extremely well. Therefore, soups are an easy addition to a menu in our home.

Now, when it comes to soups, here is the perfect opportunity to **make the ordinary extraordinary**! I enjoy the challenge of giving my soups a touch of "contrived profile", which inevitably makes the soup course "exciting". They are poured into a variety of bowls, demitasse cups, martini glasses or shot glasses. Soups arrive at our table frothed, as an eclipse, in a cappuccino style, etc. They are set on oriental stands, small framed mirrors or liners of contrasting colours and shapes. A good soup becomes exquisite (even exotic) when creatively garnished with chopped nuts, drizzles of heavy cream, skewers of grilled shrimp, handsome crab claws or sprigs of fresh herbs.

Few realize the versatility of soups. Small quantities of puréed soups, hot or cold, presented in sake cups or shot glasses, add unexpected charm to a drinks party or cocktail reception. Guests with a drink in one hand can easily manage a "canapé soup" with the other. They also can be the perfect "easy" addition to a simple coffee (or tea) gathering. And to transform cold fruit soups into extravagant desserts, just pour them into flat bowls or tall "sundae" glasses and garnish with plump berries and/or scoops of luscious ice cream!

Note: 🐇 designates a "No Time, No Talent" recipe.

---

*For this section, the only recommended "BASIC RECIPE" to have on hand is **Basic Sugar Syrup** (for balancing flavours of sweet soups). However, continuous "on hand" supplies of **finely chopped fresh garlic** as well as **peeled and grated fresh ginger** seriously reduce the time I spend on meal preparation in general!*

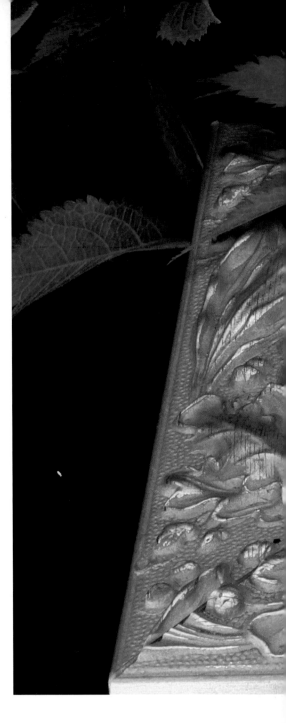

Sorrel Soup/Cappuccino (page 107)

SOUPS

GINGER STRAWBERRY SOUP (FROTHED)

Makes about 2¹/₂ cups (625 mL) or 7 to 8 servings of about ¹/₃ cup (80 mL) or
10 to 40 canapé servings

First, regardless of the guest list (children definitely included) my Ginger Strawberry Soup is certain to be a huge success! Secondly, regardless of the time of year or strawberries used, the additions of strawberry jam, cherry brandy and sugar syrup ensure that the final product will be luscious with rich strawberry flavour. There is always Ginger Strawberry Soup on hand in our freezer.

1 lb (450 g) fresh strawberries
3 tbsp (45 mL) coconut cream (canned)
3 tbsp (45 mL) strawberry jam
1 tbsp (15 mL) cherry brandy
¹/₄ cup (60 mL) milk
¹/₄ cup (60 mL) heavy cream (35% fat)
2 tsp (10 mL) finely chopped ginger in syrup*
1 to 2 tbsp (15 to 30 mL) basic sugar syrup
    (e.g., page 208), optional
1 to 1¹/₂ cups (250 to 375 mL) low fat milk (cold),
    optional

GARNISH (optional)
As required fresh strawberries or ground cherries

1 Rinse strawberries under cold running water; drain well; remove and discard stems; cut berries in half.

2 Place strawberries, coconut cream, jam and cherry brandy in a blender; purée until smooth.

3 Remove strawberry mixture from blender; add milk, heavy cream and ginger; stir well. Adjust flavours if necessary. (For a sweeter soup, add basic sugar syrup to taste. To make the soup creamier, add an additional touch of heavy cream if desired, starting with 1 tbsp or 15 mL and gradually adding more according to taste.) If possible, chill soup for at least 2 hours before serving to allow flavours to develop.

4 Stir well before serving. For each regular "meal" size serving, pour ¹/₃ cup (80 mL) of soup into individual martini glasses. If desired, froth** low fat milk and top each glass with ¹/₄ cup (60 mL) of frothed milk (cold).

5 Set each filled glass on a plate garnished with a fresh strawberry or ground cherry. Serve immediately.

* Available commercially
** If the soup is to have a frothed milk topping, a milk frother is required. **Various types of milk frothers are available** at hardware and/or kitchen stores, from inexpensive plunger types and hand-held battery operated models to more expensive electrical jug types. **Note:** The frothed milk for this particular recipe should be cold. (Many electrical models only produce a warm froth.)

MAKE-AHEAD TIP: Placed in an airtight container, the soup may be stored for up to 3 days or frozen for months. (**Note:** After it has been thawed, if necessary, place the previously frozen soup in a blender and process it until it is smooth.)

ALTERNATIVE-GARNISHING TIP (STEP 4): The soup may also be garnished with whipped cream, crème fraîche or sour cream, or it may be served ungarnished.

"WOW" TIP: I frequently arrange the soup in martini glasses for a dinner party, lunch or brunch. Sometimes I offer it as a "canapé" soup (see page 14) at a reception, garden, tea, coffee or drinks party (e.g., 3 tbsp/45 mL in individual shot glasses or 1 tbsp/15 mL in individual sake cups). Adding frothed milk carries this simple soup to an amazingly new level in terms of presentation, taste and sensual appeal!

SOUPS

HEART OF PALM CUCUMBER SOUP

Makes about 3 cups (750 mL) or 6 servings of ¹/₂ cup (125 mL) each

For originality in a quick cold soup, try this intriguing duet. Although refreshingly spiked with coriander and dill weed, it is the heart of palm and touch of wasabi that give my cucumber soup an unusual twist. The distinctive flavour is remarkably balanced by a healthy splash of heavy cream. The result is superb!

1 can (size: 14 fl oz or 398 mL) heart of palm
1 lb (450 g) English cucumber, washed and unpeeled
2 tbsp (30 mL) fresh coriander leaves, packed
¹/₃ to ¹/₂ tsp (2 to 3 mL) wasabi paste
To taste salt and crushed black peppercorns
2 tbsp (30 mL) finely chopped fresh dill weed
1¹/₂ tsp (8 mL) maple syrup
¹/₃ cup (80 mL) heavy cream (35% fat), optional

1 Drain brine (i.e., liquid) from heart of palm into a bowl and set brine aside.

2 Take only 6 oz (175 g) of drained heart of palm and set remainder aside for another purpose.

3 Coarsely chop heart of palm and cucumber; place in a blender along with ¹/₂ cup (125 mL) reserved brine.

4 Add coriander leaves and wasabi paste; process until well blended. Remove soup from blender; add salt and crushed black peppercorns to taste; stir in dill weed and maple syrup. Refrigerate to chill.

5 Before serving, stir heavy cream into soup.

(MACADAMIA) MANGO SOUP

Makes about 3 cups (750 mL) or 6 servings of 1/2 cup (125 mL) each

Our postings to Egypt and Indonesia introduced us to one of our favorite fruits, mango. Its versatility is as vast as one's imagination. In my pursuit of an extravagant soup with true mango flavour, I found that strategic additions of heavy cream, white wine, orange juice, pear liqueur, ginger in syrup and coconut extract did the trick! With the soft crunch of chopped macadamia nuts, the soup is exquisite.

*Include it in a lunch or dinner menu, or serve it as a canapé soup in shot glasses or tiny cups (e.g., sake cups) at finger food events. (**Note:** A photo appears on page 38.)*

2 very large* mangoes
2/3 cup (170 mL) heavy cream (35% fat)
1/2 cup (125 mL) white wine
3 tbsp (45 mL) orange juice
2 to 3 tbsp (30 to 45 mL) pear liqueur
1/4 cup (60 mL) coarsely chopped macadamia nuts, divided
1 tbsp (15 mL) finely chopped ginger in syrup**
2 drops*** coconut extract
2 to 6 tsp (10 to 30 mL) basic sugar syrup (e.g., page 208), optional

1 Peel mangoes, cut away flesh and discard pit.

2 Coarsely chop mango flesh and purée in a blender. Sieve into a medium-size bowl to remove any fibers.

3 Stir in cream, wine, orange juice and pear liqueur.

4 Stir in only 2 tbsp (30 mL) of macadamia nuts as well as ginger and coconut extract. (If necessary, add sugar syrup according to taste.)

5 Place in an airtight plastic container and refrigerate overnight or at least for several hours, allowing flavours to develop.

6 Serve Macadamia Mango Soup chilled. If desired, garnish with remaining chopped macadamia nuts.

* Each: 12 oz or 340 g. The mangoes must be well ripened.
** Available in health food stores, specialty food stores and some supermarkets.
*** i.e., less than 1/8 tsp or a pinch. Avoid adding too much extract.

GINGER SQUASH SOUP
(with Almond Liqueur)

*Makes 5 cups (1.25 litres) or 8 servings of about ²/3 cup (170 mL) each or
10 servings of ¹/2 cup (125 mL) each*

*If a refined soup is to be on the menu, seriously consider
this squash soup with its pleasing hints of fruit, nut and
spice. Extremely simple to prepare, the recipe can be
garnished to suit a specific menu, occasion or personal
tastes. (**Note:** In the summer, I love it "icy"cold.)*

1 small butternut squash (i.e., 2¹/4 lbs or 1 kg)
1 medium-large pear (5 oz or 150 g), peeled and cored
1 medium-small onion (about 2¹/2 oz or 75 g), peeled
1 tbsp (15 mL) crushed chicken bouillon cubes
    (or powder)
2 cups (500 mL) boiling water
1¹/2 to 2 tsp (8 to 10 mL) peeled and grated
    fresh gingerroot
¹/4 tsp (1 mL) salt
¹/3 to ¹/2 cup (80 to 125 mL) heavy cream (35% fat)
¹/4 tsp (1 mL) ground nutmeg
¹/8 tsp (4 drops) almond extract
To taste crushed black peppercorns
1 to 1¹/2 tbsp (15 to 23 mL) almond-flavoured
    liqueur (optional)*

GARNISH (3 choices, optional)
3 tbsp (45 mL) toasted sliced almonds (skins on) and
    sprigs of fresh mint or
sautéed and seasoned escargots and grains of cooked
    wild rice or
seared scallops and sprigs of fresh tarragon

1 Peel squash; remove and discard soft pulp and
seeds. (This will leave/give about 1¹/2 lbs or 675 g of
squash "flesh".)

2 Coarsely chop squash, pear and onion and place in
a medium-size saucepan.

3 Dissolve crushed chicken bouillon cubes in hot
water; add to saucepan along with ginger and salt.
Bring to a boil over medium-high heat; reduce heat to
low; simmer until squash is tender. Remove from heat;
cool until safe to handle.

4 In a blender, purée squash mixture in 2 batches
until smooth.

5 Return soup to a clean saucepan; stir in heavy
cream, nutmeg, almond extract, crushed black
peppercorns and, if desired, almond liqueur. (If
necessary, add a touch of water to bring total volume
to 5 cups or 1.25 litres and adjust flavours to taste.)

6 Serve soup hot, at room temperature or chilled.
Garnish according to taste and occasion.

* The almond liqueur gives the soup a discreet depth of flavour,
making it extraordinarily delicious.

MAKE-AHEAD TIP: Store the soup refrigerated
for up to 2 days or frozen for months in
airtight plastic containers.

**"WOW" PRESENTATION AND GARNISHING
TIPS (STEP 6):** Depending upon the rest
of the menu and my choice of bowl, I may
garnish this soup (hot or chilled) with toasted
sliced almonds and sprigs of fresh mint, or
more exotically (when served hot) with sautéed
escargots and grains of flavourful, cooked wild
rice. When serving it hot in large flat soup
bowls/dishes, I often add a pinch of tarragon to
the soup and garnish it with seared scallops
and sprigs of fresh tarragon.

SORREL SOUP/CAPPUCCINO

Makes about 5 cups (1.25 litres) or 10 servings of $^1/_2$ cup (125 mL) or 15 servings of $^1/_3$ cup (80 mL)

Perhaps not everyone is familiar with sorrel. Years ago I was able to purchase a plant which is now my faithful and generous source. It grows "like a weed" (with absolutely no attention) and comes back even after the coldest of winters. Sorrel has quite a bitter flavour, but with the careful balance of chicken bouillon, cream, nutmeg and a touch of sugar, it makes a fabulous soup. Because it is unusual as well as delicious, I frequently serve sorrel soup to "more adventurous" guests. Many have never even eaten it! I only prepare this soup in quantity (as I harvest my sorrel) and freeze it. Making the soup is an effortless task! (A photo appears on page 101.)

3 tbsp (45 mL) crushed chicken bouillon cubes
   (or powder)
4 cups (1 litre) hot water
9 oz (250 g) fresh sorrel* leaves (no stems)
$^1/_4$ cup (60 mL) butter
$^1/_2$ tsp (3 mL) finely chopped fresh garlic
1$^3/_4$ tbsp (27 mL) cornstarch
2$^1/_2$ tbsp (38 mL) milk
$^3/_4$ tsp (4 mL) ground nutmeg
1 cup (250 mL) heavy cream (35% fat)**
$^1/_4$ to 1 tsp (1 to 5 mL) granulated sugar
To taste crushed black peppercorns

GARNISH (3 choices)
heavy cream (35% fat), whipped cream or frothed milk

1 Dissolve crushed chicken bouillon cubes in hot water.

2 Thoroughly wash and drain sorrel leaves.

3 Melt butter in a large pot over medium heat; add garlic and sauté for 30 seconds. Add sorrel leaves; turn leaves constantly until wilted.

4 Add chicken bouillon and bring soup to a boil. Remove from heat; allow to cool sufficiently before transferring to a blender.

5 Purée soup (in 3 or 4 batches) until as smooth as possible. (Pass through a sieve to remove any fibers.)

6 Rinse pot, return soup to clean pot and reheat over medium-low heat.

7 Whisk cornstarch into milk until smooth. Stirring constantly, add cornstarch mixture and nutmeg to reheating soup; continue stirring until soup thickens and just begins to simmer. Reduce heat to low; add cream and reheat soup. (Do not bring soup to boil.)

8 Immediately, remove from heat. Add a pinch of sugar and crushed black peppercorns according to taste.

9 Sorrel Soup may be served hot or warm. Garnish surface of soup with drizzles of heavy cream, spoonfuls of whipped cream or frothed milk.

* Sorrel is usually available at farmers' markets.
****Option:** For a lighter soup, replace a portion of the heavy cream with an equivalent amount of lighter cream or evaporated milk. (The flavour will be less mellow and the soup less decadently delicious!)

> **MAKE-AHEAD TIP:** Store the soup refrigerated in airtight plastic containers for up to 3 days or frozen for months.

> **SUGGESTED QUANTITY TIP (STEP 9):**
> Sorrel Soup is best served in small quantities. I often serve it in demitasse cups either with drizzles of heavy cream or cappuccino style with whipped cream or frothed milk.

TARRAGON ROASTED RED PEPPER SOUP

*Makes about 6 cups (1.5 litres) or 8 servings of ³/4 cup (180 mL) each or
12 servings of ¹/2 cup (125 mL) each*

*Incredible is the only way to describe this soup — so velvety, smooth and luxuriously satisfying. The enchanting depth
of flavour is partially due to the undetectable but strategic additions of garlic, ginger, tarragon and touch of hot chili
paste. To create a "spectacular" soup, garnish it with cooked crab claws and flaked crabmeat, or even with lobster for
very special occasions.*

1¹/2 tsp (8 mL) finely chopped fresh garlic
1¹/2 tsp (8 mL) peeled and grated fresh gingerroot
2 tsp (10 mL) olive oil
¹/2 lb (225 g) leeks (white part only), cleaned well
    and sliced
1 oz or 3 tbsp (30 g/45 mL) finely chopped shallots
1³/4 tbsp (27 mL) crushed chicken bouillon cubes
    (or powder)
2 cups (500 mL) boiling water
¹/2 lb (225 g) potato, peeled and coarsely chopped
¹/2 lb (225 g) roasted red bell pepper, flesh only*
²/3 cup (170 mL) heavy cream (35% fat)
1 to 1¹/3 cups (250 to 325 mL) whole milk
1¹/2 tsp (8 mL) crushed dried tarragon leaves
¹/3 to ¹/2 tsp (2 to 3 mL) (Indonesian) hot chili paste
To taste salt

GARNISH (optional)
4 oz (115 g) cooked crab/lobster meat or 8 crab legs
    (in shell and cooked)
8 sprigs of fresh tarragon

1 In a medium-large saucepan, sauté garlic and ginger
in olive oil over medium heat for about 1 minute.

2 Add leeks and shallots; sauté gently until tender but
not browned.

3 Dissolve crushed bouillon cubes in boiling water.
Add bouillon and potatoes to saucepan. Bring to a boil;
reduce heat to low. Cover and simmer until potatoes
are soft (about 15 minutes). Remove from heat; allow
to cool.

4 Add roasted peppers; purée soup in 3 batches.

5 Return soup to a clean saucepan; add cream, milk,
tarragon and hot chili paste; season with salt (or extra
crushed chicken bouillon cubes) to taste. Stirring from
time to time, bring soup just to a boil over medium
heat. Remove from heat immediately.

6 Serve soup hot. At serving time, if desired, garnish
soup with cooked crab or lobster and sprigs of
fresh tarragon.

* For this recipe, use only the flesh of the roasted peppers after
having discarded stems, seeds and skin. To roast bell peppers,
see page 214. Because peppers vary greatly, up to 1 lb (450 g)
of fresh whole bell peppers may be required.

> **MAKE-AHEAD TIP:** Allow the soup to cool,
> then store it refrigerated in airtight plastic
> containers for up to 3 days or frozen for months.
> (If the soup has been frozen, reheat it over
> medium-low heat, whisking from time to time.
> Bring the soup almost to a boil and remove it
> from the heat immediately.)

Is there anything more refreshing on a menu than a salad? Anyone can make a good salad. Just open the refrigerator door and be creative — of course, an excellent vinaigrette or dressing is a must! Many of the salads which I would include on a dinner party menu appear under "Appetizers" simply because they are much more than a salad!

Salads at our table tend to offer an element of surprise (e.g., celery root and currants, endive and persimmon, honeydew melon and cranberries). On the other hand, with additions of fresh herbs, cheese and nuts, rather familiar salads are reinvented to offer dynamic new depths of flavour and texture. I have also developed "salad" recipes which may be used more as accompaniments in appetizers or main course dishes, or to be added to a buffet table, taken on picnics and to potluck events (e.g., Cumin Date Chickpea Salad, Blueberry Pomegranate and Almond Rice Salad, Gourmet Kasha Salad and Pine Nut Tabbouleh with Heart of Palm). Between this section on "Salads" and the section on "Appetizers", there is an irresistible choice of unique salads!

Note: designates a "No Time, No Talent" recipe.

*For this section, the only required **"BASIC RECIPE"** (not mentioned in previous sections) is **Orange Peel Dressing.***

Cranberry Melon Salad (page 113)

SALADS

BLUEBERRY/POMEGRANATE AND ALMOND RICE SALAD

Makes about 4 cups or 1 litre (5 to 6 servings)

My passion for developing versatile recipes is strategic! Doing more with basically the same recipe and reducing it to mainly an assembly process thrills me to no end. For example, I toss cooked rice with cumin, garlic and chopped fresh parsley, then moisten it with wonderful drizzles of olive oil and mayonnaise to produce the base for a myriad of rice salads. Additions of berries or chips of fruit offer the fresh taste of a particular season, while toasted slivered almonds provide a satisfying crunch.

3 cups (750 mL) cooked long grain rice
   (e.g., page 168), chilled or at room temperature
³/4 to 1 tsp (4 to 5 mL) ground cumin
¹/2 tsp (3 mL) finely chopped fresh garlic
1¹/2 to 2 tbsp (23 to 30 mL) mayonnaise
2 to 3 tsp (10 to 15 mL) olive oil (preferably
   garlic-infused)
To taste salt
1 cup (250 mL) fresh blueberries or pomegranate
   seeds* or dried cranberries
3 tbsp (45 mL) chopped fresh parsley
¹/3 cup (80 mL) toasted slivered almonds
1 to 1¹/3 tbsp (15 to 20 mL) vinaigrette, a mustard
   herb type (e.g., page 211 or commercial), optional

1 Toss rice, cumin and garlic together.

2 Whisk together mayonnaise and oil; drizzle over seasoned rice and toss to combine evenly. Add salt to taste.

3 Fold in fruit and parsley. Refrigerate for at least an hour if possible or until ready to use.

(Note: **The salad may be prepared to this point up to 8 hours** ** in advance.**)

4 Just before serving, add toasted almonds and toss. If desired, drizzle with vinaigrette according to taste and toss.

* 1¹/2 to 2 fresh pomegranates are required. Cut the fruit in half and carefully remove the seeds. Discard the skin and absolutely all bits of white pulp.
** If stored longer, the rice tends to toughen.

SERVING TIP: Serve this salad as an accompaniment to a main course recipe (e.g., chicken, pork, lamb). For buffet and "potluck" events, it imparts a tasty and original dimension to the menu.

SEASONAL TIP: Pomegranate seeds or dried cranberries are particularly appropriate for the holiday season. Blueberries create a milder but wonderfully refreshing salad particularly for summer entertaining.

CRANBERRY MELON SALAD

Makes 4 servings

When time is limited, consider this appealing salad. Just imagine cubes of succulent honeydew melon tossed with slightly tart chewy dried cranberries and drizzled with a sweetly mellow herb vinaigrette. It is a refreshing crescendo of unique flavours, textures, shapes and colours — an ideal choice for a Thanksgiving, holiday season or all-year round menu! (**Note:** *A photo appears on page 111.*)

14 oz (400 g)* honeydew melon flesh, cut into cubes
   (¹/₂ inch or 1.25 cm)
¹/₃ cup (80 mL) dried cranberries
3 tbsp (45 mL) vinaigrette, a mustard herb type
   (e.g., page 211 or commercial)
3 tbsp (45 mL) pistachio nuts, shelled and
   lightly roasted
2 oz (60 g) Parmesan cheese (block piece)

GARNISH (optional)
4 sprigs of fresh mint

1   Chill melon cubes.

2   Just before serving, drain off and discard any juice from melon cubes.

3   Combine melon cubes with cranberries, drizzle with vinaigrette and toss gently.

4   Transfer salad to serving plate(s). Sprinkle with pistachio nuts. Garnish with thick curls of Parmesan cheese and sprigs of fresh mint.

5   Serve immediately to ensure crispness of melon.

* **Note:** This weight does not include the discarded peel, seeds, cavity water and soft pulp.

DO-AHEAD TIP: Cut the **melon into cubes** up to several hours in advance and store them refrigerated in an airtight plastic container.

Bocconcini Tomato Salad with Fresh Herbs

Makes 5 cups or 1.25 litres (4 servings)

Busy days see me charming my husband or "drop-in" guests with this "fast and easy" salad served as an appetizer. I take a delectable trio of flavours (Bocconcini cheese, tomato and olives) and then dazzle the palate with a generous infusion of fresh tarragon and hints of Balsamic vinegar. The recipe is most appropriate for buffets or potluck events, providing a well-appreciated vegetarian option. Served with thick slices of fresh earthy bread, the salad makes a tasty light lunch for those "on the run"!

1¹⁄₂ cups (375 mL) red cherry/grape tomatoes
    (cut in half)
1¹⁄₂ cups (375 mL) yellow mini tomatoes* (cut in half)
1¹⁄₄ cups or 8 oz (300 mL/225 g) sliced
    Bocconcini cheese
1 cup (250 mL) marinated black olives,
    whole and unpitted
1¹⁄₃ tbsp (20 mL) fresh whole tarragon leaves**
3 to 4 tbsp (45 to 60 mL) vinaigrette, a mustard herb
    type (e.g., page 211 or commercial)
1 tsp (5 mL) balsamic vinegar
To taste salt and crushed black peppercorns

Garnish (optional)
fresh sprigs of tarragon or herbs of choice
    (e.g., chervil, dill, rosemary, mint)

1 Just before serving, toss ingredients together in a large bowl. (Be generous with fresh tarragon leaves and crushed black peppercorns.)

2 Garnish with sprigs of fresh herbs and serve.

* **Option:** Yellow or orange bell pepper (cut into ²⁄₃ inch or 1.5 cm squares); small green or yellow zucchini (sliced)
** **Option:** dill weed or herb of choice, but tarragon is by far our first choice

Do-Ahead Tip: Hours in advance of serving, the **ingredients may be prepared** (i.e., tomatoes cut, cheese sliced and tarragon leaves removed from their branches) and assembled.

Presentation Tip: I serve individual salads in large flat soup bowls/dishes with wide rims, allowing the recipe "to breathe" and to be artistically framed by the rims.

CUMIN DATE CHICKPEA SALAD

Makes 5 cups or 1.25 litres (10 to 15 servings)

Fond memories of the food and spice markets of the Middle East, Africa and Asia enchantingly invade my space as I try to toss divinely scented cumin and sticky dates with rather "reluctant" cooked chickpeas! Without question, however, it is the Orange Peel Dressing which makes this unconventional "alliance" awesome! With the dressing on hand, the salad takes 10 minutes to prepare.
(**Note:** *A photo appears on page 139 with Twin Sesame Seed-Crusted Pork Tenderloin.*)

2 cans (can size: 19 fl oz or 540 mL) chickpeas,
    drained and rinsed
1 tbsp (15 mL) cumin seeds
1¼ cups (300 mL) chopped pitted dates*
1¼ cups (300 mL) Orange Peel Dressing
    (page 211), divided

GARNISH (optional or as desired)
sprigs of fresh mint and edible flowers

1 Lightly toss together well-drained chickpeas and cumin seeds.

2 Add dates and only 2 to 3 tbsp (30 to 45 mL) of Orange Peel Dressing; combine well.

3 Refrigerate and allow salad to rest overnight or for at least several hours if possible.

4 To serve, garnish with sprigs of fresh mint and edible flowers if desired. Offer extra Orange Peel Dressing in a separate bowl at table.

* I often use the dried dates which are compressed into a block.

MAKE-AHEAD TIP: Stored in an airtight plastic container, the salad retains its quality for up to a week in the refrigerator or for months in the freezer.

PRESENTATION TIP: I serve this recipe piled high on a coloured plate (e.g., blue) as a contrast to the more monochromatic "brown-beige" nature of the salad. Sprigs of mint add enticing freshness.

ALTERNATIVE-USE TIP: The salad is ideal for **buffets**, **meze** or **potluck** events. It also makes an interesting accompaniment particularly for pork, duck, chicken and ham. (**Note:** A **meze** is an array of small Mediterranean savoury dishes designed to complement a beverage, entice taste buds and encourage diners to linger around a table chatting. Variety and originality is considered important. Ultimately, a meze table is supposed to offer a "nosh", not a meal, although it may often prove to be the latter. Indeed, my husband so loves a meze that he must restrain himself from not "filling up" before main course arrives!)

CURRANT AND CELERY ROOT SALAD

Makes about 4 cups or 1 litre (about 4 to 6 servings)

"Less is more!" The subtle but distinct flavours of chewy sweet currants and crisp savoury celery root are tastefully brought together with drizzles of a mellow herb vinaigrette. My husband judges this simple but unique salad as a "winner"!

1 large celery root (weight: 1 lb or 450 g)
1/3 cup (80 mL) currants
3 tbsp (45 mL) chopped green onions
3 tbsp (45 mL) vinaigrette, a mustard herb type
   (e.g., page 211 or commercial)
To taste salt

1 Peel celery root and cut into matchstick pieces. (This makes about 4 cups or 1 litre.)
2 In a large bowl, toss together celery matchsticks, currants and green onions.

3 Note: If a salad with tender crisp matchsticks and a blended flavour of ingredients is desired, add vinaigrette and salt, toss well and allow salad to rest refrigerated overnight (or at least several hours) in an airtight plastic container. Conversely, if very crisp celery root matchsticks are preferred, add vinaigrette and salt just before serving. (We prefer the former.)

PRESENTATION TIP: The recipe, dominated by the matchstick-cut celery root, appropriately lends itself to being served in **a "pile" formation**, resembling an unstacked wood pile.

Garlicky Feta and Pecan Spinach Salad

Makes 4 servings

When "starvation" has set in, forget the prepackaged snacks and opt for this quick, delightful salad! Fresh crisp spinach, pecans, slightly salty feta cheese and sweet cherry tomatoes are so much more satisfying, especially when tossed together with a garlicky dressing and served with thick slices of buttered bread. This tasty salad is particularly suitable for casual dining (e.g., "bistro" meals, buffets, barbecues, alfresco and family occasions).

8 cups (2 litres) baby spinach leaves (stems removed),
    washed and dried
1 cup (250 mL) coarsely crumbled feta cheese
1/4 to 1/3 cup (60 to 80 mL) coarsely chopped
    roasted pecans
20 grape or cherry tomatoes, cut in halves
To taste salt and crushed black peppercorns

DRESSING
1/4 cup (60 mL) mayonnaise
2 tbsp (30 mL) olive oil
1 1/3 tbsp (20 mL) vinaigrette, a mustard herb type
    (e.g., page 211 or commercial)
1 tsp (5 mL) finely chopped fresh garlic

1 In a large salad bowl, prepare dressing by whisking together mayonnaise, olive oil, vinaigrette and garlic.

2 Just before serving, add spinach leaves and toss to coat leaves evenly with dressing.

3 Sprinkle with feta, pecans and tomatoes; toss again, seasoning with salt and crushed black peppercorns. Serve immediately.

> **MAKE-AHEAD TIP:** Whisk together the dressing **(Step 1)** and prepare the spinach, feta, pecans and tomatoes in advance. The salad can then be quickly "tossed" at the last minute.

> **"ON-HAND" TIP:** I always have **finely chopped fresh garlic** on hand in my refrigerator. Every couple of weeks, I peel 2 heads of garlic, chop the cloves (of garlic) in a food processor and store the chopped garlic refrigerated in a small airtight plastic container. This makes about 1/2 cup or 125 mL. (**Note:** Jars of chopped, puréed or minced garlic are available commercially. However, the garlic is usually preserved in oil and its flavour is really not comparable to the original product.)

Gourmet Kasha Salad

Makes almost 5 cups or 1.25 litres (4 to 8 servings)

As a child, I loved when Mother had kasha on the stove upon our return home from school on a cold winter's day. Mother never made kasha as a salad, but she would love mine with its surprise additions of sun-dried tomatoes, nutmeg and Honey Mustard Mayonnaise. This hearty atypical "salad" is absolutely fabulous, perfect indeed for buffets and pot luck events.

2 cups (500 mL) cooked Savoury Kasha (page 206),
    room temperature or chilled
1/2 cup (125 mL) chopped green onion
2 tsp (10 mL) chopped fresh parsley
1/4 to 1/3 tsp (about 1 to 2 mL) freshly ground nutmeg
1/4 cup (60 mL) julienne-cut sun-dried tomatoes in
    seasoned oil (drained)
1 cup (250 mL) julienne-cut cooked ham*
2 tbsp (30 mL) Honey Mustard Mayonnaise
    (page 211) or mayonnaise
1 cup (250 mL) thickly sliced mushroom caps
    (cremini or white)
To taste crushed black peppercorns
1/3 cup (80 mL) coarsely chopped hazelnuts or
    toasted pecans

Garnish (optional)
fresh green onion stems or sprigs of fresh herbs
    (e.g., lemon basil, dill)

1 In a large bowl, toss lightly together cooked kasha, green onion, parsley and nutmeg.

2 Add sun-dried tomatoes, ham and Honey Mustard Mayonnaise; toss thoroughly before adding mushrooms and seasoning with crushed black peppercorns to taste.

3 If possible, let salad rest (refrigerated) overnight or for at least 30 minutes to allow flavours to develop.

4 Just before serving, toss with hazelnuts. If desired, garnish presentation artistically with stems of green onion or sprigs of fresh herbs.

* **Option:** Cooked spicy sausage or smoked turkey/chicken — or omit completely for a vegetarian version.

> **Make-Ahead Tip (Steps 1 to 3):** The **basic salad** may be prepared up to 2 days in advance.

> **Alternative-Use Tip:** This salad, served with an accompanying green salad, **can be a meal** on its own for a simple **family lunch** or **picnic**. I frequently serve it **with eggs for** a late weekend **breakfast** — hold the hash browns and bacon!

PERSIMMON ENDIVE SALAD

Makes 4 servings

A duet of sweet jelly-like persimmons and crisp mellow spears of Belgian endive orchestrates a dazzling performance of textures, flavours, colours and shapes. However, feta cheese and herb vinaigrette are also key ingredients, giving this salad its superb overall flavour.

4 or 5 heads Belgian endive, medium-small
    (i.e., length: about 5 inches or 12 cm each)
3 persimmons, very ripe (each: 5 oz or 150 g)
1¹/₄ cups (300 mL) coarsely crumbled feta cheese
¹/₂ to ²/₃ cup (125 to 170 mL) vinaigrette, a mustard
    herb type (e.g., page 211 or commercial)

GARNISH
4 sprigs of fresh rosemary (or thyme)

1 Cut off bottom of endive to release leaves.

2 Arrange leaves in a fan-like formation on a serving platter or on 4 individual plates.

3 Remove and discard blossom end, any dark spots and unripe areas of persimmons. Cut persimmons crosswise into round slices (thickness: ¹/₃ inch or 0.8 cm). Arrange slices in overlapping manner, covering base of endive stems. (**Note: The platter/ plates may be prepared to this point an hour or two before serving.** Cover with plastic wrap and refrigerate.)

4 Just before serving, sprinkle feta cheese over endive leaves and persimmon.

5 Drizzle salad with vinaigrette according to taste.

6 Garnish persimmon with sprigs of fresh rosemary. Serve immediately.

INFORMATION TIP: Persimmons are a seasonal fruit (i.e., available from October to February), so enjoy this salad as soon as the opportunity/ fruit presents itself! Persimmons should only be eaten when they are ripe (i.e., extremely soft but not mushy). Discard any "hard" areas if the persimmon is unevenly ripened. (**Note:** "Not quite ripe" persimmons ripen at room temperature in a day or two. Ripe persimmons can be stored in the refrigerator for up to 3 days.)

"WOW" PRESENTATION TIP (STEPS 2 & 3): As an alternative presentation for individual servings, you could do a more dramatic "**star presentation**". *It's easy to do, easy to visualize.* For 4 individual servings:

1 Divide the leaves into 2 piles, separating the larger leaves from the smaller ones so that there are **20 leaves in each pile.**

2 Trim the cut end of each leaf to form a point (length of point: about 1 inch or 2.5 cm).

3 On each plate, arrange 5 of the larger leaves in a star formation with the pointed cut ends in the centre of the plate.

4 Stack 2 slices of persimmon in the centre of the "star" on top of the pointed endive ends.

5 Poke the pointed cut ends of 5 of the smaller leaves between the 2 slices of persimmon in a second star formation (offset from the first). **Note:** The salad has the appearance of a lotus flower.

6 Pierce through the centre of each persimmon-endive leaf stack with a strong sprig of fresh rosemary.

PINE NUT TABBOULEH
(with optional Heart of Palm)
Makes about 3 1/2 cups or 875 mL (about 8 servings)*

Our family adopted the habit of eating tabbouleh salad while in Cairo. It is an essential element of a Middle East meze table, bringing freshness, colour and a flavour combination like no other dish. It is best eaten with (or "stuffed" into) pita bread. My basic tabbouleh also includes pine nuts, ground nutmeg and feta cheese; however, I always add heart of palm slices when serving it as a salad or a main course accompaniment**. Tabbouleh is particularly scrumptious with grilled foods (lamb, chicken, beef or fish).

1/2 cup (125 mL) bulgur wheat, fine
1/4 cup (60 mL) light olive oil
3 to 4 tbsp (45 to 60 mL) lemon juice
1/8 tsp (Pinch) salt and crushed black peppercorns
1 cup (250 mL) chopped fresh Italian
     (i.e., flat leaf) parsley
3 to 4 tbsp (45 to 60 mL) chopped onion
2 tbsp (30 mL) chopped fresh mint
1/2 tsp (3 mL) finely chopped fresh garlic
1/2 tsp (3 mL) ground nutmeg
3/4 cup (180 mL) crumbled feta cheese
2/3 cup (170 mL) finely diced tomato
     (i.e., plum tomato), seeds and juice removed
Pinch granulated sugar
1/4 to 1/3 cup (60 to 80 mL) roasted pine nuts
4 stems heart of palm* (canned), optional

GARNISH (optional or as desired)
sprigs of fresh mint
lettuce leaves
pita bread

1 Put bulgur wheat in a fine sieve and rinse with cold water; squeeze out any excess water. In a small bowl, stir together rinsed bulgur, oil, lemon juice, salt and pepper; set aside for 45 minutes.

2 In a large bowl combine parsley, onion, mint, garlic, nutmeg and cheese.

3 Just before serving, toss together bulgur wheat and parsley mixtures. Add tomato and toss again.

4 Add a pinch of sugar (to balance flavours), pine nuts and, if desired, heart of palm (cut into 1/4 inch or 0.5 cm wide slices), extra salt and crushed black peppercorns; toss.

5 Garnish Pine Nut Tabbouleh with sprigs of fresh mint and serve (according to Middle East tradition) with lettuce leaves and/or pita bread to scoop up salad. (**Note:** Leftover portions may be satisfactorily kept on hand for a couple of days.)

* Makes about 5 cups or 1.25 litres with heart of palm added
** **Option:** When serving this Pine Nut Tabbouleh as a salad or main course accompaniment, feel free to drizzle it with extra olive oil according to taste.

> **DO-AHEAD TIP (STEPS 1 AND 2):** I often prepare the **bulgur wheat** and **parsley mixtures** a day in advance, placing the two mixtures in separate airtight plastic containers and refrigerating them.

> **TIP:** The tomato is added just before serving (step 3) to avoid its loss of water.

> **ALTERNATIVE-USE TIP:** For a hearty and remarkable **hors d'oeuvre**, try my "Seductive Shrimp Tabbouleh Sandwiches" (page 75).

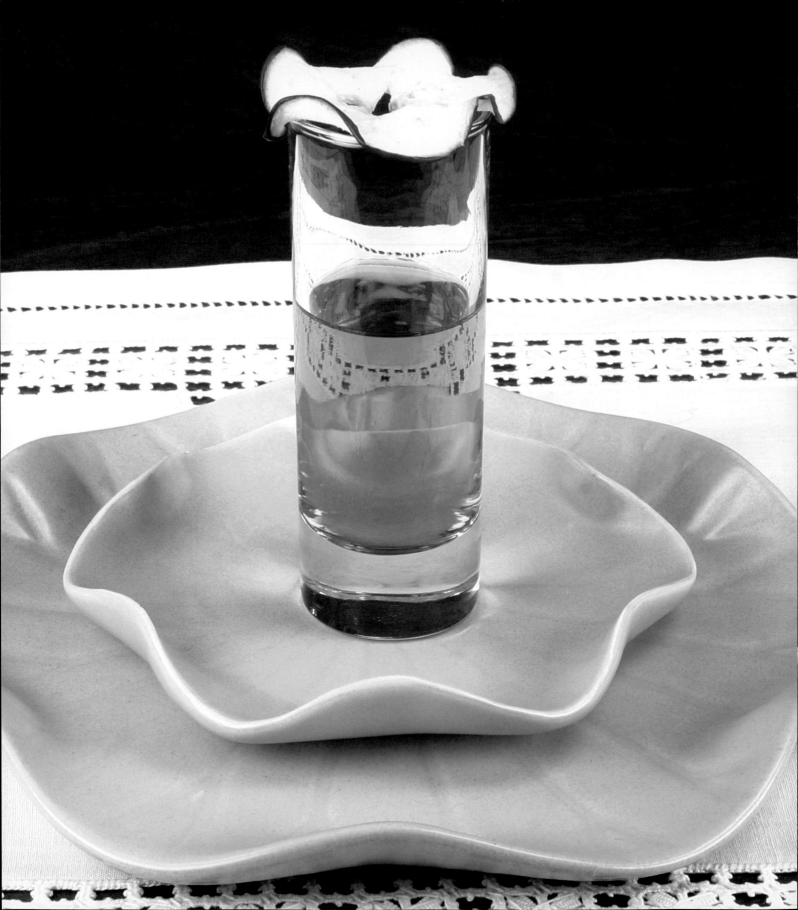

Apple Brandy Trou Normand (page 124)

Perhaps not everyone is familiar with a "Trou Normand". It is a "shot" of high proof alcohol, often Calvados, served "part way" through a copious meal — usually immediately before main course. A Trou Normand is designed to stimulate the appetite, allowing one to enjoy the array of dishes yet to come. In our home, a Trou Normand serves another important purpose. It allows me to excuse myself more comfortably from the table and assemble the main course, while guests enjoy a refreshing "taste" and a petit pause in the menu.

Traditionally, for a Trou Normand, alcohol is served "straight" or poured over ice or a sorbet — which is not always the case at our table! When I present a Trou Normand, the playful side of my character surfaces. Because quantities are small, it is fun to establish a balance by "amplifying" the ceremony! In terms of ingredients and presentation, I take "artistic licence"! (Of course, children must be included in the ceremony. They get juice or an alcohol-free version of the Trou Normand, but with the same presentation.) In this section, I have included only a couple of our favourite Trou Normands plus a fascinating sorbet which is not a Trou Normand, but is served rather as a "palate cleanser" before the main course. For family or very casual dinners, I frequently offer my mysterious but tasty "Parmesan Sorrel Oil Dip" instead of a Trou Normand.

Note: 🐇 **designates a "No Time, No Talent" recipe.**

TROU NORMANDS
& ALTERNATIVES

Apple Brandy Trou Normand
(with Dried Apple Wafer)

Makes 4 servings

*When entertaining, a trou Normand is one of my "quick and easy" techniques in adding a touch of pizzazz to casual or more formal dining. Frequently, I respect tradition and serve an apple brandy. However, to generate a certain element of excitement, I present the brandy in shot glasses and playfully lay a dried apple wafer intriguingly across the top of each glass. This "bit of drama" convincingly contributes to the perception that the trou Normand is definitely another course on the menu. (**Note:** A photo appears on page 122.)*

½ cup (125 mL) apple brandy
4 Dried Apple Wafers (page 201), optional

1 Pour apple brandy into 4 tall thin shot* glasses.

2 If desired, lay a single Dried Apple Wafer horizontally across rim of each glass to represent a lid.

3 Set each glass on a liner and serve.

* **Option:** Liqueur glasses of choice

Parmesan Sorrel Oil Dip

Makes almost 1¼ cups (300 mL) or about 12 servings

As a tasty novel touch to a dinner, serve individual tiny dishes of Parmesan Sorrel Oil along with slices or chunks of baguette. This is a fun way to keep the table animated between courses before main course is served. I find that small Chinese sauce dishes (diameter: about 2¾ inches or 7 cm) set on plates work well for individual servings of sorrel oil.

3 to 4 baguettes (preferably whole wheat)

PARMESAN SORREL OIL
1 cup (250 mL) olive oil
6 tbsp (90 mL) pregrated Parmesan cheese
¾ oz (23 g)* fresh sorrel leaves
1 tsp (5 mL) Dijon mustard
⅛ tsp (Pinch) crushed black peppercorns
¼ tsp (1 mL) granulated sugar
To taste salt (optional)

1 To make the Parmesan Sorrel Oil, process oil, cheese, sorrel leaves and mustard in a blender.

2 Add crushed black peppercorns and sugar to taste and, if desired, salt.

3 Place oil in a sterilized, well-sealed jar and store refrigerated for up to a week (or frozen for months). **Note:** If oil does not remain liquid, allow it to rest at room temperature for a few minutes before using.

4 Stir (or shake) well. For individual servings, pour about 1½ tbsp (23 mL) of Parmesan Sorrel Oil into small shallow dishes and place on separate, larger plates along with slices or chunks of baguette.

* This is about 10 medium-size leaves.

HERB AND SPICE SORBET

Makes 3 cups or 750 mL (12 to 16 servings)

I risk saying that nobody will correctly guess what is in this sorbet! The agreeably competing flavours of the rosemary and cinnamon playfully confuse the palate and conceal the true identity of the ingredients. Without a doubt, the refreshing and fascinating nature of this sorbet is always appreciated! I like to make my servings "petit"; however, do what suits you.

4 cups (1 litre) key lime sorbet* (commercial),
    softened slightly
2 tsp (10 mL) finely chopped fresh** rosemary leaves
3/4 tsp (4 mL) cinnamon extract

GARNISH (optional)
sprigs of fresh rosemary

1 Place slightly softened sorbet in a large chilled bowl and break sorbet apart.

2 Sprinkle with rosemary and cinnamon extract. Using a dinner fork, thoroughly combine ingredients.

3 Place sorbet in an airtight plastic container, covering surface of sorbet closely with plastic wrap; freeze.

4 Scoop sorbet into previously chilled shot glasses (preferably not crystal) or small glasses/dishes of choice, adding 3 to 4 tbsp (45 to 60 mL) per glass/dish. (**Note:** To avoid melting, definitely use **chilled glasses** and only **fill them a few at a time**.)

5 Cover glasses individually with plastic wrap and return to freezer until ready to serve.

6 If sorbet is frozen solid, transfer filled glasses to refrigerator about 10 minutes before serving. (Remove plastic wrap.)

7 If desired, serve with a sprig of fresh rosemary poked into top of sorbet.

MAKE-AHEAD TIP (STEPS 1 TO 3): The sorbet may be prepared and kept on hand frozen for months.

MAKE-AHEAD TIP (STEPS 4 AND 5): The glasses of sorbet may be prepared several days in advance.

PRESENTATION TIP (FOR STEP 7): If using shot glasses, balancing a long-handled teaspoon or parfait spoon horizontally across the top of each glass makes for an artistic presentation.

* **Option:** Sherbet
** **Option:** If fresh rosemary is not available, use chopped dried leaves.

Cinnamon-Scented Pomegranate Seeds

Makes 1 cup or 250 mL (8 servings)

Are you eager to serve something desperately novel as a "modified" trou Normand? Pomegranate seeds tossed with cinnamon-flavoured liqueur are certain to provoke abundant and favourable comments. When pomegranates are available, this enticing unorthodox recipe is "a refreshing must"!

1 cup (250 mL) fresh pomegranate seeds*
3 tbsp (45 mL) cinnamon-flavoured liqueur
   (e.g., Goldschlager)
1/8 tsp (Pinch) cinnamon extract (or lime juice)

Garnish (optional)
8 thin cinnamon sticks (length: 31/2 inches or 9 cm)

1   Mix ingredients together.

2   Store refrigerated in an airtight plastic container, stirring occasionally to ensure even flavouring of seeds.

3   Allow mixture to rest for at least several hours (but preferably for a day or 2) before serving.

4   Serve chilled pomegranate seed mixture in liqueur glasses, dividing seeds and liquid evenly between glasses (e.g., 2 tbsp or 30 mL per serving). Poke a slender cinnamon stick into each glass as a garnish.

* 11/2 to 2 fresh whole pomegranates are required. Cut the fruit in half and carefully remove the seeds. Discard the skin and absolutely all bits of white pulp. (**Note:** I choose "leathery skin" fruit of the darkest burgundy colour possible.)

Make-Ahead Tip (Steps 1 to 3): The pomegranate seeds may be prepared and soaked up to 3 or 4 days in advance.

"WOW" Hoarding Tip: Pomegranates are usually **available from October to November** in North America. However, I generally purchase a half dozen or so at the end of the season and store them loose/unwrapped in the fruit drawer of the refrigerator. Although their leathery skins may shrink, I have juicy pomegranates for up to another couple of months.

The main course, the most strategic part of a menu, should be a memorable experience! To achieve this, my recipes are a creative composition of interesting ingredients offering unforgettable flavours. Balanced and appealing colours, textures, shapes, heights and arrangement all play a role in the final recipe. However, when preparing the main course, focus must be maintained on cooking the meat, chicken, fish, etc., to the correct degree of doneness. No matter how fabulous flavours, combinations and presentations are, all will suffer if the principle item is not appropriately cooked. You will notice that I give special attention and complete details on cooking in all my recipes. (**Note:** Meat, chicken, fish, etc., are usually just below room temperature at time of cooking.)

As for my repertoire of chosen main course recipes, it includes a variety from beef, chicken, pork to lamb, quail, seafood, escargots and pasta. Amazingly delicious recipes have been developed using the simplest of ingredients. Understanding that the depth of flavour is the "key" to culinary success, I use various cooking techniques — roasting, poaching, sautéing, searing and frying, or even a combination of these. Many recipes offer alternative-cooking techniques to suit personal preferences, resources, skills, situations, convenience, time of year and weather. Definitely, marinades, rubs, drizzles, sauces and toppings are critical. I have a passion for designing recipes that are "stuffed", "crusted", "glazed", "stacked", "seared" and certainly, "barbecued/grilled"! Introducing an element of intrigue into my recipes excites me (e.g., Decadent Lamb Medallions with Seared Pâté, Springtime Filets Mignons with Fiddleheads and Wild Garlic, and Escargots and Orzo in Portobello Dish)!

Being of Ukrainian background and having traveled the world for 28 years, do I need to say that international flavours, spices, herbs, ingredients and techniques are part of my culinary make-up? Asian and middle-east influences probably dominate. My food styling, presentation and decor are equally affected.

As a final comment, I strongly believe that plates should "breath" (i.e., not be overcrowded) and that food carefully and artistically arranged is always more tempting. Touches of fresh herbs, shoots, salad leaves, edible flowers and "drizzles" are essential in bringing life to my plates.

Note: 🐇 designates a "No Time, No Talent" recipe. designates the recipe may be barbequed/grilled.

*For this section, the recommended **"BASIC RECIPES"** (not mentioned in previous sections) to be made in advance/kept on hand, include **Pesto** and a variety of savoury sauces (i.e., **Roasted Red Pepper Cream Sauce, Asian Cashew Sauce/Dressing** and **Cognac White Wine Cream Sauce**). Note: Some commercial options exist and may be used/modified to suit the purpose.*

Decadent Lamb Medallions (page 142)

MAIN COURSES

PORTOBELLO DELUXE STUFFED CHICKEN BREASTS

Makes 4 servings

*This chicken is exquisite in flavour as well as visually stunning with its layered filling of spinach, portobello mushrooms, cheese and oven-dried tomatoes. It is the perfect main course solution for many occasions: an elegant dinner, lunch, barbecue, buffet, finger food reception or pot luck event. (**Note:** Organize/prepare your ingredients before you begin, and the rest is a matter of assembly. **After you have done the recipe once, it becomes simple**.)*

ACCOMPANIMENT TIP: Pasta (e.g., spinach tortellini) works well with this recipe. (**Note:** Asparagus spears and Roasted Red Pepper Cream Sauce are included in the recipe.)

1 very large portobello mushroom cap (3 oz or 85 g), sliced (thickness: 1/3 inch or 0.8 cm)
3 to 4 tbsp (45 to 60 mL) herb garlic butter (e.g., page 205) or butter
To taste salt and crushed black peppercorns
1 cup (250 mL) (well-packed) fresh spinach leaves (stems removed)
4 single chicken breasts, boneless with skin (each: 6 oz or 175 g)
1 1/2 tsp (8 mL) dried crushed tarragon leaves
4 oz (115 g) Oven-Dried Tomatoes*
1 1/2 oz (45 g) mozzarella cheese, sliced
1/3 cup (80 mL) lightly spiced flour (e.g., page 206)
2 tbsp (30 mL) vegetable oil
1 1/4 cups (300 ml) Roasted Red Pepper Cream Sauce (page 214)

GARNISH (optional)
spears of freshly cooked asparagus

1 Sauté mushroom slices briefly in herb garlic butter in a large preheated skillet over medium-high heat. Season with salt and crushed black peppercorns; transfer to a platter.

2 Place spinach leaves on a large microwave-proof plate. Place in a microwave oven at high heat, turning leaves a couple of times, until spinach is only slightly wilted (less than one minute). Remove from oven and season with salt and crushed black peppercorns.

3 Slit chicken breasts horizontally to form a pocket. (Definitely avoid piercing top or bottom of breasts in order to prevent contents, particularly cheese, from escaping during cooking process.)

4 Sprinkle interior of pocket with salt, crushed black peppercorns and tarragon. On one interior surface of pocket, arrange 1/4 of Oven-Dried Tomatoes, top with 1/4 of cheese, mushrooms and spinach. (**Note:** For an attractive "layered effect" of the filling in the final presentation, arrange/stack the ingredients in the order outlined above **on the side of the pocket to which the skin is attached.**)

5 Close breasts around filling and secure edges together with strong wooden toothpicks/cocktail picks or fine metal skewers. (**Note:** Be consistent in using the same number of picks/skewers per stuffed breast to avoid confusion when removing them later.)

6 Dust stuffed breasts carefully with lightly spiced flour. Place breasts (skin side down) in hot oil in a preheated large skillet or grill pan over medium to medium-high heat; brown all surfaces.** Reduce heat to medium-low or lower; cover pan loosely and cook until chicken is tender and done. (Total cooking time: about 20 to 24 minutes. Juices run clear when chicken is pierced with a fork and meat thermometer registers 170°F or 77°C.)

7 Remove picks/skewers while chicken is still warm (counting them carefully to ensure that all have been removed).

8 Serve with Roasted Red Pepper Cream Sauce and garnish with cooked asparagus spears.

* To make Oven-Dried Tomatoes, cut ¹/2 lb (225 g) of whole tomatoes (e.g., plum) horizontally in half; arrange on a baking sheet (cut side up), drizzle with 1¹/2 tsp (8 mL) of olive oil and season with salt and crushed black peppercorns. Bake in a 225°F (110°C) oven until the tomatoes are reduced to about half of their original size (about 2¹/2 to 3 hours). Cool and store refrigerated.

** Note: Alternatively, at this time, transfer the chicken to a parchment-lined baking tray and place it in a preheated oven (350°F or 180°C) until done.

MAKE-AHEAD TIP: The stuffed chicken breasts can be prepared in advance (**i.e., Steps 1 to 5**) and cooked shortly before serving, or they can even be cooked in advance (**i.e., Steps 1 to 7**) and served warm or cold.

ALTERNATIVE-COOKING TECHNIQUE/TIP (FOR STEP 6): Instead of using a grill pan or skillet, place the chicken breasts on a very well-oiled, preheated (medium-high) **barbecue grill**. Cook over direct heat with the lid down (as much as possible), reducing the heat to medium (or lower) once the breasts have browned. (**Note:** When cooking the chicken on a barbecue, do not dust the stuffed breasts with flour.)

"WOW" PRESENTATION TIP (FOR STEP 8): I tend to cut each breast diagonally in half (crosswise) and present one piece propped up against the other (with skin side up), exposing the tempting filling. Drizzles of Roasted Red Pepper Cream Sauce dramatically decorate the plate.

QUICK CHINESE SPICED WINGS/DRUMSTICKS

Makes 4 main course servings or 10 to 12 hors d'oeuvre cocktail buffet servings

*Oriental flavours can be absolutely addictive. These quick spicy wings are no exception! Feel free to adjust the recipe (i.e., garlic, ginger, chili paste and peppercorns) to meet your preferred "level of hot and spicy"! The sesame-infused Balsamic Red Wine Drizzle makes an excellent sauce; however, the chicken is also fabulous on its own. (**Note:** Chicken drumsticks* may be used instead of wings.)*

> **ACCOMPANIMENT TIP:** For a match made in heaven, serve this recipe with Oriental Mango Rice (page 165) or Korean Mixed Vegetables and Noodles (page 164). My Honey Nutmeg Fiddleheads (page 163) and corn on the cob also work well!

3 lb (1.3 kg) chicken wings* (tips removed and discarded)
3 tbsp (45 mL) soya sauce
1¹/₂ tbsp (23 mL) peeled and grated fresh gingerroot
1¹/₂ tbsp (23 mL) white sesame seeds
1 tbsp (15 mL) granulated sugar
1 to 1¹/₂ tsp (5 to 8 mL) Chinese Five Spice
¹/₃ to ³/₄ tsp (2 to 4 mL) (Indonesian) hot chili paste
¹/₃ tsp (2 mL) crushed black peppercorns
¹/₂ cup (125 mL) sesame oil, divided
¹/₃ cup (80 mL) Balsamic Red Wine Drizzle/Sauce (page 213), optional

1 Cut chicken wings into 2 sections at joints; place in a large strong resealable plastic bag. (**Note:** If marinating drumsticks, use 2 bags.)

2 In a small bowl, whisk together soya sauce, ginger, sesame seeds, sugar, spice, chili paste, crushed black peppercorns and only 1¹/₂ tbsp (23 mL) of sesame oil. Pour marinade into bag with chicken wings; seal bag securely and "massage" marinade into wings. Refrigerate overnight or up to 36 hours, turning bag occasionally to redistribute marinade.

3 If wings are to be served with a sauce/drizzle, whisk ¹/₃ cup (80 mL) of sesame oil into Balsamic Red Wine Drizzle/Sauce. Set sauce aside.

4 Line 2 rimmed baking trays with aluminum foil and spray with oil. Add wings arranged in a single layer.

5 Bake in centre of a preheated 400°F (200°C) oven for about 20 minutes* until juices run clear when thickest areas are pierced with a fork.

6 Transfer wings to a very well-oiled preheated (medium) barbecue and grill both sides for a minute or 2 until wings are brown and crisp. (**Broiler Option:** Broil wings under a preheated broiler element for a minute or 2 per side, turning the wings once.)

7 If desired, arrange wings on a bed of fresh coriander leaves. Serve drizzled with sesame Balsamic Red Wine Drizzle/Sauce and pass extra sauce at table.

* Drumsticks take about 25 minutes to cook. (**Note:** I do the final grilling of the drumsticks under the broiler in order to keep the skin intact.)

Amazing Cajun Roast Chicken

Makes 6 servings

*In response to that spontaneous craving for succulent roasted chicken, try this "no time, no talent" recipe. The generously spiced, crisp skin locks in the juices resulting in a very moist chicken. With the exquisite seasoning also emanating from the cavity of the bird, every mouthful is seductive! (**Note:** Although I roast this chicken in the oven, it could also be done on a barbecue rotisserie.)*

ACCOMPANIMENT TIP: A salad (simple or exotic) and virtually any sauce (even purchased cranberry) make perfect accompaniments. My choices usually include a Blueberry/Pomegranate and Almond Rice Salad (page 112).

2 chickens (each: 3 lb or 1.3 kg)
2 to 3 tsp (10 to 15 mL) coarse salt
1/2 tsp (3 mL) crushed black peppercorns
2 to 3 tsp (10 to 15 mL) Cajun seasoning
2 tbsp (30 mL) olive oil (preferably garlic-infused)
1½ cups (375 mL) Cognac White Wine Cream Sauce
    (page 213) or sauce of choice

GARNISH (optional)
sprigs of fresh herbs and/or watercress

1 Rinse chickens well (interior and exterior); drain and pat dry with paper towels.* Remove excess fat from interior of chickens.

2 Sprinkle salt and crushed black peppercorns evenly over exterior and lightly over interior of chickens; repeat with Cajun seasoning.

3 Arrange each chicken on its back; tuck wings under backs; tie legs together loosely with kitchen string.

4 Cover 2 baking sheets with aluminum foil (shiny side up) and line with parchment paper if desired.**

5 Set chickens on individual baking sheets. Place uncovered in middle of a preheated 400°F (200°C) oven. After 30 minutes, remove from oven and drizzle all exterior surfaces of chickens with oil. Return chickens to oven until done. (Juices run clear and meat thermometer inserted into thigh registers 180°F or 82°C. This takes about 50 to 60 minutes.)

6 Tent chickens with foil (shiny side in); let rest for 10 minutes before transferring to a carving board. Remove string and carve.

7 If desired, serve Cajun Roast Chickens with Cognac White Wine Cream Sauce (or a sauce of choice) and garnish with fresh herbs or watercress.

* The skin of the chickens should not be "paper" dry. It must be sufficiently moist so that the seasoning adheres.
** Cover the baking sheets with foil to assist in the clean-up. The parchment paper allows for easy removal of the chickens.

ORIENTAL GRILLED QUAIL

Makes 4 servings

Oriental Grilled Quail (pictured on page 37) is definitely one of our favourite recipes! I seriously believe that quail is best when marinated in thick Asian sauces and grilled to perfection, caramelizing the sauces deep into the flesh of the quail. Drizzled with my seductive sesame balsamic vinegar sauce, this recipe is definitely #1 on my list of favorites! Virtually all of the preparation can be done in advance. It is quick and easy to cook.

ACCOMPANIMENT TIP: I always serve the quail with Double Sesame Quinoa (page 161), steamed baby bok choy and if available, fresh red currants. The flavours, colours, shapes and textures are truly fantastic.

8* quail (each: 5 oz or 150 g), partially deboned and butterflied/spatchcocked**

MARINADE
1/2 cup (125 mL) oyster sauce
1/2 cup (125 mL) hoisin sauce
3 tbsp (45 mL) balsamic vinegar
1 1/3 tbsp (20 mL) sesame oil (first addition)
2 tsp (10 mL) finely chopped fresh garlic
2 tsp (10 mL) peeled and grated fresh gingerroot
1 1/2 tsp (8 mL) anise seed

SAUCE
1/3 cup (80 mL) Balsamic Vinegar Syrup (page 204)
1/3 cup (80 mL) sesame oil (second addition)

GARNISH
sprigs of fresh thyme
4 small clusters of fresh red currants (optional)

1 In a small bowl, combine marinade ingredients. (Makes about 1 1/4 cups or 300 mL.) Brush all surfaces of quail with marinade. Cover and refrigerate for 2 to 6 hours, turning occasionally. (Allow quail to rest at room temperature for 30 minutes before grilling.)

2 Whisk together Balsamic Vinegar Syrup and sesame oil; set sauce aside.

3 Remove quail from marinade. Place on a very well-oiled preheated hot barbecue grill with skin side down; reduce heat immediately to medium or medium-high. With hood down, cook for 2 to 3 minutes per side until meat springs back slightly when touched and flesh is pink and moist. **Note:** If not serving immediately, transfer to a couple of baking sheets, cover loosely with aluminum foil (shiny side in) and place in a warm oven (150°F or 73°C).

4 For individual servings, 2 quail may be presented in a vertical "headstand" position (with mashed potatoes holding them together). Drizzle with sesame balsamic vinegar syrup sauce. Garnish with sprigs of fresh thyme and clusters of red currants.

* **Note:** If quail are significantly larger than the suggested weight, 6 quail may be sufficient, allowing 1 1/2 quail per serving.
** If necessary, to partially debone and butterfly quail, use heavy kitchen shears to cut out the neck and backbone. Place quail in an open/flat position (skin side down) on a clean work surface. Loosen the breast bone by slipping your fingers along both sides of the rib cage and pulling the rib cage away from the flesh. (Leave the breasts attached together.) Cut the wishbone away from the meat and remove it. (Keep the wings and the legs intact and attached to the body.)

ALTERNATIVE-TO-BARBECUING TIP (FOR STEP 3): Arrange the quail, *skin side down*, on a broiler pan and place them in the oven 4 inches (10 cm) under a preheated **broiler**. Cook the quail in a similar manner to the method outlined above, turning them once. (**Note:** If grill marks are desired, place the quail briefly on a well-oiled preheated grill pan over medium heat; turn once.)

KOREAN BULGOGI

Makes 4 regular servings (or about 8 cocktail buffet servings)

From our stay in Korea, I can well recall the flavours of my two favourite dishes. The first is Bulgogi, very thin slices of sweetly marinated beef barbecued over hot coals and sprinkled with toasted sesame seeds. One bite only invites another! Bulgogi must be served with a tasty stir-fry of Korean mixed vegetables and noodles. Because the thin slices of beef take only minutes to grill, Bulgogi is a perfect (and original) recipe for a barbecue event; however, it can be grilled effectively in a large heavy grill pan or skillet.

ACCOMPANIMENT TIP: As mentioned, Korean Mixed Vegetables and Noodles (page 164) are essential. If desired, garnish the Bulgogi with water chestnuts (tossed with a touch of sweet-and-sour hot sauce), and/or cooked mini cobs of corn rubbed with sesame oil. Fresh enoki mushrooms drizzled with a mustard herb vinaigrette and cooked broccoli florets are also wonderful.

1 lb (450 g) flank steak or beef tenderloin*
1/4 cup (60 mL) soya sauce
1/3 cup (80 mL) finely sliced green onions
1/4 cup (60 mL) granulated sugar
11/2 tbsp (23 mL) sesame oil
3 tbsp (45 mL) medium dry sherry or red wine
11/2 tsp (8 mL) finely chopped fresh garlic
1/2 tsp (3 mL) peeled and grated fresh gingerroot
1/2 tsp (3 mL) crushed black peppercorns
1 to 2 tsp (5 to 10 mL) liquid smoke (optional)**

GARNISH
11/2 tbsp (23 mL) (total) black and toasted white sesame seeds

1 Using a sharp straight-edged knife, cut slightly thawed beef* into 1/8 inch (0.3 cm) thick slices.

2 To make marinade, mix together soya sauce, green onions, sugar, sesame oil, sherry, garlic, ginger and crushed black peppercorns.

3 Drizzle 11/2 tbsp (23 mL) of soya marinade over bottom of a large glass baking dish. Add a single layer of beef slices and drizzle with more of marinade; add another layer of beef and repeat process using remaining beef and marinade. Allow beef to marinate for at least 1 hour at room temperature or up to 8 hours refrigerated.

4 Just before serving, if desired, very carefully brush liquid smoke evenly over surface of beef slices. ("A little goes a long way!")

5 Working in batches, sear beef slices (arranged in a single layer) on a well-oiled preheated (medium-high) grill, grill pan or skillet for a matter of seconds per side; transfer to a clean platter.

6 Serve sprinkled with toasted sesame seeds.

* To facilitate slicing and handling, freeze the beef and slice it when the beef is only (very) slightly thawed.
** Liquid smoke is available at some supermarkets and specialty food stores.

"WOW" PRESENTATION TIP: For extra excitement and pleasure, I adore serving a Korean/Asian meal in individual bento boxes. (**Note: Bento boxes** are thin metal or lacquered wooden boxes divided into compartments. They are used in Japan to hold different dishes that would make up a meal for one individual. Bento boxes are available at or can be ordered from Asian home decor shops.)

ALTERNATIVE-USE TIP (STEP 6): If serving Bulgogi for a "stand up" event, cut slices into shorter lengths of about 21/2 inches or 6 cm.

SPRINGTIME FILETS MIGNONS
(with Fiddleheads and Wild Garlic)

Makes 4 servings

*Spring is the only time of year that nature produces two of its most exotic "wild products" — fiddleheads and wild garlic. As a salute to the happy arrival of our "Canadian" spring, I have designed a filet mignon recipe where my Sesame Honey Mustard Cognac Sauce plays a critical role in the successful orchestration of the various elements. Served with a mushroom wild rice, the recipe is particularly flavourful as well as intriguing and attractive. (**Note:** At other times of the year, when fiddleheads and wild garlic are not available — or if you have yet to develop a taste for the "exotic wild", use asparagus spears. To serve, lay two cooked and buttered asparagus spears arranged in a criss-cross manner over individual filet mignon steaks.)*

> **ACCOMPANIMENT TIP:** The accompaniments are included in the recipe. Anything else would distract from the amazing combination.

4 thick filet steaks (each: 5 oz or 150 g)
4 strips of bacon
1¹/₃ tbsp (20 mL) teriyaki marinade/sauce (commercial)
1 tbsp (15 mL) olive oil (preferably garlic-infused)
10 oz (280 g) fresh fiddleheads
¹/₄ cup (60 mL) milk
4 cups (1 litre) water
To taste salt
1 tsp (5 mL) peppercorn steak spice
¹/₂ cup (125 mL) Sesame Honey Mustard Cognac
    Sauce (page 214), divided
3 cups (750 mL) mushroom wild rice
    (e.g., page 167), optional

GARNISH
8 stems wild garlic (stem and bulb attached), roots
    trimmed off

1 Wrap each steak with a single strip of bacon. (Secure bacon in position with a toothpick.)

2 Rub exterior of steaks with teriyaki marinade/sauce and then olive oil. Let steaks rest at room temperature for 20 minutes.

3 Rinse fiddleheads several times in plenty of cold water, swirling to remove brown feathery portions; drain. Trim off brown ends.

4 To cook, add fiddleheads and milk to salted boiling water in a large size saucepan. Bring contents back to a boil and cook fiddleheads for 10 minutes. (**Note:** This minimum cooking time is important as a food safety precaution.) Drain, rinse a couple of times and drain very well again. Place fiddleheads between paper towels and pat gently to remove extra water.

5 Just before serving, season steaks with peppercorn steak spice and place in a lightly oiled preheated grill pan (heavy skillet or on a barbecue grill*) over medium heat. Cook to desired degree of doneness, reducing heat if required and turning once (e.g., rare: about 2 to 2¹/₂ minutes per side; medium-rare: about 3 minutes per side). Turn steaks on their sides; rotate (i.e., roll) to sear bacon wrapping.

6 Transfer to a plate, remove toothpicks and hood loosely with aluminum foil (shiny side in).

7 Meanwhile, toss heated (and drained again if necessary) fiddleheads with 1¹/₃ tbsp (20 mL) of Sesame Honey Mustard Cognac Sauce to glaze evenly.

8 For individual servings, if desired place about ²/₃ cup (170 mL) of mushroom wild rice in centre of 4 individual oversized dinner plates and top with a grilled steak.

9 Drizzle each steak with 1 tbsp (15 mL) of Sesame Honey Mustard Cognac Sauce, top with glazed fiddleheads and crown with 2 wild garlic stems arranged in a criss-cross manner. Garnish plates with drizzles of remaining sauce.

* If using a barbecue grill, place the steaks on a well-oiled, medium-high preheated grill and immediately reduce the heat to medium.

> **MAKE-AHEAD TIP (STEPS 3 & 4):** The **fiddleheads** may be cooked, placed in an airtight plastic container and stored refrigerated for up to 2 days.

ALTERNATIVE-COOKING TECHNIQUE (FOR STEP 5): Quickly sear both sides of fillet steaks in a lightly oiled preheated grill pan/skillet or on a barbecue grill. **Transfer them to** a baking sheet, place in a **400°F (200°C) preheated oven** and cook to the desired degree of doneness (e.g., medium-rare: about 5 minutes in the oven).

INFORMATION TIP: Fiddleheads are the edible, tightly coiled tops of young ostrich-fern leaves. Their flavour is often compared to that of asparagus but with an "earthy" or "swamp-like" (slightly bitter) edge. Cooking fiddleheads with milk reduces the bitterness. Fiddleheads with longer stems are sweeter and more tender than short-stemmed ones.

Twin Sesame Seed-Crusted Pork Tenderloin

Makes 4 to 6 servings

No question, this remarkably tender pork tenderloin is always a hit! The lemon zest and Asian flavours sealed in an exotic crust of roasted sesame seeds mesmerizes taste buds. I tend to roast an extra tenderloin to have in the freezer for the assembly of quick, hearty and tasty hors d'oeuvres. **Note:** *The recipe is easy to prepare.)*

ACCOMPANIMENT TIP: I highly recommend serving the pork tenderloin with "Cumin Date Chickpea Salad" (page 116) and "Perfect Rice" (page 168) tossed with toasted slivered almonds. The entire ensemble of delightful flavours is astonishingly simple to put together and may be one of your "best meals ever"! Just ask my husband!

2¹/₄ lbs (1 kg) pork tenderloin (2 or 3 tenderloins)
¹/₄ cup (60 mL) Dijon mustard
3 tbsp (45 mL) (total) mixed black and roasted white
    sesame seeds
1 cup (250 mL) Lemon Mustard Sour Cream Sauce
    (page 92)

MARINADE
¹/₃ cup (80 mL) oyster sauce
1¹/₂ tbsp (23 mL) honey
1¹/₂ tbsp (23 mL) frozen concentrated orange
    juice, thawed
1 tbsp (15 mL) finely chopped fresh garlic
1 tbsp (15 mL) peeled and grated fresh gingerroot
1 tbsp (15 mL) grated lemon zest
³/₄ tsp (4 mL) sesame oil

GARNISH
1 bunch fresh coriander sprigs
As desired fresh edible flowers

1 In a small bowl, mix together all marinade ingredients.

2 Place tenderloins in a resealable plastic bag; add marinade and seal bag.

3 Refrigerate for up to 24 hours or at least overnight, turning bag from time to time.

4 Drain tenderloins well, discarding only marinating liquid (but not lemon zest, garlic and ginger clinging to meat).

5 Spread Dijon mustard over all surfaces. Sprinkle sesame seeds over top and sides, pressing to secure in position.

6 Transfer tenderloins to parchment paper-lined* baking sheet. Place in centre of a preheated oven at 375°F or 190°C until cooked to medium-well** to almost well done (about 12 to 19 minutes, depending on size of tenderloin). Be careful to avoid overcooking.

7 Remove roasted tenderloins from oven, transfer to a cutting board and tent with aluminum foil (shiny side in). Allow to rest about 5 minutes before cutting into slices (thickness: ¹/₄ to ¹/₃ inch or 0.6 to 0.8 cm). Keep slices together in a single loin formation (to retain heat) until ready to serve.

8 If desired, serve slices in an overlapping manner on a bed of fresh coriander sprigs and garnish with edible flowers. Drizzle plates/platter with Lemon Mustard Sour Cream Sauce. Pass extra sauce at table.

* This facilitates the removal of the cooked tenderloins and reduces the amount of clean up.
** Only cook the pork to "medium-well" if that degree of doneness is approved by your local department of food and health guidelines.

TIP: To check the **degree of doneness** of meat, I generally use an **instant-read meat thermometer**. Remember, cooking continues after food has been removed from the heat, so you may want to remove the food a bit sooner.

PESTO BUTTERFLIED LEG OF LAMB
(Barbecued and Roasted)

Makes 4 to 6 servings

By combining a variety of ingredients not normally presented together (Dijon mustard, pesto and nutmeg), I have developed a delightfully innovative recipe for a butterflied leg of lamb. As a marinade and coating, they enhance the flavour of the lamb in a subtle and intriguing manner. The aroma and colour are most appealing. This is always a very successful "No Time, No Talent" recipe! (Of course, it is best to start with good quality lamb.)

    *I have perfected a few different methods of cooking a butterflied leg of lamb depending on the situation and/or time of year. It may be roasted in the oven or grilled on the barbecue. I also use 2 barbecuing techniques. Do what suits you or try all my recommendations. My preferred method of cooking a butterflied leg of lamb is to divide/cut it into its thicker and thinner sections (2 of each) and grill them on the barbecue. (**Note:** This latter barbecue technique is very practical for single people or couples who do not want to cook an entire leg of lamb at once.)*

> **ACCOMPANIMENT TIP:** To really impress, serve the lamb with Middle East Rice Pilaf (page 166) or Nutmeg Mashed Potatoes (page 165) and a medley of grilled vegetables or my Garlicky Feta and Pecan Spinach Salad (page 118).

1 leg of lamb, butterflied (3¹/₃ lb or 1.5 kg)*
1¹/₃ tbsp (20 mL) finely chopped fresh garlic
¹/₄ cup (60 mL) Dijon mustard
¹/₂ cup (125 mL) basil pesto (e.g., page 206 or commercial), divided
2 tsp (10 mL) ground nutmeg
To taste salt
1 cup (250 mL) mustard mint sauce (e.g., page 213)

GARNISH (optional)
¹/₃ to ¹/₂ cup (80 to 125 mL) roasted pine nuts
As desired sprigs of fresh herbs (e.g., thyme, basil, rosemary)

1 Trim excess fat, sinew and most of the "silver" muscle sheath from butterflied leg of lamb, keeping flesh attached to fatty skin side as much as possible. Score fat side.

2 In a small bowl, combine garlic and mustard. Rub all surfaces of lamb with mustard mixture.

3 Apply ¹/₃ cup (80 mL) of pesto evenly over mustard-painted surfaces and sprinkle with nutmeg. If possible, refrigerate and allow lamb to marinate for up to 36 hours (or for at least several hours).

4 Let lamb stand at room temperature for 30 minutes before grilling (or roasting). Season with salt just before cooking. (**Note:** If necessary, hold butterflied leg together with metal or "water-soaked" wooden skewers.)

5 To barbecue lamb, preheat a well-oiled grill to high and *cook according to one of the following 2 methods*. (**Note:** During grilling, watch for flare-ups and douse any flames with a spray of water.)

Method I: *If thick areas of lamb are to be just medium-rare and thin areas are to be well done*, place entire butterflied leg of lamb on a well-oiled preheated (hot) grill (fat side down) and sear for 2½ minutes with hood down. If necessary, brush top of lamb lightly with oil and turn; sear second side for 2½ minutes. Reduce heat to medium; continue to grill meat (with hood down) for about another 4 to 5 minutes per side or until an instant-read meat thermometer just registers about 135°F (57°C) or medium-rare when inserted in thickest areas of meat. (Total cooking time is about 14 to 20 minutes.*) Remember, the internal temperature will rise several more degrees while it "rests". (**Note:** Alternatively, if desired, cut away thinner portions as they reach the appropriate degree of doneness.)

Method II (my preferred method): *If all parts are to be cooked to same degree of doneness (and/or for better control of final degree of doneness of all areas)*, divide/cut butterflied leg of lamb into sections in order to separate thinner and thicker areas of meat (i.e., 2 thinner and 2 thicker sections). Place all sections on a well-oiled preheated (hot) barbecue grill at once. (This ensures searing of all pieces). Cook as directed in Method I, gradually removing thinner and then thicker pieces as they are cooked to degree of doneness desired. (Avoid overcooking.) **For medium-rare:** Total cooking time for thin pieces (1 inch or 2.5 cm thick) is about 5 to 7 minutes; for thicker pieces (2 inches or 5 cm), total time is about 14 to 16 minutes or so depending upon thickness. **For rare,** the cooking times are less.

6 Transfer meat to a platter and cover with aluminum foil (shiny side in). Allow meat to rest for 10 minutes to retain juices.

7 To carve, place a sharp knife at a slight angle at one corner of roast (or grilled pieces) and cut meat against grain into attractive thin diagonal slices.

8 To serve, drizzle lamb slices with remaining pesto, sprinkle with roasted pine nuts and garnish with sprigs of fresh herbs. Pass mustard mint sauce at table.

* **Note:** Cooking time will vary with weight of butterflied leg of lamb and the extent to which the leg has been butterflied.

ALTERNATIVE-TO-BARBECUING TIP (STEP 5):

To oven roast a butterflied leg of lamb, place the lamb (fat side up) on a wire rack in a shallow roasting pan. Roast in a preheated 450°F (230°C) oven for 15 minutes; reduce the heat to 350°F (180°C) and continue to cook until the meat reaches the degree of doneness desired. **Note:** If thick areas are to be medium-rare and thin areas medium-well done, the roasting time will be about 20 to 25 minutes.* However, if all the meat is to be medium-rare, cut off the thinner areas and remove them from the oven as they are cooked (i.e., starting after about 12 to 15 minutes).

DECADENT LAMB MEDALLIONS
(with Seared Pâté)

Makes 4 servings

Stop! This recipe can be rated "outstanding"! My grilled medallions of lamb layered with crusty seared pâté squares and drizzled with a stunning Balsamic Red Wine Drizzle/Sauce is one of those perfectly divine combinations of flavours, textures and forms. Everyone adores it — children included.

ACCOMPANIMENT TIP: My Fruit and Nut Buckwheat/Quinoa Pilaf (page 162) and buttered mini vegetables (e.g., sunburst squash, cauliflower, zucchini or asparagus spears) make delightful accompaniments. When I am in a hurry, fresh watercress drizzled with an herb vinaigrette replaces the mini-veggies!

4 oz (115 g) pâté*, cut into 8 squares (1¼ inches or 3 cm; thickness: about ⅓ inch or 0.8 cm)
2 tbsp (30 mL) all-purpose flour
8 lamb medallions** (each: about 2⅓ oz or 70 g), thickness: ¾ inch or 2 cm
2½ tbsp (38 mL) olive oil (preferably garlic-infused)
To taste crushed black peppercorns
¾ cup (180 mL) Balsamic Red Wine Drizzle/Sauce (page 213)

GARNISH (optional)
4 sprigs of fresh rosemary
2 oz (60 g) fresh enoki mushrooms
3 tbsp (45 mL) vinaigrette, a mustard herb type (e.g., page 211 or commercial)

1 Coat all exterior surfaces of pâté squares lightly with flour; arrange on a wax paper-lined tray and refrigerate for at least 30 minutes (so that flour clings more effectively to pâté).

2 Half an hour before serving, rub lamb medallions with olive oil, season with crushed black peppercorns and leave at room temperature.

3 Just before serving, place medallions on a well-oiled preheated (medium-high) barbecue grill; immediately reduce heat to medium. With lid down, grill medallions for about 2 minutes per side for medium-rare or longer for greater degree of doneness. **Note:** An instant-read meat thermometer inserted into thickest part of flesh is very helpful in accurately determining degree of doneness (e.g., medium rare: 135°F or 57°C).

4 Immediately transfer grilled medallions to a baking sheet and cover loosely with aluminum foil (shiny side in). If necessary, place in a slightly warm oven (150°F or 73°C) until ready to serve.

5 Meanwhile, in a preheated, medium-size, nonstick skillet over medium-high heat, quickly sear flour-coated and chilled pâté squares (for a matter of seconds per side) until golden brown and slightly crisp; transfer to a plate.

6 Place one lamb medallion on each of 4 plates; drizzle each with 2 tsp (10 mL) of Balsamic Red Wine Drizzle/Sauce; top with 1 square of seared pâté. Add a second medallion and square of pâté, then drizzle entire stack with another 2 tsp (10 mL) of Balsamic Red Wine Drizzle/Sauce and pierce with a sprig of fresh rosemary.

7 Artistically garnish plate with fresh enoki mushrooms drizzled with vinaigrette.

8 Serve immediately. Pass remaining Balsamic Red Wine Drizzle/Sauce at table.

* **Note:** I use an affordable commercial pâté. Although we prefer a cognac pork and ham or a chicken liver pâté, the choice is up to you.
** Diameter: about 2½ inches or 6 cm. There are lamb medallions available commercially. Generally each medallion comes wrapped with a thin strip of fat much like bacon-wrapped beef filets mignons.

MAKE-AHEAD TIP (FOR STEP 1): The **floured pâté squares** may be prepared in advance, placed in an airtight container and stored refrigerated for up to a day or frozen for weeks.

ALTERNATIVE-TO-BARBECUING TIP (FOR STEP 3): Place the medallions in a well-oiled preheated **grill pan** or **skillet** over medium heat; immediately reduce the heat slightly. Cook for about 2 minutes per side for medium-rare.

"WOW" TIME-SAVING TIP: With the **Balsamic Red Wine Drizzle/Sauce** and **floured pâté squares** prepared in advance, the lamb can be grilled, the pâté seared and the recipe assembled at the last minute while guests are seated at the table.

SEED-CRUSTED RACK OF LAMB

Makes 4 to 6 servings

Imagine the exceptional overall flavour and texture: coriander and mustard seeds combined with fresh rosemary leaves, mixed together with Dijon mustard, balsamic vinegar and a touch of buckwheat honey! "Fantastic" describes this extremely simple recipe.

> **ACCOMPANIMENT TIP:** My Deluxe Sweet Potato Cream (page 160) is magnificent with this recipe. Also, in my "WOW" Presentation TIP, I like to poke a few spears of freshly cooked asparagus into the centre of the interlocked ribs, artistically securing them between the bones.

3 lb (1.3 kg) frenched* racks of lamb,** trimmed
To taste salt

COATING PASTE
1/3 cup (80 mL) grainy Dijon mustard
3 tbsp (45 mL) balsamic vinegar
2 tbsp (30 mL) freshly crushed coriander seeds
2 tbsp (30 mL) chopped fresh rosemary leaves
1 1/2 tbsp (23 mL) buckwheat honey
1 1/2 tbsp (23 mL) finely chopped fresh garlic
2 tsp (10 mL) whole mustard seeds
2/3 cup (170 mL) Mustard Mint Sauce/Drizzle
     (page 213 or commercial)

GARNISH (optional)
As desired colourful young salad leaves and/or
     fresh herbs

1 In a small bowl, mix together coating paste ingredients.

2 Apply paste evenly over lamb flesh but not over exposed bones. (**Note:** The racks may be prepared to this point several hours in advance and refrigerated until 20 minutes before roasting.)

3 Twenty minutes to half an hour before serving (depending on size of racks and degree of doneness desired), arrange racks of lamb on a parchment-lined baking sheet, fat side up. Place in middle of preheated 450°F (230°C) oven for 10 minutes. Reduce heat immediately to 350°F (180°C) and continue to roast racks of lamb until desired degree of doneness is reached. **Note:** Use an instant-read meat thermometer inserted into thickest part of flesh to determine doneness (e.g., medium-rare: 135°F or 57°C). **FLASH:** If chops are very small and are to be served rare or medium-rare, check their internal temperature just 8 minutes after having put them in oven. They may be done.

4 Remove lamb from oven, tent with aluminum foil (shiny side in) and allow to rest 5 minutes.

5 Arrange racks or chops artistically on plates/platter. If desired, garnish with drizzles of Mustard Mint Sauce and colourful young salad leaves or fresh herbs.

6 Serve. Pass a bowl of extra Mustard Mint Sauce at table.

* "Frenched" racks of lamb have the meat cut away from the ends of the ribs so that part of the bones are exposed.
** **Note:** Usually, I use frozen spring lamb (i.e., 4 racks, each weighing about 11 oz or 310 g) which is conveniently available at many supermarkets. It is generally more affordable, cooks quickly (total time: about 8 to 12 minutes) and is very tender. (Be careful to remove all of the thin "silver" membrane before applying the coating paste.) The small racks of spring lamb also provide more (but smaller) chops per serving which better suit my particular presentation technique. If larger racks are used, the cooking time will be longer.

> **MAKE-AHEAD TIP (STEP 1):** The **coating paste** can be done a week in advance and kept on hand refrigerated.

"WOW" PRESENTATION TIP (STEP 5): For this recipe, I prefer to use small racks of lamb (see **), roasting them and then cutting them into sections/pieces of 3 ribs each. (**Note:** Two sections are required for each serving.) For individual servings, arrange **two sections on a plate facing one another, with bones pointing inward and interlocking together.**

CHILI-CRUSTED SALMON
(with Macadamia Aïoli Shrimp Topping)
Makes 4 servings

Neither skill nor much time are necessary for this delectable recipe! Chili and sugar are caramelized into the flesh of grilled salmon before it is generously garnished with an absolutely decadent macadamia shrimp topping. Prepare one serving or dozens, on a barbecue grill, in a grill pan or skillet. Results will be consistently superb! You may want to put this recipe on the menu for your next "hassle-free" barbecue event!

ACCOMPANIMENT **TIP:** This recipe is wonderful on its own. It doesn't need much in terms of accompaniments. A simple baked potato on a side dish is usually my choice.

4 salmon fillet pieces, skin on and boneless
   (each: 7 oz or 200 g; 1¼ inches or 3 cm thick*)
2 tsp (10 mL) peeled and grated fresh gingerroot
2 tbsp (30 mL) chili powder (not "hot" variety)
2 tbsp (30 mL) granulated sugar
1 tbsp (15 mL) lemon juice
2/3 cup (170 mL) chiffonade (i.e., thinly sliced) of
   romaine lettuce
1 cup (250 mL) Zesty Ginger Mayonnaise
   (page 212), optional

MACADAMIA AÏOLI SHRIMP TOPPING
½ cup (125 mL) coarsely diced shrimp
   (peeled and cooked)
¼ cup (60 mL) coarsely chopped macadamia nuts
2 tsp (10 mL) chopped fresh chives
½ to 1 tsp (3 to 5 mL) finely chopped fresh garlic
½ tsp (3 mL) lemon juice
¼ tsp (1 mL) (Indonesian) hot chili paste, optional
2 tbsp (30 mL) mayonnaise
To taste salt

GARNISH
As desired sprigs of fresh herb (e.g., dill or
   personal choice)

1 To make the Macadamia Aïoli Shrimp Topping, toss together shrimp, nuts, chives, garlic, lemon juice (i.e., ½ tsp or 3 mL) and chili paste. (**Note:** ***The topping can be prepared to this point up to a day in advance and stored refrigerated in an airtight plastic container.***)

2 To make romaine chiffonade, wash and dry lettuce leaves. Layer leaves and slice thinly to create very thin strips of romaine.

3 Before serving, add mayonnaise and salt to shrimp aïoli; toss gently. (Makes about ¾ cup or 180 mL.)

4 Wipe fillets dry with paper towels. Rub flesh with ginger.

5 Combine chili powder and sugar on a flat plate. Press surface of fish fillet (flesh sides only, not skin side) into chili sugar mixture to coat well.

6 Place fillets, flesh side (sugar coated) down, on a well-oiled, preheated (hot) barbecue grill. With lid up, grill first side for 1½ minutes. Using a long broad metal spatula, turn salmon over (i.e., skin side down) and grill second side for 1 minute.

7 Immediately, close lid**, reduce heat to medium and cook **until central core is still translucent** (about another 3 minutes). **Note:** Total cooking time: about 5½ minutes. Avoid overcooking.

8 Pushing spatula under entire fillet, immediately and carefully transfer salmon to a tray/platter. (Don't worry if skin is left behind.) **Promptly cover salmon closely with aluminum foil** (shiny side in) for at least 4 minutes to keep in heat and to allow for more even cooking.

9 Serve salmon fillets with sugar-crusted surface up. Lightly drizzle with lemon juice (according to taste), sprinkle with lettuce (chiffonade), crown with Macadamia Aïoli Shrimp Topping and garnish with sprigs of fresh herbs. If desired, artistically drizzle plates with Zesty Ginger Mayonnaise and pass extra at table.

* If the fillets are not 1¼ inch or 3 cm thick, it is important to adjust the cooking time accordingly.
** Alternatively, at this point, transfer them to a parchment-lined baking tray (skin side down) and place in a preheated 350°F or 180°C oven until done (e.g., 3 minutes).

ALTERNATIVE-TO-BARBECUING TIPS (STEPS 6 TO 8): Use a well-oiled preheated **grill pan** (or **skillet**) placed over medium-high heat. Sear the salmon (sugar-coated side down) for 1½ minutes until brown grill marks appear. Turn and grill second side for 1 minute. Transfer the seared salmon to a parchment-lined baking tray and place in a preheated oven (350°F or 180°C) until the central core is still translucent (about another 3 minutes). Remove from oven and cover with aluminum foil for 4 minutes to allow for more even cooking.

Quick Grilled Salmon Steaks/Fillets
(with Nutty Mango Salsa)

Makes 4 servings

For many, grilled salmon is irresistible, particularly if it is cooked to perfection. With this in mind, I have developed grilling techniques which work wonderfully for me whether I use the barbecue, a grill pan or heavy skillet, on their own or in combination with oven baking. Remember, regardless of the method, avoid overcooking the salmon. Remove it from the heat when the central core is still translucent as the salmon will continue to cook.

*With a little imagination, this perfectly cooked salmon could be the basis for a quick but extraordinary meal. Nutty Mango Salsa is a stunning melange of nuts, fresh mango and coriander, with seductive notes of honey and spice. Grilled salmon topped with this "10 minute" salsa is certainly on my repertoire of "fast, impressive" recipes! It's great with wild salmon as well! (**Note:** The recipe is equally appealing served hot, warm or at room temperature!)*

ACCOMPANIMENT TIP: This recipe requires only the simplest of accompaniments such as baked or mashed potatoes (e.g., page 165) and some broccoli or asparagus.

4 salmon steaks* (thickness: at least 1 inch or 2.5 cm; weight: 8 oz or 225 g)
1¹/3 tbsp (20 mL) olive oil (preferably citrus-infused)
1 tbsp (15 mL) peeled and grated fresh gingerroot
To taste salt and crushed black peppercorns
1¹/3 cups (325 mL) Cognac White Wine Cream Sauce (page 213), optional

NUTTY MANGO SALSA
1¹/2 cups (375 mL) diced (¹/4 inch or 0.6 cm) mango
2¹/2 tbsp (38 mL) chopped fresh coriander leaves
1 tbsp (15 mL) finely diced onion (peeled)
³/4 tsp (4 mL) (Indonesian) hot chili paste
1¹/2 tsp (8 mL) honey
¹/3 cup (80 mL) coarsely chopped macadamia nuts
3 tbsp (45 mL) coarsely chopped pecans

GARNISH (optional)
4 Petit "Plate" Bouquets of Fresh Herbs and/or Edible Flowers (page 202)

1 To make Nutty Mango Salsa, with a fork, toss together mango, coriander leaves and onions; set aside.

Note: **The salsa may be prepared to this point up to 12 hours in advance and stored refrigerated in an airtight plastic container.**)

2 Rub salmon with olive oil and ginger; allow to rest at room temperature for 20 minutes.

3 Season with salt and crushed black peppercorns; place salmon on a well-oiled and preheated very hot barbecue grill over direct heat with lid up. Grill first side for 1¹/2 minutes until brown grill marks appear. Turn salmon over and grill second side for 1 minute. Immediately, close lid, reduce heat to medium and cook **until central core is still translucent** (about another 3 minutes). (Avoid overcooking.)

4 **Remove from heat and promptly cover salmon closely with aluminum foil** (shiny side in) for at least 4 minutes to keep in heat and to allow for more even cooking.

5 Add chili paste, honey and nuts to mango salsa; toss. (Makes almost 2 cups or 500 mL.)

6 Top salmon with Nutty Mango Salsa and if desired, garnish with Petit "Plate" Bouquets of Fresh Herbs and/or Edible Flowers.

7 Serve promptly with Cognac White Wine Cream Sauce, if desired.

* **Option:** Salmon fillets (7 oz or 200 g each and at least 1 inch or 2.5 cm thick) may be cooked in a similar manner. (**Note:** Sear flesh side first, and if finishing the cooking in the oven, arrange the fillets skin side down on baking tray.)

ALTERNATIVE-TO-BARBECUING TIP: Use a well-oiled preheated **grill pan** (or **skillet**) set over medium-high heat. Sear the salmon exactly as outlined in **Step 3**. Immediately transfer it to a parchment paper-lined baking tray and **complete the cooking in a preheated 350°F (180°C) oven** until the central core is still translucent (e.g., about 3 minutes). Continue with **Step 4.**

ALTERNATIVE-COOKING TECHNIQUE TIP (FOR STEP 3): **After searing the salmon** on both sides (i.e., after 2¹/₂ minutes) on the barbecue, transfer the salmon to a parchment-lined baking tray. **Place it in a preheated 350°F (180°C) oven** until the central core is still translucent (e.g., about 3 minutes). **Note:** This is a useful technique when limited time is available for supervising the barbecue or when preparing large quantities of grilled salmon.

Coconut Cream Kaffir Lime Shrimp
(with "Salmon" Alternative)

Makes 4 servings

Dried kaffir leaves give the recipe its unique and appealing flavour, with water chestnuts and cashew nuts providing the crunch! The sauce, which is a principal element of this astonishingly simple dish, may be prepared in advance and even frozen. For special occasions, I use colossal shrimp to offer a truly exceptional dining experience.

ACCOMPANIMENT TIP: This recipe must be served with rice (e.g., page 168). Include a fresh vegetable of choice (e.g., Brussels sprouts) or a simple salad (e.g., mâche, mesclun).

1 small can (8 fl oz/227 mL) water chestnuts, drained and sliced
1 lb (450 g) jumbo shrimp, peeled (with tails attached) and deveined

SAUCE
2 tsp (10 mL) cornstarch
1/2 cup (125 mL) coconut milk
2 to 3 tsp (10 to 15 mL) peeled and grated fresh gingerroot
2 tsp (10 mL) finely chopped fresh garlic
1 1/2 tbsp (23 mL) vegetable oil
1 cup (250 mL) finely chopped onion
2 to 3 tsp (10 to 15 mL) Thai red curry paste*
1 1/2 cups (375 mL) coconut cream**
1 1/2 to 2 tsp (8 to 10 mL) crushed*** dried kaffir lime leaves
1/3 tsp (2 mL) salt
Pinch granulated sugar

GARNISH
1/2 cup (125 mL) roasted whole cashew nuts
sprigs of fresh herbs (e.g., coriander, lemon basil)

1 Whisk cornstarch into coconut milk; set aside.

2 In a large deep skillet, stirring constantly, sauté ginger and garlic in hot oil over medium heat for less than a minute.

3 Add onion; stir frequently and cook until translucent but not brown. Add curry paste; stir constantly to combine well, cooking mixture for two minutes.

4 Add coconut cream and crushed dried kaffir lime leaves; blend well. (**Note:** I freeze any "left over" portions of curry paste, coconut milk and cream for future use, in labeled airtight plastic containers.)

5 Whisk in coconut milk mixture and bring to a boil. Reduce heat and allow sauce to simmer for a few minutes, stirring frequently. Add salt and sugar. (This makes about 2 1/2 cups or 625 mL of sauce.)

6 Just before serving, add water chestnuts and shrimp to heated kaffir lime coconut sauce over medium-low heat. Turning constantly, cook shrimp for a few minutes until shrimp are pink and centres are barely opaque (about 2 1/2 minutes). (Avoid overcooking.) If necessary, adjust consistency and/or flavour of sauce by adding a touch of coconut milk or cream.

7 Transfer shrimp and sauce to serving bowl(s)/ plates; garnish with roasted cashew nuts and sprigs of fresh herbs.

* There are several varieties of Thai red curry paste. Some are fibrous in consistency, others are more starchy. I use the fibrous type which tends to be stronger in flavour. If using the starchy type, you may have to increase (even double) the quantity of Thai red curry paste recommended in this recipe.

** **Option:** For a lighter sauce, substitute a portion of the coconut cream with coconut milk. Using a "light" variety of coconut milk is not recommended as the flavour is reduced.

*** Dried kaffir lime leaves are available at oriental food stores. Crush the leaves in a spice grinder before transferring them to a large sieve set over a large bowl. Rub the crushed leaves through the sieve; discard all hard ribs and bits remaining in the sieve. Use only the tender crushed leaves that pass into the bowl.

MAKE-AHEAD TIP (STEPS 1 TO 5): The **sauce** may be prepared in advance, placed in an airtight plastic container and refrigerated for up to 2 days or frozen for months.

"WOW" TIP: For a **quick meal**, with the sauce on hand (refrigerated or frozen), it is just a matter of adding the water chestnuts and poaching the shrimp for a few minutes.

"WOW"! SALMON STEAK ALTERNATIVE RECIPE/TIP: Instead of the shrimp, add 4 salmon steaks (each: 8 oz/225 g) to the heated kaffir lime coconut sauce in a very large deep skillet over medium-low heat. Bathe the salmon with the sauce, cover and poach gently. Turning the salmon once halfway through the cooking process, cook until the thickest part of the flesh is slightly translucent (about 6 minutes). **Note:** Bathe the salmon well with sauce and avoid overcooking. Serve immediately.

"WOW" COMBINATION: Serve these salmon steaks topped with Coconut Cream Kaffir Lime Shrimp!

EXTRAORDINARY SUN-DRIED TOMATO SHRIMP
(on Squid Ink Pasta)

Makes 4 servings

Who isn't determined to "charm" palates? In this recipe, the delicate flavour of sautéed butterflied shrimp is graciously empowered by sun-dried tomatoes and a devastating Garlic Wine Butter Sauce. **Preparation is surprisingly quick and definitely easy.** *(FLASH: The sauce is simple to make — just follow the instructions!) (A photo appears on page 34.)*

20 colossal shrimp, deveined and unpeeled
    (each: at least 1 oz or 30 g)
8 oz (225 g) squid ink fettuccini
To taste salt
4 tbsp (60 mL) herb garlic butter (e.g., page 205) or
    butter, divided
1 recipe Garlic Wine Butter Sauce*
To taste crushed black peppercorns
1/2 cup (125 mL) julienne-cut sun-dried tomatoes in
    seasoned oil (drained)

GARNISH (optional)
4 clusters of fresh basil leaves (preferably lemon basil)

1 Peel shrimp, keeping tails intact; butterfly** and set aside.

2 Cook fettuccini in an abundant amount of boiling salted water until al dente (about 6 minutes). Drain well and toss with 2 tbsp (30 mL) of garlic butter; set aside. (Makes more than 4 cups or 1 litre.)

3 Prepare Garlic Wine Butter Sauce* to point of blending in heavy cream; remove from heat.

4 **Just before serving**, in a large heavy skillet, sauté shrimp in remaining 2 tbsp (30 mL) of garlic butter over medium heat, seasoning with salt and crushed black peppercorns. Cook until almost done (i.e., centres are still slightly translucent.) Remove from heat.

5 To finish Garlic Wine Butter Sauce, place small skillet with partially prepared sauce over medium-low heat and warm sauce; whisk in butter a few cubes at a time. Remove from heat promptly; season with salt and crushed black peppercorns.

6 Add sun-dried tomatoes and Garlic Wine Butter Sauce to sautéed shrimp in large skillet; toss.

7 Serve immediately (3 to 5 shrimp per serving) over hot squid ink fettuccini. Garnish with clusters of fresh basil leaves.

* To make the Garlic Wine Butter Sauce, in a small skillet over low heat, combine 1/3 cup (80 mL) of chopped green onion, 2 1/2 tbsp (38 mL) each of raspberry vinegar and dry white wine, 2/3 tsp (3.5 mL) each of grated fresh gingerroot (peeled) and finely chopped fresh garlic and 1/3 tsp (2 mL) of powdered mustard. Cook the mixture until only about 1 1/3 tbsp (20 mL) of the liquid remains in the skillet. Blend in 2 1/2 tbsp (38 mL) of heavy cream (35% fat); set aside. Immediately before serving, using almost 1/2 cup (125 mL) of room temperature unsalted butter (cut into cubes), whisk in the butter, a few pieces at a time, until it is completely incorporated. Promptly remove the sauce from the heat, add salt and crushed black peppercorns to taste and combine with shrimp/seafood.
** To "butterfly", cut the entire length of the shrimp deeply along the deveining line but not all the way through. The opened shrimp resemble a "butterfly" shape.

MAKE-AHEAD TIP (STEPS 1 TO 3):
The **shrimp** may be **peeled, butterflied** and refrigerated up to a day in advance. The **fettuccini** may be **cooked** and the **Garlic Wine Butter Sauce partially prepared** an hour before guests arrive.

CAUTION TIP (STEP 5): The **butter** must be **whisked into the sauce immediately before serving**, and the sauce must **not** be **reheated** because it may separate.

Aromatic Asian Seafood Noodles

Makes 4 servings

*I put together this flavourful Asian noodle salad to appease my personal craving for an absolutely satisfying experience of oriental tastes. This recipe may be served warm or cold, and is ideal as a main course for lunch or even for a picnic. (**Note:** The list of ingredients is rather long; however, the recipe is not complicated. **Much of the preparation for this recipe may be done a day in advance and the final dish tossed together just before serving.**)*

9 oz (250 g) vermicelli bean noodles
    (i.e., fine "glass" type)
12 cups (3 litres) boiling water
5 tbsp (75 mL) sesame oil
2¹/₂ tbsp (38 mL) rice vinegar
2¹/₂ tbsp (38 mL) oyster sauce
1¹/₂ tbsp (23 mL) finely chopped fresh garlic
2 to 3 tsp (10 to 15 mL) (Indonesian) hot chili paste
2 to 2¹/₂ tsp (10 to 13 mL) peeled and grated
    fresh gingerroot
4 oz (115 g) peeled carrot
4 oz (115 g) snow peas
2 tbsp (30 mL) toasted white sesame seeds
¹/₃ cup (80 mL) fresh coriander leaves (torn into
    individual leaves)
8 oz (225 g) crabmeat, flaked
¹/₂ to ²/₃ cup (125 to 170 mL) whole cashew nuts
14 oz (400 g) peeled shrimp (large or jumbo),
    deveined with tails left on
1¹/₂ tbsp (23 mL) herb garlic butter (e.g., page 205)
    or butter
To taste salt and crushed black peppercorns
1 cup (250 mL) Zesty Ginger Mayonnaise (page 212),
    optional

Garnish (optional)

12 cherry or grape tomatoes, artistically cut
As desired sprigs of fresh coriander
4 clusters fresh basil leaves

1 Drop vermicelli noodles into a very large pot of boiling water over medium heat. Stir noodles gently to loosen and reduce heat to the lowest setting. Allow noodles to soak until tender but firm (about 4 to 7 minutes). Drain; rinse with cold water until cool and drain well again. (Makes about 7 cups or 1.75 litres.)

2 In a small bowl, combine thoroughly sesame oil, rice vinegar, oyster sauce, garlic, hot chili paste and ginger; set aside.

3 Cut peeled carrots into fine matchstick pieces.

4 Place snow peas in a shallow glass baking dish and cover with boiling water to blanch (about 30 seconds); drain and immediately cool in ice water; drain well. Cut off and discard tips (i.e., end pieces); cut snow peas diagonally into long narrow slices/sticks (width: ¹/₄ inch or 0.6 cm); set aside.

5 Shortly before serving, place drained noodles in a large bowl; drizzle with spicy sesame oil mixture; toss gently but thoroughly. Sprinkle with sesame seeds and toss. Add coriander leaves; toss thoroughly. Add carrot and snow pea pieces, flaked crabmeat and cashew nuts; toss. Season with salt and crushed black peppercorns to taste.

6 Adjust flavours if necessary. (Add touches of extra oyster sauce, rice wine vinegar, sesame oil, garlic and hot chili paste to taste.)

7 Just before serving, sauté shrimp in hot garlic butter over medium heat, seasoning with salt and crushed black peppercorns.

8 To serve, garnish noodles with shrimp and if desired, tomatoes and sprigs of fresh herbs. At table, pass Zesty Ginger Mayonnaise as a side sauce.

> **MAKE-AHEAD TIP:** The **ingredients in Steps 1 to 4** may be prepared a day in advance and stored refrigerated in 4 separate airtight plastic containers. (**Note:** If the noodles toughen, soak them briefly again in boiling water; drain, rinse with cold water and drain them well again.)

SEARED TUNA
(with Sesame Balsamic Vinegar Sauce)
Makes 4 servings

To be perceived as an executive chef or as a "cutting-edge" home cook, you must serve seared tuna. Offered as an hors d'oeuvre, appetizer or main course, it never ceases to impress! In this recipe, Balsamic Vinegar Syrup whisked with an equal quantity of sesame oil plays a critical role. Wasabi and pickled ginger arranged in isolated areas of the plate to be used as desired (if at all) offer the choice of more traditional tuna accompaniments.

> **ACCOMPANIMENT TIP:** Along with the sushi rice, I often serve fresh, crisp Sesame Zucchini "Noodles" (page 169) with this recipe. (**The zucchini may be grated and the sushi rice prepared up to a day in advance.**)

1¹/2 lbs (675 g) fresh tuna steaks, skin removed
   (thickness: 1 inch or 2.5 cm)
3 tbsp (45 mL) sesame oil, divided
1¹/3 tbsp (20 mL) granulated sugar
To taste salt and crushed black peppercorns
2 tsp (10 mL) vegetable oil
3 cups (750 mL) cooked sushi rice (e.g., page 207), warm

SAUCE
¹/2 cup (125 mL) Balsamic Vinegar Syrup (page 204)
¹/2 cup (125 mL) sesame oil

GARNISH (optional)
stems of fresh chives, fresh herbs of choice and
   edible flowers
¹/2 cup (125 mL) pickled ginger
2 tsp (10 mL) wasabi paste

1 To make the sauce, whisk together Balsamic Vinegar Syrup and ¹/2 cup (125 mL) of sesame oil; set sauce aside. (**Note:** The sauce naturally separates; stir well before using.)

2 Rub all surfaces of tuna with about 2 tbsp (30 mL) of sesame oil; sprinkle with sugar, salt and crushed black peppercorns.

3 Brush grill pan (heavy skillet or grill) with vegetable oil and heat (medium-high).

4 Sear tuna on both sides and all edges. (Total searing time: about 1 to 2 minutes. Surfaces should only be seared to a depth of ¹/6 inch or 0.4 cm. Tuna will continue to cook to some degree once steaks have been removed from grill pan.)

5 Transfer seared steaks to a cutting board. Cut across grain into thin slices (thickness: ¹/4 inch or 0.6 cm) and divide into 4 portions.

6 Toss heated sushi rice with about 1 tbsp (15 mL) of sesame oil.

7 For individual servings, place sushi rice (about ²/3 cup or 170 mL) in an even layer (thickness: ¹/2 inch or 1.25 cm) on each of 4 oversized plates and drizzle lightly with sesame balsamic vinegar sauce (e.g., about 2 tsp or 10 mL).

8 Arrange one portion of seared tuna slices in a slightly overlapping manner on rice and drizzle with additional sauce (e.g., 1 tbsp or 15 mL).

9 Garnish tuna artistically with chive stems, fresh herbs and edible flowers. Accent vacant areas of plate with a mound of pickled ginger and drops of wasabi paste.

10 Pass remaining sauce and pickled ginger at table.

> ### "WOW"! MY SECRET TIPS:
> **1** Start with good or "sushi" quality tuna steaks.
> **2** Devote 100% of your attention to absolutely nothing else when searing the tuna.
> **3** Serve it with a drizzle of sauce that makes even top quality tuna taste many times better!

FRAGRANTLY POACHED MUSSELS

Makes 2 "main course" servings or 4 "appetizer" servings

Here is a fantastic and oh so easy recipe! Although mussels can be a perfect "quick meal" formula impressing both family and guests, not everyone has included them in a repertoire of personal recipes. The thick flavourful sauce makes this dish outstanding. (Feel free to adjust the seasoning to suit your own taste.)

> **ACCOMPANIMENT TIP:** I like to serve individual portions of rice (e.g., page 168) in small covered dim sum baskets which have been lined with lettuce leaves. This is always a big hit!

2 lbs (900 g) mussels
1 can plum tomatoes (can size: 14 fl oz or 398 mL)
2/3 cup (170 mL) dry white wine
1/2 cup (125 mL) tomato sauce*
1/4 cup (60 mL) tomato paste*
1 1/2 to 2 tsp (8 to 10 mL) finely chopped fresh garlic
1 tsp (5 mL) fines herbes (or mixed herbs)
1 tsp (5 mL) dried tarragon leaves
1/2 to 3/4 tsp (3 to 4 mL) peeled and grated
    fresh gingerroot
1/4 to 1/3 tsp (1 to 2 mL)** (Indonesian) hot chili paste
1/3 cup (80 mL) heavy cream (35% fat)
3 tbsp (45 mL) chopped fresh parsley
2 tbsp (30 mL) chopped fresh dill weed
1/2 tsp (3 mL) granulated sugar
To taste salt and crushed black peppercorns

GARNISH (optional or as desired)
sprigs of fresh herbs

1 Before cooking, scrub mussels (if necessary) and pull off any beards; rinse and drain well. Place any mussels that are not closed in a bowl of cool water and stir them. **Discard all that do not close after a minute.**

2 Cut tomatoes into quarters; put tomatoes and juice into a large pot. Add wine, tomato sauce, tomato paste, garlic, fines herbes, tarragon, ginger and chili paste.

3 Shortly before serving, bring contents of pot to a boil over medium-high heat. Add mussels and bring back to a boil, turning mussels frequently and into sauce. Cover, reduce heat to medium-low and cook for 5 minutes.

4 Add cream, parsley and dill; turn mussels in sauce; reduce heat to low. Add sugar; season with salt and crushed black peppercorns according to taste. **Discard any mussels that do not open.**

5 Serve mussels with their sauce in large flat bowls. Garnish with sprigs of fresh herbs as desired. **Place an empty bowl on table to catch discarded shells.**

* **Note:** When using a commercial product, generally only partial bottles/cans are needed for this recipe. I freeze the "left over" portions in labeled airtight plastic containers for future use.
** **Option:** To adjust the "hot" spicy flavour of this dish, decrease or increase the quantity of the (Indonesian) hot chili paste according to taste. (The amount of garlic, ginger and crushed black peppercorns may also be adjusted.)

MAIN COURSES

ESCARGOTS AND ORZO IN PORTOBELLO DISH

(with Instant Goat's Cheese Sauce)

Makes 4 servings

I have introduced an unusual quartet of exotically simple ingredients (i.e., portobello mushrooms, orzo, escargots and goat's cheese) to design a dramatically original dish. Together, these elements offer an exciting myriad of flavours, textures and shapes while my "stack" presentation contributes to the artistry and immediate appeal of the recipe. Try it as a main course for lunch or brunch or even for a light dinner. Basically this is an "assembly" recipe where many of the components may be prepared a day or longer in advance.

ACCOMPANIMENT TIP: What might be considered as accompaniments are already included in the recipe.

3 cans escargots (can size: 4 oz or
   115 g drained weight)
3 tbsp (45 mL) butter (first addition)
1¹/₂ tsp (8 mL) finely chopped fresh garlic
1¹/₂ tsp (8 mL) peeled and grated fresh gingerroot
1 tbsp (15 mL) crushed beef bouillon cubes
   (or powder)
To taste crushed black peppercorns
1 cup (250 mL) orzo
¹/₃ cup (80 mL) herb garlic butter (e.g., page 205)
   or butter, divided
To taste salt
4 portobello mushroom caps, large and undamaged
   (diameter: 4¹/₂ inches or 11 cm)
7 oz (200 g) fresh spinach leaves (stems removed)
3 tbsp (45 mL) Zesty Ginger Mayonnaise (page 212)
   or mayonnaise

INSTANT GOAT'S CHEESE SAUCE
5 oz (150 g) soft unripened goat's cheese
¹/₂ tsp (3 mL) crushed chicken bouillon cubes
   (or powder)
¹/₂ cup (125 mL) hot water

GARNISH (optional)
3 cups (750 mL) mesclun or young salad leaves
2 to 3 tbsp (30 to 45 mL) vinaigrette, a mustard herb
   type (e.g., page 211 or commercial)

1 Drain and rinse escargots; drain well again; check for and discard any pieces of shell.

2 Melt butter (first addition) in a large skillet over medium heat. Add garlic and ginger; stirring constantly, cook for 1 minute.

3 Add escargots; sauté for another minute; sprinkle with crushed bouillon cubes and crushed black peppercorns; cook for 2 or 3 more minutes stirring frequently. Cover, remove from heat and allow escargots to rest about 10 minutes to absorb flavours.

4 Cook orzo in an abundant amount of salted boiling water over medium heat until al dente (almost 8 minutes); drain. (Makes about 2¹/₂ cups or 625 mL.) Toss with just 1 tbsp (15 mL) garlic butter and salt to taste; set aside.

5 Meanwhile, to make the Instant Goat's Cheese Sauce, break up goat's cheese in a small bowl. Dissolve crushed chicken bouillon cubes in hot water and gradually add, **as required (i.e., about 6 tbsp or 90 mL)**, to the goat's cheese to form a smooth creamy sauce. If necessary, add an extra touch of bouillon or water to thin the sauce. (Makes about 2/3 cup or 170 mL.)

6 In a couple of large skillets or on a griddle, over medium heat, sauté whole portobello mushroom caps in remaining garlic butter. Season with salt and crushed black peppercorns; cook until about 2/3 done; remove from heat. Transfer sautéed mushroom caps (underside up) to serving plates/platter. Drizzle mushroom drippings into inverted caps.

7 Heat spinach leaves in a microwave oven (or on a lightly oiled skillet) only to soften slightly. (Spinach should still look fresh.) Divide spinach between (and place in) mushroom caps; drizzle with Zesty Ginger Mayonnaise; top with warm orzo (about 1/2 cup or 125 mL per cap); crown with heated escargots.

8 Warm (only) Instant Goat's Cheese Sauce over low heat, stirring constantly. (Avoid overheating.) Drizzle escargots with sauce.

9 If desired, garnish plates with mesclun and drizzle with vinaigrette.

MAKE-AHEAD TIP: The **sautéed** and **seasoned escargots (i.e., Steps 1 to 3)** and **orzo (Step 4)** may be prepared in advance, placed in airtight plastic containers and stored refrigerated for up to 3 days or frozen for months. (**Note:** Normally, I only freeze small "left over" portions of orzo in order to have it on hand for the preparation of hors d'oeuvres.)

CAUTION TIP (FOR STEP 5): Avoid overcooking the portobello caps. They will definitely continue to cook after they have been removed from the skillets/griddle.

ALTERNATIVE-USE TIP: The **sautéed** and **seasoned escargots (i.e,. Steps 1 to 3)** can be used for a **multitude of other purposes** (e.g., pasta recipes, hors d'oeuvres, appetizers and garnishes). This recipe is **considered a "Basic Recipe" in our home.**

ROASTED TOMATO AND GOAT'S CHEESE FUSILLI

Makes 4 servings

Quick tasty comfort food is certain to be a part of everyone's culinary repertoire. In this exquisitely satisfying pasta recipe, I toss freshly cooked fusilli with flavour-rich oven-dried grape tomatoes and goat's cheese. Strategic additions of garlic, hot sauce and fresh parsley add the zip and freshness not always associated with comfort food!

ACCOMPANIMENT AND PRESENTATION TIPS: This recipe is best served in bistro bowls along with something simple such as cumin-scented pork chops (boneless), sausage, ham or a bit of chicken — whatever is convenient and suits the situation!

1/3 cup (80 mL) **soft unripened goat's cheese (first addition)**
1/4 cup (60 mL) **heavy cream (35% fat), first addition**
1/4 cup (60 mL) **water**
2 tsp (10 mL) **finely chopped fresh garlic**
1/3 to 1/2 tsp (2 to 3 mL) **(Indonesian) hot chili paste**
1 lb (450 g) **fusilli (i.e., little "spring-like" pasta)**
1 tbsp (15 mL) **butter**
8 oz (225 g) **oven-dried grape (or cherry) tomatoes***
1/2 cup (125 mL) **chopped fresh parsley**
To taste **salt and crushed black peppercorns**
1/4 to 1/3 cup (60 to 80 mL) **heavy cream (35% fat), second addition (optional)**
2 to 4 tbsp (30 to 60 mL) **goat's cheese (second addition)**

GARNISH (optional)
sprigs of fresh herbs (e.g., tarragon, dill, parsley)

1 In a small bowl, whisk together goat's cheese, cream (first addition), 1/4 cup (60 mL) of water, garlic and chili paste; set aside.

2 About 15 to 20 minutes before serving, in a large pot, cook pasta in an abundant amount of salted boiling water, stirring from time to time, until al dente. Drain well, **reserving 1 cup (250 mL) of water**. Return pasta to pot, toss with butter; set aside.

3 Virtually at time of serving, place pot over medium-low heat and heat pasta, adding a touch of reserved water as necessary.

4 Add goat's cheese mixture and toss to distribute evenly through pasta.

5 Promptly, add tomatoes, toss and allow mixture to heat through.

6 Sprinkle with parsley; season with salt and crushed black peppercorns according to taste.

7 Immediately (i.e., within seconds) before transferring to serving dish(es), if desired, stir in more cream (second addition), another 2 to 4 tbsp (30 to 60 mL) of goat's cheese (second addition) and if necessary, a touch more of reserved water. (**Note:** The pasta should be "saucy", not pasty.)

* To make 8 oz (225 g) of oven-dried grape/cherry tomatoes, cut 1 lb (450 g) of grape/cherry tomatoes horizontally in half; arrange on a baking sheet (cut side up), drizzle with 1 tbsp (15 mL) of olive oil and season with salt and crushed black peppercorns. Bake in a 225°F (110°C) oven until the tomatoes are reduced to about half of their original size (about 1 1/2 to 2 hours). If not using immediately, cool and store the oven-dried tomatoes refrigerated for up to 3 days or frozen for a couple of weeks.

MAKE-AHEAD TIP: With the **oven-dried tomatoes*** prepared in advance (e.g., during a small pocket of time), **dinner is ready in a matter of minutes!** FLASH: With other ingredients also assembled in the required amounts, the **recipe is perfect for occasions which demand "make ahead" casual recipes** (i.e., visit of family or house guests).

Recipes for Main Course Accompaniments might well be a book on their own! I adore them, particularly with the wide variety of incredible vegetables readily available all year round. However, I have restricted myself to presenting only those recipes which are absolutely essential for the main courses presented in this book and which one might not find in other books.

Experimenting in my kitchen, I am delighted to "come up with" new accompaniment recipes which truly please the palate and perfectly compliment the main course. All the following recipes are unique or offer a "special twist" to more traditional versions. My deliberate use of a myriad of ingredients makes dining not only more interesting but perhaps even more nourishing. Quinoa, kasha, wild and flavoured rices, pilafs, sweet and white potatoes, oriental noodles and fresh vegetable "noodles", chickpeas, fiddleheads, etc., are part of our regular everyday menus. Several of the recipes listed under "Salads", make delightful main course accompaniments. I am convinced that many of the following recipes will become versatile favourites for readers as they mix and match them with other main course recipes beyond the pages of this book.

Note: 🐇 designates a "No Time, No Talent" recipe.

For this section, I recommend having a supply of "toasted slivered almonds" on hand to add to the list of "BASIC RECIPES" mentioned in previous sections.

ACCOMPANIMENTS

DELUXE SWEET POTATO CREAM

Makes 2¹/3 cups or 575 mL (4 servings)

Here is an "exquisite" recipe for sweet potatoes. The real magic comes from the touch of Dijon mustard and the dash of hot chili paste which accentuate the infusion of sautéed chives, fresh ginger and garlic. Serve the sweet potato cream as a welcome accompaniment for a myriad of main course dishes (e.g., lamb, chicken, turkey, duck, goose, game).

2 lbs (900 g) sweet potatoes
3 tbsp (45 mL) butter
3 tbsp (45 mL) finely chopped fresh chives
1¹/2 tsp (8 mL) peeled and grated fresh gingerroot
¹/2 tsp (3 mL) finely chopped fresh garlic
2 tsp (10 mL) Dijon mustard
¹/2 tsp (3 mL) raspberry vinegar (or red wine vinegar)
To taste salt
¹/4 tsp (1 mL) (Indonesian) hot chili paste (optional)*

1 Scrub sweet potatoes clean; with tines of fork, prick skins in several places.

2 Bake** until soft. As soon as potatoes are cool enough to handle, remove and discard skins.

3 While sweet potatoes are still warm, mash flesh (or press through a "ricer") to form a smooth purée. (**Note:** If "mashed" purée is fibrous, using a heavy rubber spatula, rub purée through a coarse mesh sieve.)

4 In a small skillet over medium heat, melt butter. Add chives, ginger and garlic; cook until chives soften slightly.

5 Stir chive mixture into sweet potato purée. Add Dijon mustard, vinegar, salt and if desired, hot chili paste; blend well with a fork/rubber spatula/spoon. (**Note:** Do not use a blender as the potato mixture may become too soft and/or "gummy".)

6 Serve warm.

* Add if an interesting "zip" is desired.
** Sweet potatoes can be baked quickly (about 12 to 15 minutes) and conveniently in a microwave oven set at high heat.
*** When using the recipe as a filling for ravioli, add more flavouring if desired (i.e., slightly more ginger, garlic, hot chili paste).

MAKE-AHEAD TIP: Store the Deluxe Sweet Potato Cream refrigerated in an airtight plastic container for up to 3 days. (It may be stored frozen for months; however, previously frozen sweet potato cream tends to be slightly softer.)

ALTERNATIVE-USE TIP: As I say, let your imagination and palate be your guide. Add the sweet potato cream to the bottom of pastry cups for creative **hors d'oeuvres** or use it as a **component in an appetizer** (e.g., ravioli***, stacks).

DOUBLE SESAME QUINOA
(with "Buckwheat" Alternative)
Makes about 3 cups or 750 mL (4 to 6 servings)

Quinoa ("keen-wa") is an ancient grain originally cultivated in the mountains of South America. This unique "less is more" recipe frequently proves to be the perfect accompaniment for certain main course dishes. A strategic balance of sesame enhances the nutty flavoured quinoa without overwhelming it. I am quietly amused by the significant role designated to the tiny black sesame seeds. They add an appealing contrast in colour, size and texture while harmonizing with the shape of the individual grains of quinoa.

1 cup (250 mL)* quinoa**
2 cups (500 mL) cold water
1¹/3 to 1²/3 tbsp (20 to 25 mL) sesame oil
2 to 3 tsp (10 to 15 mL) black sesame seeds
To taste salt and crushed black peppercorns

1   To cook quinoa, rinse a couple of times and drain well.

2   Place in a medium-size saucepan along with cold water, cover and bring to a boil over high heat.

3   Immediately, reduce heat to simmer; allow quinoa to cook until tender and almost translucent (8 to 12 minutes). (Be careful! Avoid overcooking.)

4   Remove from heat immediately, pour into a large wire sieve and thoroughly drain off any extra liquid.

5   Quickly transfer cooked quinoa to a large platter. Turn hot quinoa gently with a fork to stop cooking process, to separate grains and allow excess moisture to escape.

6   Toss cooked quinoa with sesame oil and seeds; season with salt and crushed black peppercorns. If not using immediately, store refrigerated for up to 2 days.

* **Note:** To make larger quantities, it is NOT recommended to more than double this recipe at once.
** Quinoa is available in health food stores as well as some supermarkets and specialty food stores.

MAKE-AHEAD TIP (STEPS 1 TO 5): The quinoa may be cooked, placed in an airtight plastic container and stored refrigerated for up to 2 days or frozen for several months. (**Note:** Although I freeze cooked quinoa, I only tend to freeze "left over" portions of Double Sesame Quinoa.)

TIP (ALTERNATIVE TO QUINOA): Double Sesame *Buckwheat Groats* may be prepared by substituting 3 cups (750 mL) of cooked **buckwheat groats** (see: Fruit and Nut Buckwheat Pilaf, page 162) for the cooked quinoa.

ALTERNATIVE-USE TIP: With a little ingenuity and experimentation, the recipe may also be used as a **component in hors d'oeuvres, appetizers** and **salads.**

FRUIT AND NUT BUCKWHEAT PILAF
(with Quinoa Alternative)

Makes 3 1/2 cups or 875 mL (5 to 6 servings)

> **"WOW" FACTOR:** This simple but exquisite recipe is a real **"winner"**! It **placed first** in the buckwheat groats' category in The Birkett Mills International Association of Culinary Professionals' buckwheat competition.

With its exciting flavours and textures, the myriad of uses for this currant and nut buckwheat pilaf is remarkable. Fresh chives and a mustard herb vinaigrette add an interesting "zip", allowing the pilaf to marry extremely well with poultry and meats (e.g., lamb, pork, game) as well as with scallops. Take it on a picnic; make it part of your next dinner, barbecue or buffet! Served warm, cold or at room temperature, it is always a treat. With cooked buckwheat groats on hand, the recipe can be tossed together in minutes! (**Note:** *A photo appears on page 143 with the Decadent Lamb Medallions.*)

2 tbsp (30 mL) **crushed chicken bouillon cubes**
    (**or powder**)
2 cups (500 mL) **hot water**
1 cup (250 mL) **whole buckwheat groats***
2/3 cup (170 mL) **currants**
1/2 cup (125 mL) **chopped hazelnuts or pecans**
1/4 cup (60 mL) **finely chopped fresh chives**
2 1/3 tbsp (35 mL) **vinaigrette, a mustard herb type**
    (**e.g., page 211 or commercial**)
To taste salt and crushed black peppercorns
Pinch granulated sugar (optional)

1 In a medium saucepan, dissolve crushed bouillon cubes in hot water; place over high heat and bring to a boil.

2 Stir in buckwheat groats, bring back to a boil and immediately reduce heat to low, covering saucepan tightly. Simmer until groats are just tender (about 15 to 18 minutes); avoid overcooking.

3 Pour cooked groats into a large wire sieve; turn gently with a fork and drain extremely well.

4 Immediately, spread groats on a couple of large plates. With a fork, gently turn kernels to stop cooking process and to allow extra moisture to escape. Let groats cool and rest for at least 30 minutes before using or refrigerating. (This makes about 2 1/2 cups or 625 mL of cooked groats.) **Note:** *Groats become drier (i.e., less sticky) and firmer (i.e., not "mushy") as they cool and rest.*

5 To make Fruit and Nut Buckwheat Pilaf, toss together cooked buckwheat groats, currants, hazelnuts, chives, vinaigrette, salt and crushed black peppercorns. If desired, add a pinch of sugar to strategically balance the acidic flavour of the vinaigrette.

6 Let pilaf rest at least an hour to allow flavours to develop.

7 Serve pilaf at room temperature or cold.

* These are dehulled, unroasted buckwheat kernels. They are available in health food stores as well as some supermarkets and specialty food stores.

> **TIP (ALTERNATIVE TO BUCKWHEAT):**
> A Fruit and Nut *Quinoa Pilaf* may be prepared by substituting 2 1/2 cups (625 mL) of cooked **quinoa** (see: Double Sesame Quinoa, page 161) for the cooked buckwheat groats.

Honey Nutmeg Fiddleheads

Makes about 3 cups or 750 mL (6 to 8 servings)

When fiddleheads appear on the market in Canada, it is a sure sign that spring has arrived. Since they are only available for a few weeks, we take full advantage. In the process, I have learned some "tricks"! First, fiddleheads could tend to taste a bit earthy (i.e., "swampy") if not rinsed well and prepared with a careful balance of other ingredients.
I find that additions of butter, buckwheat honey and nutmeg work wonders in maintaining the flavour of the fiddleheads while camouflaging any less appealing "edge"! Also, to reduce the slight bitterness, add a little milk to the water when cooking the fiddleheads.
(***Note:** A photo appears on page 137.*)

1 lb (450 g) fresh fiddleheads*
¹/₃ cup (80 mL) milk
1¹/₂ tbsp (23 mL) butter
1¹/₂ tbsp (23 mL) buckwheat honey
To taste ground nutmeg, salt and crushed
  black peppercorns

1 Rinse fiddleheads several times in plenty of cold water, swirling to remove brown feathery portions; drain.

2 Trim off brown ends.

3 When ready to cook, add fiddleheads and milk to an abundant amount of salted boiling water in a large saucepan. Bring contents back to a boil and cook fiddleheads gently for at least 10 minutes. (This is important to meet recommended health standards.) Drain and rinse very well.

4 Immediately before serving, if necessary reheat fiddleheads; drain off any liquid, toss with butter and honey, and season with nutmeg, salt and crushed black peppercorns.

* Fiddleheads are the edible, tightly coiled tops of young ostrich-fern leaves; thus, they are usually only available "fresh" for a few weeks in the spring. Their flavour has been compared to that of asparagus, however with a slightly bitter and "earthy" edge. Fiddleheads with longer stems are sweeter and more tender than short-stemmed ones.

MAKE-AHEAD TIP (STEPS 1 AND 2):
  Fiddleheads may be **rinsed and cleaned** a day or two before cooking.

MAKE-AHEAD TIP (STEP 3): The fiddleheads may be cooked, placed in an airtight plastic container and stored refrigerated for up to 2 days.

Korean Mixed Vegetables and Noodles

Makes 4¹/₂ cups or more than 1 litre (4 regular servings or about 8 to 10 cocktail buffet servings)

*As delicious and irresistible as the barbecue beef dish, Korean Bulgogi, may be, I believe that it must be served with a colourful and rich array of stir-fried sliced vegetables tossed with noodles and lacquered with soya sauce and hot chili paste. This vegetable-noodle combination is one of those dishes that, regardless of its temperature, is always a treat for the palate! Serve it as an accompaniment for other recipes, particularly grilled chicken (e.g., "Quick Chinese Spiced Wings/Drumsticks", page 132), or pack it in a picnic basket. (**Note**: Despite the number of steps, **this recipe is easy!**)*

8 dried shiitake mushroom caps
4 oz (115 g) vermicelli bean noodles
10 cups (2.5 litres) boiling water
3¹/₂ oz (100 g) fresh spinach leaves, stems removed
4 tbsp (60 mL) vegetable oil, divided
To taste salt
¹/₂ tsp (3 mL) finely chopped fresh garlic
¹/₂ tsp (3 mL) peeled and grated fresh gingerroot
²/₃ cup (170 mL) peeled and sliced onion
¹/₂ cup (125 mL) julienne-cut carrot (peeled)
¹/₂ red bell pepper (medium size), very thinly
    sliced (vertically)
¹/₄ cup (60 mL) sliced green onion
To taste crushed black peppercorns
2 tbsp (30 mL) soya sauce
1 tbsp (15 mL) sweet soya sauce/paste
1 tsp (5 mL) sesame oil
1 tsp (5 mL) granulated sugar
¹/₂ tsp (3 mL) (Indonesian) hot chili paste
1 tsp (5 mL) toasted white sesame seeds
¹/₃ cup (80 mL) whole cashew nuts (optional)

1 Soak dried mushrooms in lukewarm water until soft (about 50 minutes). Squeeze out and discard liquid; cut mushroom caps into thin slices.

2 Drop vermicelli noodles into a large pot of boiling water. Stir noodles gently to loosen and reduce heat to lowest setting. Allow noodles to soak until tender but firm (about 5 to 7 minutes). Drain; rinse with cold water until cool and drain well again. (Makes about 2¹/₂ cups or 625 mL.) If not using until later, place noodles in an airtight plastic container lined with a triple layer of paper towels and refrigerate.

(**Note**: When serving the Korean Mixed Vegetables and Noodles at a "stand up" event, cut the noodles into shorter lengths of 3 inches or 8 cm.)

3 If spinach leaves are large, tear them into somewhat smaller pieces. In a large skillet/wok over medium heat, sauté spinach leaves in 1 or 2 teaspoons (5 to 10 mL) of vegetable oil until leaves wilt. (It may be necessary to do this in 2 batches.) Transfer wilted leaves to a large platter; season with salt and set aside.

4 Return large skillet/wok to medium heat. Sauté garlic and ginger in hot vegetable oil (2 tbsp or 30 mL) for about 30 seconds. Add onion and carrots; stir-fry for about 30 seconds. Add red pepper, green onions and mushrooms; stir-fry until red pepper is tender crisp (about another 2 minutes), seasoning with salt and crushed black peppercorns. Transfer to platter with spinach. Toss ingredients evenly together.

5 Combine soya sauces, sesame oil, sugar and chili paste in a small bowl.

6 Just before serving, heat remaining vegetable oil (i.e., more than 1 tbsp or 15 mL) in wok over medium to medium-low heat. Add noodles and quickly drizzle with soya sauce mixture; toss to coat noodles evenly.

7 Add stir-fried vegetables, toss lightly together and adjust seasoning if necessary; heat through. (Avoid overcooking.)

8 Sprinkle with sesame seeds and cashew nuts; serve.

MAKE-AHEAD TIP: With Steps 1 to 5 done up to a day in advance and refrigerated, the recipe may be quickly stir-fried together just minutes before serving.

NUTMEG MASHED POTATOES

Makes about 2¹/4 cups or 550 mL (4 servings)

In my Nutmeg Mashed Potatoes, there is a magnificent creaminess punctuated by the discreet flavour of nutmeg. As a remarkably versatile accompaniment, the recipe enhances both mild-flavoured poultry or fish as well as more robust meats and game. Beware, these mashed potatoes can be addictive!

1¹/2 lb (675 g) potatoes (e.g., Russet)
To taste salt
3 tbsp (45 mL) butter
3 tbsp (45 mL) sour cream or heavy cream (35% fat)
¹/3 to ¹/2 tsp (2 to 3 mL) ground nutmeg

1 Peel potatoes and cut into wedges.

2 Place in a medium-size saucepan, cover with cold water and add salt to taste.

3 Cover saucepan, place over high heat and bring to a boil. Reduce heat immediately and cook potatoes at a gentle boil until soft. Drain well.

4 Promptly, add butter, sour cream and nutmeg; mash to a smooth consistency. (If necessary, add an extra touch of butter, sour cream/heavy cream, nutmeg and salt according to taste.) Serve hot.

MAKE-AHEAD TIP: The recipe may be prepared and refrigerated up to 2 days in advance. Reheat the potatoes (loosely covered) in a microwave oven at "high" heat (or in a preheated moderate oven) until heated through.

ORIENTAL MANGO RICE

Makes 4²/3 cups or more than 1 litre (6 to 8 servings)

*Simple additions of mango, fresh coriander and sesame oil redefines cooked rice as an elegant and refreshing side dish. Served hot or cold, Oriental Mango Rice brings a symphony of delicate notes to a menu. It's fabulous with chicken, pork, lamb, seafood, fish and game as well as tofu and a variety of vegetarian choices. Remember to include it on a buffet and in a picnic basket. (**Note:** A photo appears on page 132 with Quick Chinese Spiced Wings/Drumsticks.)*

4 cups (1 litre) cooked long grain rice (e.g., page 168)
1 tsp (5 mL) finely chopped fresh garlic
¹/3 cup (80 mL) chopped fresh coriander leaves
3 tbsp (45 mL) Honey Mustard Mayonnaise (page 211)
2 to 3 tbsp (30 to 45 mL) sesame oil
1¹/3 cups (325 mL) diced (¹/3 inch or 0.8 cm) fresh
    mango (flesh only)
To taste salt
¹/4 cup (60 mL) toasted slivered almonds

1 Toss together rice (hot, cold or at room temperature) and garlic. Add coriander leaves and toss again.

2 Whisk together Honey Mustard Mayonnaise and sesame oil; drizzle over rice mixture and toss.

3 Fold in mango. If necessary, season with salt to taste.

4 Just before serving, fold in almonds.

MAKE-AHEAD TIP (STEPS 1 TO 3): If serving cold or at room temperature, the Oriental Mango Rice may be prepared (except for the addition of the almonds) several hours in advance and refrigerated.

MAIN COURSE ACCOMPANIMENTS

MIDDLE EAST RICE PILAF

Makes more than 3½ cups or almost 1 litre (4 to 6 servings)

One of my very favorite dishes is a highly fragrant middle east rice pilaf. In this recipe, I combine the sweet flavours of raisins, sautéed onion and garlic with a multitude of spices including cardamom, cinnamon and cumin, as well as orange zest and pistachios. The dish is quick and easy to make. Serve it with meat, fish and poultry. The stunning yellow colour of this pilaf studded with the green pistachios and brown raisins makes it completely irresistible!

1 cup (250 mL) basmati rice
1¾ tbsp (27 mL) crushed chicken bouillon cubes
   (or powder)
1 cup (250 mL) hot water
⅓ cup (80 mL) finely chopped white onion
2 tbsp (30 mL) butter, divided
¾ tsp (4 mL) whole cumin seeds
½ tsp (3 mL) turmeric
½ tsp (3 mL) finely chopped fresh garlic
¼ tsp (1 mL) ground decorticated* cardamom
2 cinnamon sticks (length: 3 inches or 8 cm),
   broken into 3 pieces
6 whole cloves
3 bay leaves
¼ cup (60 mL) dark raisins
1½ tsp (8 mL) grated orange zest
To taste salt
⅛ tsp (Pinch) crushed black peppercorns
¼ cup (60 mL) pistachio nuts (shelled)

1 Rinse rice several times in cold water. Place in a medium size pot; cover generously with cold water. (Water should cover rice by 1½ inches or 3.5 cm.) Soak for 45 minutes; drain rice very well and discard water.

2 Meanwhile, dissolve crushed bouillon cubes in hot water; set aside.

3 Stirring frequently, sauté onion in 1 tbsp (15 mL) of melted butter in a heavy medium-size nonstick saucepan over medium heat until tender. Add cumin seeds, turmeric, garlic, cardamom, cinnamon sticks, cloves and bay leaves; stir constantly for about a minute.

4 Increase heat to medium-high, add drained rice; stirring constantly, roast mixture for a couple of minutes. Add bouillon and raisins; bring to a boil. Reduce heat to lowest setting; stir mixture, cover saucepan tightly and cook for 12 minutes without removing lid.

5 Check for doneness. If tender, gently fluff rice with a fork and carefully fold in remaining tablespoon (15 mL) of butter, along with orange zest, salt, crushed black peppercorns and pistachios.

6 If desired, add a touch of extra ground decorticated cardamom according to taste (e.g., ⅛ tsp or a pinch).

7 Remove from heat.

* Cardamom seeds are encapsulated in small pods about the size of a cranberry. With the pod removed and discarded, the seeds are then referred to as "decorticated cardamom".

MAKE-AHEAD TIP: Although this recipe is best served shortly after having been cooked, it may be prepared up to 12 hours in advance. Allow the pilaf to cool and store it refrigerated in an airtight plastic container. Immediately before serving, reheat the pilaf in a large covered nonstick skillet over medium-low heat. Add a few drops of water (as required) to prevent the pilaf from sticking and turn frequently until hot.

MUSHROOM WILD RICE

Makes 3¹/₂ cups or almost 1 litre (4 to 6 regular servings or about 10 cocktail buffet servings)

With its additions of garlic, ginger and crunchy almonds, this recipe gives a broader dimension of flavours and textures to the typical stellar combination of wild rice and mushrooms! Yes, my Mushroom Wild Rice is a delectable accompaniment for virtually everything — seafood, fish, game, beef, poultry and pork. Featuring one of Canada's navtive food products (i.e., wild rice), it disappears quickly when placed on a buffet table! The recipe certainly is a smart choice for a potluck event.

1 tsp (5 mL) finely chopped fresh garlic
1 tsp (5 mL) peeled and grated fresh gingerroot
¹/₄ cup (60 mL) butter
¹/₄ cup (60 mL) peeled and diced shallots
2¹/₂ cups or 8 oz (625 mL or 225 g) sliced
    mushroom caps
To taste salt and crushed black peppercorns
2 cups (500 mL) cooked tasty wild rice
    (e.g., page 207)
¹/₄ cup (60 mL) toasted slivered almonds

1 In a large skillet over medium-low heat, sauté garlic and ginger in hot butter for about 1 minute. Add shallots and sauté carefully until translucent.

2 Add mushrooms, seasoning with salt and crushed black peppercorns; sauté over medium-high heat until just tender and slightly browned. Remove from heat.

3 Shortly before serving, heat mushroom mixture over medium-low heat. Stir in cooked wild rice; combine thoroughly and heat through, adding a few drops of water to keep mixture slightly moist. If necessary, adjust flavours by adding a touch of butter/ garlic butter, salt and/or crushed black peppercorns. Cover and remove from heat immediately. (**Note of Caution:** *Avoid overheating rice and/or holding it for more than a few minutes as the grains may open too much.*)

4 Stir in toasted almonds and serve.

MAKE-AHEAD TIP (STEPS 1 & 2):
The recipe may be prepared to this point up to 2 days in advance, cooled and stored refrigerated in an airtight plastic container. (**Note:** The wild rice may also be prepared days in advance.)

PERFECT RICE

Makes more than 6 cups or 1.5 litres (6 to 10 servings)

*I have developed this recipe using an Iranian technique where the rice is soaked in cold water, then partially cooked in an abundant amount of boiling water before finally being steamed with butter over low heat. The cooked grains are tender and remain separate — Perfect Rice! (**Note:** A photo appears on page 139 with Twin Sesame Seed-Crusted Pork Tenderloin.)*

2 cups (500 mL) basmati* or long grain rice
8 cups (2 litres) hot water
1¼ tbsp (19 mL) salt
4 tbsp (60 mL) herb garlic butter (e.g., page 205) or butter, melted and divided

1 Rinse rice several times in cold water. Place in a large pot; cover generously with cold water. (Water should cover rice by 1½ inches or 3.5 cm.) Soak for 45 minutes; drain rice and discard water.

2 Bring hot water to a boil in a large pot; add salt. Pour drained rice in a steady stream into boiling water. Boil, uncovered, until grains of rice are about ¾ cooked (approximately 5 to 6 minutes), stirring occasionally.

3 Using a large sieve, drain rice very well and rinse pot.

4 Place only 2 tbsp (30 mL) of melted garlic butter in bottom of pot. Add drained rice, shaping it into a cone. Drizzle remaining melted garlic butter over surface of rice. Cover pot tightly.

5 Place over lowest heat possible and cook rice until just tender (about 3 to 6 minutes depending on "fluffiness" desired).

6 Remove from heat and toss rice lightly with a fork.

* If using other types of long grain rice, the boiling and final cooking times may vary.

TIP: If the rice is perfectly cooked but it is to be served later, spread it on a platter to stop the cooking process. (If the rice could be slightly more tender, keep the pot covered and off any heat; toss the rice every few minutes and check for doneness.)

MAKE-AHEAD TIP: Rice is best served shortly after having been cooked; however, it may be cooled and stored refrigerated in airtight plastic containers for up to 3 days. To reheat the rice, immediately before serving, steam the quantity required in a wire sieve suspended above a small amount of simmering water in a covered pot.

CAUTION TIP: "Perfect Rice" (unlike cooked wild rice) does not freeze well.

ALTERNATIVE-RECIPE TIP: Often, I serve a **combination of this rice and Tasty Wild Rice** (page 207), preparing the 2 rice recipes separately and then folding them together.

SESAME ZUCCHINI "NOODLES"

Makes 2 cups or 500 mL (4 to 6 servings)

It takes only 5 minutes to prepare this out of the ordinary, "garden fresh" vegetable side dish! The crisp, sesame-scented strands of zucchini noodles surprise and delight everyone! Their flexibility enables them to be served with a variety of dishes from meat to seafood. They are excellent drizzled with Lemon Mustard Sour Cream Sauce.

2 zucchini, medium size and whole
    (each: about 6 oz or 175 g)
1 tbsp (15 mL) sesame oil
3/4 tsp (4 mL) black sesame seeds
3/4 tsp (4 mL) roasted white sesame seeds
To taste salt (optional)

GARNISH (optional)
1/4 to 1/3 cup (60 to 80 mL) Lemon Mustard Sour
    Cream Sauce (page 92)

1 Cut off and discard ends of zucchini.

2 Using a **coarse grater***, grate zucchini into long, strong, "noodle-like" strands.

3 Just before serving, toss zucchini "noodles" with sesame oil and sesame seeds. If desired, add salt to taste at the last minute.

4 If appropriate, serve drizzled with a touch of Lemon Mustard Sour Cream Sauce.

* **Note:** If a fine grater is used, the zucchini noodles may be "watery" and slightly "mushy".

> **MAKE-AHEAD TIP (STEPS 1 & 2):** The zucchini may be grated up to 2 days in advance and stored refrigerated in an airtight plastic container.

For most people, dessert is the "pièce de résistance" of a meal. And if you are not a dessert fan, read on! You are guaranteed to be enticed, charmed and persuaded to try some of my personal creations. An array of fresh berries and fruit, ice cream, chocolate, pastry, mousses, meringues, sauces — even goat's cheese and wasabi — is all there!

Being the last course served at the table, desserts must be special and could be fun! It is the grand finale, so give it your "best shot"! I like my desserts to surprise and to look particularly attractive, inviting and tempting. Although "we eat with our eyes", desserts should also offer an appealing balance of flavours and, if possible, textures, colours, shapes and heights. Flashes of freshness and bursts of the "unexpected" are always well appreciated.

All my desserts are rather original. Many are absolutely decadent (e.g., Caramel Mousse Chocolate Cups, Decadent Chocolate Mint Ice Cream and Orange-Infused Lava Cakes); however, portion sizes are definitely reasonable. Others are certain to be a first-time experience (e.g., Blackberry Butterscotch Cocktail Fondue, Mini Flowerpots of Chocolate Mint Ice Cream and The Ultimate Coffee Spoons). Some will leave the diner happily perplexed (e.g., Berries and Cream Exotic Straw Sandwiches and Tiramisu Wasabi Ice Cream Parfaits). A number may be conveniently served as intriguing "taster desserts" at drinks parties or stand-up receptions.

FLASH: All the desserts in this book with the exception of "Orange-Infused Chocolate Lava Cakes" are basically assembly desserts. And of these, excluding the making of Kataifi Straw Disks and the baking of phyllo squares, they all are also "No Time, No Talent" recipes.

Note: designates a "No Time, No Talent" recipe.

For this section, with regards to "BASIC RECIPES", I highly recommend maintaining a supply of the 3 Sweet Sauces (i.e., Creamy Butterscotch Dessert Sauce, Decadent White Chocolate Sauce and Easy Caramel Sauce) plus Velvety Lemon Curd. Commercial options are available for all except for the Decadent White Chocolate Sauce; however, I encourage readers to make my "homemade" versions of all 4 cited recipes. They are so easy to prepare, so extraordinarily delicious and store well for months!

Ice Cream Meringue Nests (page 181)

DESSERTS

BERRIES AND CREAM EXOTIC STRAW SANDWICHES

Makes 4 servings

*Imagine the delightfully curious reaction of guests when what might first appear to be a "straw" sandwich is placed in front of them for dessert! My deep fried circles of kataifi pastry dough are the basis of this extravaganza of flavours and textures. The recipe is refreshingly original, very attractive, simple, quick to assemble — and to eat! Of course, you could do a similar type of stack, although less adventurous, with circles of cake, phyllo or regular pastry. (**Note:** A photo appears on page 47.)*

1 cup (250 mL) heavy cream (35% fat), chilled
2¹/2 tbsp (38 mL) icing sugar
1¹/2 tbsp (23 mL) whisky (optional)
1¹/2 cups (375 mL) berries (e.g., blackberries,
    raspberries or sliced fresh strawberries)
1 tbsp (15 mL) orange-flavoured liqueur (optional)
¹/2 cup (125 mL) caramel sauce (e.g., page 215 or
    commercial variety)
8 Kataifi Straw Disks (page 209)

GARNISH (optional or as desired)
sprigs of fresh mint
edible flowers

1 Whip cream in a chilled medium-size bowl with chilled beaters until cream begins to thicken. Add sugar and beat until soft peaks form. Add whisky and beat until peaks are firm. (Makes 2 cups or 500 mL.) Refrigerate (in bowl) until ready to use.

2 Immediately before serving, toss berries with orange-flavoured liqueur and set aside.

3 Drizzle centre of 4 individual oversized plates with a little caramel sauce (about ¹/2 tsp or 3 mL per plate), add one Kataifi Straw Disk and secure in position on sauce.

4 Drizzle each disk with more caramel sauce (about 1 tsp or 5 mL); top with whipped cream (about ¹/3 cup or 80 mL); sprinkle with berries (¹/4 of total); drizzle again with caramel sauce (1 tsp or 5 mL); add more whipped cream (about 2¹/2 tbsp or 38 mL) and crown with a second straw disk.

5 Artistically drizzle straw stacks and plates with additional caramel sauce and garnish with sprigs of fresh mint and edible flowers. Serve.

> **MAKE-AHEAD TIP (STEP 1):** The **cream** may be **whipped** hours in advance. If it softens even slightly, rebeat it briefly (i.e., a matter of seconds) with chilled beaters just before using.

> **"WOW" FACTOR:** A mesmerizing unique tangle of crisp kataifi "straw", berries, cream and decadent caramel sauce makes this recipe an exotic adventure! It is an elegant dessert which offers sophisticated flavours plus great fun!

AN ICE CREAM CONE FIX

Makes 4 servings

Here's a combination that should satisfy everyone's passion for an "ice cream" fix! (A photo appears on page 200.)

4 ice cream cones, preferably "sugar" type
1½ cups (375 mL) Decadent Chocolate Mint
    Ice Cream (page 186)
¾ cup (180 mL) Addictive Coffee Ice Cream (below)
⅔ cup (170 mL) Macadamia Cinnamon Chocolate
    Ice Cream* (page 179)

GARNISH (optional)
4 Chocolate Curl Sticks (page 200) or chocolate
    sticks/sculptures

1 Scoop ice cream equally between cones in sequence given above. Poke a Chocolate Curl Stick into top of each ice cream cone as a garnish.

2 Serve!

* **Option**: Another gourmet variety of chocolate ice cream.

> **TIME-SAVING TIP:** My ice creams are fabulous; however, there are also wonderful **commercial** versions of these flavours on the market.

> **MAKE-AHEAD TIP (STEP 1):** Cones may be prepared up to several days in advance and stored frozen in a vertical position in empty spice jars. (**Note:** If not serving cones within 8 hours, instead of inserting the Chocolate Curl Sticks, simply make suitable deep holes with a skewer and freeze the filled cones until the ice cream is firm. Cover the firm cones individually with an airtight piece of plastic wrap. Just before serving, remove the plastic wrapping and insert the chocolate curl sticks into the prepared holes.)

ADDICTIVE COFFEE ICE CREAM

Makes 3 cups (or 750 mL)

*Our home has a well-developed reputation for the array of homemade ice creams to be found in its freezer! My distinctively rich coffee ice cream is rated # 2 in popularity (after Decadent Chocolate Mint, page 186) among adults and children alike. The secret to this "signature" recipe lies in my addition of both coffee paste and maple syrup. (**Note:** A photo appears on page 188 with the Ultimate Coffee Spoons or on page 187 with the Taster Dessert Plates.)*

4 cups (1 litre) vanilla ice cream
1⅔ tbsp (25 mL) maple syrup
2 tsp (10 mL) Coffee Paste (page 208)

1 Place slightly softened ice cream into a large bowl.

2 Using an electric mixer, beat in maple syrup and then (according to taste) Coffee Paste until well blended.

3 Immediately transfer ice cream to chilled airtight plastic containers, covering surfaces of the ice cream closely with plastic wrap. Secure lids and freeze for up to several months.

> **CAUTION TIP:** *The intensity of both flavour and colour will increase slightly when the ice cream is frozen.*

BLACKBERRY BUTTERSCOTCH COCKTAIL FONDUE

Makes 18 to 25 cocktail servings (or 4 regular servings*)

*Will chocolate fondue ever lose its popularity? Personally, I am particularly fond of butterscotch. In my determination to offer simple but innovative alternatives to traditional favorites, I have come up with my own personal Butterscotch Fondue. Guests refer to it as "a sensuous experience" as they continue to dip tart fresh blackberries into a creamy butterscotch sauce with uncontrollable enthusiasm! The stunning balance between sour and sweet mesmerizes absolutely everyone — including children and those who are not dessert fans! (**Note**: This is another assembly, "No Time, No Talent" recipe!)*

2 cups (500 mL) fresh large blackberries, whole
    and clean
3/4 cup (180 mL) Creamy Butterscotch Dessert Sauce
    (e.g., page 214 or commercial variety**), chilled

GARNISH (optional or as desired)
fresh mint
edible flowers

1 Creatively arrange a bowl/dish of blackberries and another with butterscotch sauce* on a serving tray.

2 Place a cup or glass with cocktail picks or heavy toothpicks on tray along with a second empty cup/glass to catch used picks.

3 If desired, garnish tray with fresh mint and edible flowers.

4 Using cocktail picks/toothpicks, securely pierce berries one at a time and dip into butterscotch sauce. Place used picks in empty cup/glass.

* **Option:** Individual portions could be prepared (using small bowls and cocktail forks) and served to guests as dessert at the table.

** **Option:** If desired, whisk a small quantity (according to taste) of heavy cream (35% fat) into a commercial variety of butterscotch sauce in order to give it a creamier flavour. (If the sauce becomes too thin, heat it and thicken it with a little cornstarch mixed into a touch of heavy cream.)

> **TIP:** I serve my "fondue" with the **sauce taken directly from the refrigerator** or after having allowed it to rest briefly at room temperature. (The colder the sauce, the thicker it will be.)

> **CONVENIENCE TIP:** I find elegant "**corn picks/holders**" to be most appropriate for piercing the berries.

175

LEMON PHYLLO NAPOLEONS

Makes 4 servings

"Unquestionably popular" clearly defines the slightly tart lemon curd cream piled between crisp buttery layers of phyllo pastry. It is light with phenomenal flavour, texture and visual appeal. For a quick touch of pizzazz, top the Napoleons with a delicate dusting of icing sugar and drizzles of melted bittersweet chocolate.

2 sheets phyllo pastry*
2 tbsp (30 mL) unsalted butter, melted
2 tbsp (30 mL) granulated sugar

LEMON CREAM FILLING**
1 cup (250 mL) heavy cream (35% fat), chilled
2¹/₂ tbsp (38 mL) icing sugar (first addition)
**1 cup (250 mL) lemon curd (e.g., page 210 or
    commercial), chilled**

GARNISH (optional)
2 tbsp (30 mL) icing sugar (second addition)
1¹/₂ oz (45 g) bittersweet chocolate, melted

1 Place one sheet of phyllo pastry on a clean work surface with long side in horizontal position; brush with melted butter. Lay another sheet on top of first and brush with butter. Cut phyllo horizontally into 3 equal strips and then vertically into 4 equal portions to produce 12 "squares" (**Note:** Each square is made up of a double thickness of phyllo pastry and is almost "square" in shape!). Sprinkle top of phyllo squares evenly with granulated sugar.

2 Transfer phyllo squares (sugar side up) to parchment paper-lined baking sheets. Bake in a preheated 400°F (200°C) oven until golden and crisp (about 2¹/₂ to 4 minutes). Remove from oven; transfer to wire cooling rack.

3 Beat cream in a medium-size chilled bowl with chilled beaters until cream begins to thicken. Add icing sugar; continue beating until firm peaks form.

4 Place lemon curd in a second medium-size bowl. With a rubber spatula, carefully fold whipped cream into lemon curd and combine thoroughly to produce a Lemon Curd Filling. (Makes about 3 cups or 750 mL.) If not using immediately, refrigerate.**

5 Just before serving, add 1 tsp (5 mL) of Lemon Cream Filling to centre of 4 individual oversized plates. (**Note:** This will hold the Napoleon in place on the plate.) Then top each with one baked phyllo square (sugar side up). Add ¹/₄ cup (60 mL) of Lemon Cream Filling to each square and spread evenly to about ¹/₃ inch (0.8 cm) from edges of square. Top each portion with another phyllo square. Repeat process crowning with a third phyllo square. (**FLASH: For smaller appetites, use only a total of 2 phyllo squares with ¹/₃ cup or 80 mL of filling per serving.**)

6 To complete each presentation, dust Lemon Phyllo Napoleon and plate with icing sugar (shaken through a fine sieve) and decorate with piped lines of melted chocolate. For best results, serve as soon as possible so that phyllo pastry remains crisp.

* Size: About 16¹/₂ × 12¹/₄ inches (41 × 30.5 cm)
** The Lemon Cream Filling is firmest the first day once it has been chilled; however, leftover quantities usually retain their quality for several days. (If the filling softens, re-beat it in a chilled bowl with chilled beaters until firm. This may take several minutes.)

MAKE-AHEAD TIP (STEPS 1 & 2): The **phyllo squares** may be prepared several weeks in advance. Place them in a wax paper-lined covered metal container, separating layers with wax paper, and store them in a cool dry place. (**Note:** Very large shallow metal cookie boxes work well.) I usually have a reserve of phyllo squares on hand to eliminate the stress that planning desserts can bring!

CARAMEL MOUSSE CHOCOLATE CUPS

Makes 4 filled chocolate cups

Caramel, chocolate, hazelnuts and cream are a divine combination for almost every palate. These being among my favorite tastes, I decided to put them all into one dessert! Imagine a cloud of ultra light caramel mousse happily restrained in a chocolate cup, with its heavenly smoothness sporadically interrupted by caramel-bathed roasted hazelnuts! To "heighten" the drama, I poke one of my signature Chocolate Curl Sticks into each dessert before serving.

²/₃ cup (170 mL) heavy cream (35% fat), chilled

¹/₂ cup (125 mL) caramel sauce* (e.g., page 215 or commercial variety), chilled and divided

¹/₃ to ¹/₂ cup (80 to 125 mL) whole dry roasted filberts (i.e., hazelnuts), skinless

4 chocolate dessert cups/shells** (diameter: 2¹/₂ inches or 6 cm), commercial or page 209

GARNISH (optional)
4 Chocolate Curl Sticks (page 200) or chocolate sticks edible flowers (e.g., pansies, violas)

1 Whip cream in a medium-size chilled bowl with chilled beaters until soft peaks form. Add just ¹/₄ cup (60 mL) caramel sauce and continue whipping until firm peaks form. Refrigerate caramel "mousse" in its bowl until ready to use. (Makes about 1²/₃ cups or 400 mL.)

2 Coat hazelnuts with caramel sauce (about 1¹/₂ tbsp or 23 mL); divide into 4 portions.

3 Starting with 2 tsp (10 mL) of caramel mousse, prepare chocolate cups by layering mousse with only a few caramel-coated hazelnuts until cups are generously filled. (Finish with hazelnuts.)

4 Secure one filled chocolate cup on individual plates with a touch of caramel sauce; artistically drizzle plates with remaining caramel sauce. Poke a Chocolate Curl Stick into each filled cup and garnish with edible flowers.

* I much prefer my homemade Easy Caramel Sauce. (**Note:** If the refrigerated sauce is too firm to be whipped into the cream, let it rest briefly at room temperature. This will not be necessary for commercial varieties.)
** Volume: About ⅓ cup or 80 mL. Commercial chocolate dessert cups or shells of various shapes (e.g., bear paws) are available at many large supermarkets, chocolate shops and bakeries.

MAKE-AHEAD TIP (STEP 1): The **caramel mousse** may be prepared hours in advance. If the mousse should lose some of its stability during storage, re-beat it briefly with chilled beaters.

"WOW" FACTOR: On many occasions, guests have vowed that this has been the best dessert they had ever eaten!

SEDUCTIVE CHOCOLATE ICE CREAM PARFAITS

Makes 4 servings

*The touch of cherry brandy makes my already exotic Macadamia Cinnamon Chocolate Ice Cream with its subtle additions of raspberry jam truly seductive! You might want to have extra servings of this dessert in the freezer! (**Note:** I suggest keeping individual portions small with the option of offering "seconds".)*

2 tbsp (30 mL) cherry brandy
1⅓ cups (325 mL) Macadamia Cinnamon Chocolate Ice Cream*
½ cup (125 mL) Whisky Whipped Cream (page 210) or whipped cream

GARNISH (optional)
4 Chocolate Curl Sticks (page 200) or chocolate sticks

1 Pour 1½ tsp (8 mL) of cherry brandy into each of 4 fluted Champagne glasses (or glasses of choice).

2 Add ⅓ cup (80 mL) of slightly softened Macadamia Cinnamon Chocolate Ice Cream, pressing it gently into each glass.

3 Place filled glasses in freezer.

4 About 10 minutes before serving, transfer prepared glasses of chocolate ice cream to refrigerator.

5 Just before serving, top ice cream with Whisky Whipped Cream.

6 If desired, garnish each dessert with a Chocolate Curl Stick poked vertically into whipped cream topping.

* To make the Macadamia Cinnamon Chocolate Ice Cream, slightly soften 2 cups (500 mL) of chocolate ice cream in a medium bowl. Working quickly, add ½ tsp (3 mL) of both ground cinnamon and cinnamon extract; beat until the mixture is well blended and the ice cream is smooth. Using a fork, first incorporate 2 tbsp (30 mL) of coarsely chopped macadamia nuts and then swirl in 1 tbsp (15 mL) of seedless raspberry jam. (Avoid overmixing.) Immediately transfer the ice cream to a chilled airtight plastic container, cover the surface of the ice cream closely with plastic wrap, secure the lid and freeze. (Makes about 1½ cups or 375 mL.)

MAKE-AHEAD TIP (FOR STEPS 1 TO 3): The parfaits may be virtually prepared several days in advance of serving (except for the final topping of whipped cream and the chocolate stick garnish). To maintain the quality, cover the surface of the ice cream in each glass closely with plastic wrap before freezing.

GOAT'S CHEESE-STUFFED FRESH FIGS

(with Anise-Infused Lemon Syrup)

Makes 4 servings

I have designed a goat's cheese and fresh fig recipe for those who are not normally tempted by desserts and would undoubtedly opt for a piece of cheese or fruit. The culinary finesse of the final plate lies in the drizzle of Anise-Infused Lemon Syrup which pairs exquisitely with both the fresh figs and the soft unripened goat's cheese.

8 fresh whole figs, ripe
1/2 cup (125 mL) soft goat's cheese, unripened
1/4 cup (60 mL) Anise-Infused Lemon Syrup* or
   drizzle of choice

GARNISH
sprigs of fresh herbs (e.g., lavender) and/or
   edible flowers

1   Wipe figs clean with a soft cloth. Cut figs vertically in half through stem to base.

2   Lay out fig halves in matching pairs on a clean flat surface; with a finger press an indentation into centre of each half. (Avoid cracking outer edge of fig.)

3   Place 1 tbsp (15 mL) of goat's cheese in indentation of one fig half of each pair; bring fig halves together, reassembling individual figs.

4   Smooth cheese filling to follow contour of figs. Set figs in a "standing" position with stem end "up". (Note: **The figs may be prepared to this point hours in advance of serving**. Place them in an airtight plastic container and refrigerate until shortly before serving.)

5   To serve, arrange cheese-stuffed figs artistically on a platter or individual plates; drizzle with Anise-Infused Lemon Syrup (about 1 1/2 tsp or 8 mL per fig).

6   Garnish platter/plates with whole star anise (from syrup) and sprigs of fresh lavender.

* To make the Anise-Infused Lemon Syrup, in a small saucepan over medium heat, stir together 1 cup (250 mL) of granulated sugar and 1/2 cup (125 mL) of lemon juice until sugar dissolves and syrup comes to a boil. Immediately reduce heat to lowest setting. Add 6 whole star anise, cover saucepan and allow syrup to rest for 5 minutes. Remove syrup from heat and stir in 3/4 tsp (4 mL) of grated lemon zest. Let cool. Store syrup refrigerated in a well-sealed jar for up to several months. (Makes almost 1 cup or about 200 mL.) **Note:** Whole star anise is available at oriental food stores as well as some health food and specialty food stores.

"WOW" TIP: Anise-Infused Lemon Syrup* only takes minutes to prepare! Serve it chilled or warm. I generally use it directly from the refrigerator, when it is enticingly thick.

ALTERNATIVE-RECIPE TIP: Drizzle the stuffed figs with a Mustard Herb Vinaigrette (page 211) instead of the syrup and serve them as an **appetizer** with sprigs of fresh basil.

ICE CREAM MERINGUE NESTS
(with Honey Mustard Dessert Vinaigrette)

Makes 4 servings

My unusual dessert vinaigrette can ultimately claim the credit for the success and originality of this recipe. The vinaigrette's sweet, tart, sharp dimensions graciously counterbalance the sweetness of the ice cream and baked meringue while enhancing the natural flavour of the berries. (A photo appears on page 171.)

4 meringue nests (diameter: 3 inch or 8 cm),
    commercial or homemade
2 tsp (10 mL) hazelnut chocolate spread
1¹/3 cups (325 mL) maple walnut ice cream,
    homemade* or commercial
¹/4 cup (60 mL) Honey Mustard Dessert Vinaigrette**
    (room temperature)
1 cup (250 mL) fresh berries (i.e., blueberries,
    blackberries or raspberries)

GARNISH (optional)
edible flowers or sprigs of fresh mint

1 To make individual servings, secure one meringue nest on each of 4 large dinner plates with a small dab of hazelnut chocolate spread. (Note: *This may be done hours in advance of serving.*)

2 Just before serving, fill each meringue nest with ice cream (¹/3 cup or 80 mL), drizzle lightly with Honey Mustard Dessert Vinaigrette (1 tbsp or 15 mL) and sprinkle with fresh berries. Garnish plates with edible flowers and sprigs of fresh mint. Serve immediately.

* To make the Maple Walnut Ice Cream, mix ¹/3 cup (80 mL) of coarsely chopped walnuts with 1 tbsp (15 mL) of maple syrup; set aside. Beat 1 tbsp (15 mL) of maple extract into 2 cups (500 mL) of softened vanilla ice cream; fold in the chopped walnuts and freeze. The ice cream retains its quality for months.

** To make the Honey Mustard Dessert Vinaigrette, in a small bowl, carefully whisk together until smooth ¹/4 cup (60 mL) each of buckwheat honey and lemon juice as well as 3 tbsp (45 mL) of olive oil (extra light tasting) and ³/4 tsp (4 mL) of sandwich mustard. (This makes more than ¹/2 cup or about 150 mL.) Store the vinaigrette refrigerated in a well-sealed jar until 20 minutes before required. Whisk it well before using.

"NO TIME, NO TALENT" TIP: With the meringue nests and ice cream on hand (both of which could be purchased products), this recipe is virtually reduced to making the simple vinaigrette and assembling. (**Note: I tend to prepare the vinaigrette in advance**.)

BE INSPIRED TIP: Design your own recipe using an ice cream, fruit and sauce (e.g., chocolate, butterscotch, fruit purée or Anise-Infused Lemon Syrup, page 180) of choice. (**Note:** You may want to **"taste test" a sample** to ensure that your combination works before serving it.)

CARAMEL MANGO TARTS
(with "Sugar Stencil Art")

Makes 4 servings

No time? No talent? This recipe is basically one of assembly. The combination of pastry, caramel, fresh mango and whipped cream is formidable! Use homemade or commercial tart shells (or arrange larger amounts of diced mango directly on dessert plates, in bowls or glasses, top with whipped cream and drizzle with caramel sauce). Other types of bases/edible containers may be used including phyllo cups or Kataifi Straw Disks (page 209). Be inspired! To add a "dusting" of pizzaz, I often decorate the dessert plates in advance with "Sugar Stencil Art" (page 202).

1/4 cup (60 mL) heavy cream (35% fat), chilled
2 tsp (10 mL) icing sugar
1 tsp (5 mL) whisky (optional)
4 baked tart shells (diameter: 2¹/2 inches or 6 cm)*, commercial or homemade
1/3 cup (80 mL) caramel sauce (e.g., page 215) or commercial variety
1 large mango**, peeled and diced
1¹/2 tsp (8 mL) orange-flavoured liqueur (optional)

GARNISH (optional)
4 Dark Chocolate Toffee Butterflies (page 194)
fresh mint leaves

1 Whip cream in a small chilled bowl with chilled beaters until it begins to thicken. Add sugar and beat until soft peaks form. Add whisky and continue beating until firm peaks form. If not using immediately, refrigerate (in its bowl) until ready to use.

2 Shortly before serving, spoon caramel sauce into empty tart shells to cover bottom generously (about 2 tsp or 10 mL per shell).

3 Toss diced mango with orange-flavoured liqueur; fill tart shells.

4 Top mango with whipped cream. If desired, garnish with chocolate butterflies and fresh mint leaves.

5 To serve, drizzle 4 dessert plates with caramel sauce and add one filled tart to each plate (securing it in/on sauce).

* **Option:** Size of choice. Adjust other ingredients accordingly. If desired, use recipe for Delicately Tender Pastry (page 208) to make your own tart shells.
** About 10 oz or 280 g

> **MAKE-AHEAD TIP (STEP 1):** Remember, the **whipped cream** may be prepared hours in advance of serving. If it softens even slightly, re-beat it briefly with chilled beaters just before using.

MINI FLOWERPOTS OF CHOCOLATE MINT ICE CREAM

Makes 16 canapé taster desserts (or 6 regular size servings*)

As one of my signature creations, these mini* flowerpots are always an unexpected treat regardless of time of year, guest list or occasion - drinks parties, cocktail receptions and garden parties. Business associates, friends and family are all particularly thrilled to see my decadently "chocolate" mint ice cream make its appearance. Its smooth and crunchy texture, its tantalizing colour and flavour — not to mention the presentation — never disappoint! This "potted" temptation proves completely irresistible when a chocolate butterfly is comfortably perched on top of the ice cream! (A photo appears on page 40.)

3 cups (750 mL) Decadent Chocolate Mint Ice Cream (page 186 or commercial variety)
16 mini flowerpots* (top diameter: 2 inches or 5 cm)

GARNISH (optional)
16 Dark Chocolate Toffee Butterflies (page 194) or chocolate sticks (commercial)

1 Select cups (e.g., sake cups) that fit perfectly into mini flowerpots and chill.

2 Scoop 3 tbsp (45 mL) of ice cream into each cup. Securely perch a chocolate butterfly on top of (or poke a chocolate stick into) each serving of ice cream.

3 Place in freezer for up to several days, until ready to serve.

4 To serve, drop ice cream-filled sake cups into individual mini flowerpots. Serve immediately with small spoons.

* **Option:** Prepare 6 dessert size servings of 1/2 cup (125 mL) each presented in individual small flowerpots (top diameter: about 2³/4 inches or 7 cm). **Note:** I fit small disposable plastic glasses (3 fl oz or 90 mL) into the flowerpots as a liner.

TIPS ON CHOOSING FLOWERPOTS: Small flowerpots are available at landscape stores, garden centres or some craft stores. The size of flowerpots is one of personal preference. I usually use mini pots (top diameter: 2 inches or 5 cm) for canapé taster desserts.* The only challenge this recipe presents is finding the little containers that will fit into the flowerpots as a liner to hold the ice cream. Generally, small oriental porcelain sake cups fit perfectly into the mini flowerpots.

MAKE-AHEAD AND STORAGE TIP (FOR STEPS 1 TO 3): Prepare the ice cream-filled sake cups and place them in clean empty egg cartons (with lids removed). Cover the cartons of ice cream cups loosely (but in an airtight manner) with a hood of plastic wrap and place them in the freezer.

ALTERNATIVE-USE TIP: Mini Flowerpots of Ice Cream may also be arranged along with other petit bites (e.g., chocolate-dipped strawberries, mini tarts, liqueur-soaked fruit) to create tempting individual **Taster Dessert Plates** (see page 187).

ORANGE-INFUSED CHOCOLATE LAVA CAKES

Makes 7 to 10 servings

While in Indonesia, hundreds of volcanoes (many of which are still active) inspired me to design my very own personal version of warm petit chocolate cakes with fluid centres. The infusion of orange (i.e., orange zest and orange-flavoured liqueur) makes these lava cakes amazingly delectable whether they are served warm or cold! The recipe is surprisingly easy to prepare — just follow the directions carefully. (A photo appears on page 52.)

2 tbsp (30 mL) **unsalted butter** (to butter ramekin dishes)
1¹/2 tbsp (23 mL) **cocoa powder** (to dust ramekin dishes)
2 whole **eggs** (room temperature)
2 **egg yolks** (room temperature)
³/4 cup (180 mL) **icing sugar**
¹/2 cup less 1 tbsp (110 mL) **cake/pastry flour**
¹/2 cup less 1 tbsp (110 mL) **unsalted butter**
3¹/2 oz (100 g) **bittersweet chocolate, chopped**
2 tsp (10 mL) **orange-flavoured liqueur** (optional)
1¹/3 tbsp (20 mL) **grated orange zest, divided**

GARNISH*
³/4 cup (180 mL) **Decadent White Chocolate Sauce** (page 215)
1 to 1¹/2 cups (250 to 375 mL) **Whisky Whipped Cream** (page 210) or whipped cream
¹/2 cup (125 mL) **fresh berries** (e.g., blackberries or raspberries)
As desired **fresh mint leaves**

1 Butter extravagantly 10 **small** porcelain ramekin dishes (i.e., volume: ¹/3 cup or 80 mL); dust interior of dishes evenly with sifted cocoa powder; set aside.

2 Place eggs and egg yolks in a medium bowl; add sugar and beat with electric mixer on high speed until very pale yellow (about 3 minutes). Carefully fold in flour only until barely incorporated.

3 Place butter and chocolate over barely simmering water in a double boiler until butter melts and chocolate starts to soften. Remove from heat; stir until chocolate melts and mixture is well blended.

4 Carefully fold warm chocolate mixture into egg and flour mixture just to combine evenly. (**Note:** Add orange-flavoured liqueur and 1¹/2 tsp or 8 mL of grated orange zest during final stages of folding.)

5 Place ¹/4 cup (60 mL) of batter into each prepared ramekin dish. (Avoid adding more than the specified amount of batter as it may overflow during baking.)

6 Place filled dishes, well separated, on a large baking tray. Bake cakes in middle of a preheated 425°F (220°C) oven until central area of top crust is half done (about 5¹/2 to 6¹/2 minutes). (Avoid over-baking; cakes will continue to bake when removed from oven. **Note:** Centres should still be fluid when cakes are served.)

7 Remove from oven; transfer ramekin dishes from baking tray to a wire cooling rack; allow cakes to rest for 5 minutes.

8 Run tip of a small sharp knife around edges of each cake. Invert each ramekin dish over an individual dessert plate and turn out cake.

9 If desired, brush exterior of cakes with a touch of **extra** orange-flavoured liqueur*.

10 Drizzle cakes with Decadent White Chocolate Sauce; sprinkle with remaining orange zest; garnish with Whisky Whipped Cream, fresh berries and mint leaves. Serve immediately.

* These ingredients are optional; however, they make the dessert truly irresistible!

"WOW" DRINK TIP: As an accompanying beverage, offer 1 to 1¹/2 fluid ounces (30 to 45 mL) of a **good quality chilled whisky** served directly from the freezer.

PRUNES IN PORT
(with Chestnut Mousse)

Makes about 20 prunes (4 to 6 servings)

Memories of our short posting to Austria have inspired this recipe where "Less is More"! Exceedingly quick and easy to prepare, it is graciously appealing in all its simplicity! Just soak ordinary pitted prunes in Port for a few days, whip a little cream, fold in some chestnut purée (if desired) and dessert is ready! However, it is the presentation that makes all of the difference!

20 pitted prunes (about 7 oz or 200 g)
1/2 cup (125 mL) Port (red)

CHESTNUT MOUSSE*
1/2 cup (125 mL) heavy cream (35% fat), chilled
1/4 tsp (1 mL) ground cinnamon
1/2 cup (125 mL) chestnut purée with vanilla**, chilled

GARNISH
1/3 cup (80 mL) toasted sliced almonds

1 Rinse prunes, drain very well and place in a single layer in an airtight plastic container. Cover prunes completely with Port and store refrigerated for at least several days (or up to several months). Turn occasionally.

2 Whip cream and cinnamon in a small chilled bowl with chilled beaters until firm peaks form. Fold in chilled chestnut purée to create a Chestnut Mousse. (Makes about 1 1/3 cups or 325 mL.) Store refrigerated until ready to use (or for up to 3 days).

3 Shape individual prunes into little "nest" shapes (with slit at top centre).

4 Just before serving, fill prunes generously with Chestnut Mousse (or whipped cream) and crown with toasted slivered almonds.

5 For individual portions, serve only 3 filled prunes. (An extra couple of prunes per person remain, if "seconds" are desired.)

* Option: Simply serve the prunes with the whipped cream or cinnamon whipped cream (sweetened to taste) and crowned with toasted sliced almonds.
** This is a commercial product (sweet) available at many supermarkets (or specialty food stores) in the canned fruit section. (**Note:** Leftovers freeze well.)

"WOW" PRESENTATION TIP: I artistically present the **dark prunes in an isolated manner on a stark white plate. Note:** Sometimes instead of filling the prunes, I simply plate them and serve the Chestnut Mousse (or whipped cream) separately either on the individual plates or in a bowl to be passed at the table.

ALTERNATIVE-USE TIP: Serve a plate of Prunes in Port (with Chestnut Mousse) as an impressive **"Finishing Touch" for a "special occasion" breakfast or brunch.** (Do this in much the same way you might serve chocolates after dinner.)

DECADENT CHOCOLATE MINT ICE CREAM

Makes 3¹/2 cups (almost 1 litre)

*My Decadent Chocolate Mint Ice Cream is "outrageously" enticing — and so easy that children can make it! No question, this is by far the most popular ice cream/dessert in our home, an undisputed treat for adults and children of all ages (family or guests). There is always a supply in our freezer. When preparing the ice cream, the trick is to add the mint flavour and green colouring in intensities that suit you. A touch of crème de menthe liqueur takes this ice cream to a "gourmet level"! (**Note:** A photo appears on page 40 with the Mini Flowerpots of Chocolate Mint Ice Cream.)*

2 oz (60 g) bittersweet chocolate (first addition),
    cut into thick slivers*
4 cups (1 litre) vanilla ice cream
2 tsp (10 mL) mint/peppermint extract
1 to 1¹/4 tsp (5 to 6 mL) green food colouring
1 tbsp (15 mL) crème de menthe liqueur (optional)
2 oz (60 g) bittersweet chocolate (second addition),
    coarsely chopped*

1 Place **chocolate slivers** in freezer to chill for at least 30 minutes.

2 Allow ice cream to soften slightly; place in a large bowl. Using an electric mixer, beat in mint extract, food colouring and, if desired, crème de menthe liqueur. (**Note of Caution:** *The intensity of flavour and colour will both increase slightly when the ice cream is frozen.*)

3 Meanwhile, partially melt **coarsely chopped chocolate** over barely simmering water in a double boiler (or in a microwave oven at **medium-low** heat). Remove from heat; stir until chocolate is completely melted and smooth. (**Note:** If necessary, transfer the chocolate to another bowl in order to cool it.)

4 With mixer operating on low speed, quickly add melted chocolate to ice cream and beat only to break up chocolate. (Avoid overbeating.)

5 Using a fork, immediately but carefully, stir in **chilled chocolate slivers**.

6 Promptly transfer ice cream to chilled airtight plastic containers; cover surface of ice cream closely with plastic wrap; secure lids and freeze for up to several months.

* **Note:** Two different forms of chocolate (i.e., slivers and chopped) are used in this recipe.

> **"WOW" FACTOR:** At the end of a "finger food" event (e.g., reception, cocktail or garden party), serve this irresistible treat in mini flowerpots (or mini ice cream cones) with a chocolate butterfly comfortably perched on top!

> **"WOW" TIP:** I tend to keep several mini cones "loaded" with Decadent Chocolate Mint Ice Cream in our freezer. Suspended in individual empty spice bottles, they are my husband's regular evening treat once he has done the dinner dishes!

TASTER DESSERT PLATES

As an option to traditional desserts, my "Taster Dessert Plates" thrill guests with an exciting selection of signature tastes!

A mini pot of ice cream* (e.g., Addictive Coffee, page 173; Decadent Chocolate Mint, page 186)
A chocolate* or two (e.g., Maple Marzipan Pearls, page 195; Macadamia Nut Clusters/Pearls, page 195)
An oriental porcelain spoon of mousse* (e.g., Lemon Cream Filling, page 177; Caramel Mousse, page 178)
Fresh berries of choice

1 Using individual plates (of an interesting shape if possible), artistically arrange a sampling of "sweets" which may include petit treats such as those listed above.

*** Option:** Commercial products may be used.

The Ultimate Coffee Spoons

Makes 12 petit ice cream spoons

Even if you don't usually require a coffee spoon, you will want to have a few of these — filled of course! Mouthfuls of coffee ice cream become a really "cool" surprise when arranged on petit oriental porcelain spoons and encrusted with a delicate shell of dark chocolate. Certainly simple and devastatingly tempting, these Ultimate Coffee Spoons are perfect as a unique Finishing Touch to any event (particularly a drinks, cocktail, tea/coffee party or light lunch), or as part of a Taster Dessert Plate.

12 small oriental porcelain* spoons
1¹/₂ tsp (8 mL) maple syrup
¹/₂ cup (125 mL) Addictive Coffee Ice Cream
**   (page 173 or commercial variety)**
1¹/₃ tbsp (20 mL) chocolate "shell" topping
**   (commercial product)****

1 Arrange porcelain spoons on a tray with bowls facing upwards. Spread ¹/₈ tsp (pinch) of maple syrup over bottom of bowl of each spoon. (This enables ice cream to slip off spoon when consumed.)

2 Place tray with spoons in freezer to chill.

3 Once spoons are thoroughly chilled, remove spoons from freezer a few at a time. Using a small ice cream scoop or melon baller (2 tsp or 10 mL capacity), add a level scoop of ice cream to each spoon (with dome of ice cream facing up).

4 Return ice cream-filled spoons to freezer until the ice cream becomes firm.

5 Using a tiny spoon, carefully pour (in a steady stream) ¹/₃ tsp (2 mL) of fluid chocolate "shell" topping over top of each petit dome of ice cream, allowing it to drip over and to cover (as much as possible) ice cream dome. Immediately transfer chocolate-coated ice cream spoons to freezer.

6 When ready to serve, remove filled spoons from freezer and arrange on a presentation tray. Remember to include an empty vessel (e.g., oversized cognac glass) on serving tray to catch empty spoons.

* These are 2 tsp (10 mL) in capacity. It may be difficult to find this particular size, so use the smallest porcelain spoons available. As an option to the oriental spoons, you could use good quality small plastic spoons. **Metal spoons are not appropriate.**
** This is a fluid commercial product which must be stored at room temperature. When chilled, it becomes brittle. It is generally available in the "ice cream toppings" section of super-markets. **Note:** As a compromised option, use some melted (but cooled and very fluid) bittersweet chocolate.

MAKE-AHEAD TIP: The Ultimate Coffee Spoons may be prepared several days in advance of an event and carefully stored (in a single layer) in airtight plastic containers.

Tiramisu-Wasabi Ice Cream Parfaits

Makes 4 servings

I take "artistic licence" and welcome the adventurous to indulge themselves in one of my "East Meets West" desserts. Intriguing? — Definitely! Delicious? — Of course! Simple? Few desserts could be simpler. When I developed my Wasabi Ice Cream (below), I wanted to incorporate it into a recipe that would entice people to gobble it down without focusing on what they were actually consuming! Taking a popular Italian dessert, I put a simple but memorable "Dickenson" spin on it. The dusting of both coffee and cocoa adds another element of surprise to my mysterious ice cream version of tiramisu. (A photo appears on page 51.)

2 tbsp (30 mL) instant coffee crystals* (preferably freeze dry), divided
1¹/2 tsp (8 mL) cocoa powder

WASABI ICE CREAM
3 cups (750 mL) vanilla ice cream, commercial or homemade
2/3 tsp (3.5 mL) wasabi paste

1 To make the Wasabi Ice Cream, place slightly softened ice cream in a medium bowl. Take a couple of tablespoons of ice cream, blend wasabi paste thoroughly into it and return the mixture to bowl. With an electric mixer, beat the ice cream thoroughly. Immediately transfer to a chilled airtight plastic container and freeze. (Makes about 2¹/2 cups or 625 mL.)

2 Take only 1¹/2 tsp (8 mL) of instant coffee crystals, **crush slightly and set aside**. Press remaining coffee crystals through a fine sieve, **reducing coffee to a powder**.

3 Place 4 parfait-type glasses (3/4 cup or 180 mL capacity) in freezer. Working with only two chilled glasses at a time to prevent ice cream from melting, sprinkle a small amount of instant **coffee powder** (about ¹/4 tsp or 1 mL) and cocoa powder (¹/8 tsp or a pinch) into bottom of each glass. Add 2¹/2 tbsp (38 mL) of ice cream, press gently into glass and level surface. (Try to keep upper part of glass clean.)

4 Repeat process until you have 3 layers of ice cream. (**Flash: For smaller appetites**, *2 layers of ice cream may be sufficient*. In that case, use smaller glasses with a ¹/2 cup or 125 mL capacity.)

5 Clean inner rims of glasses carefully (with a tissue). Place filled glasses in freezer.

6 About 5 to 10 minutes before serving, transfer ice cream parfaits to refrigerator. Immediately before serving, sprinkle top surface of ice cream in each glass with just a pinch of **"crushed"** instant coffee crystals. (**Note of Caution:** *This is not the "sieved" instant coffee powder which is "dusty" in nature and could be uncomfortably inhaled.*)

* **Option:** regular or caffeine-free.

DO-WHAT-SUITS-YOU TIP: First, for those who are not yet ready for the "Wasabi Ice Cream" experience, **regular vanilla ice cream** may be used. Secondly, instead of making individual parfaits, **prepare the dessert in a glass serving dish/bowl**, increasing the quantity prepared and adjusting the recipe as required.

MAKE-AHEAD TIP (STEPS 1 TO 5): The ice cream parfaits may be prepared up to several days in advance (except for the final "sprinkling" of crushed instant coffee crystals). Cover individual glasses with plastic wrap before freezing.

Before guests leave any event, my husband and I offer a final "sweet" taste — a "Finishing Touch". It may be served with coffee after a meal or simply as the last item(s) on the menu of a drinks or cocktail party. Most frequently, I offer a variety of homemade chocolates spilling out of a decorative ethnic box. Everyone adores this final display of warm hospitality. However, I must be perfectly honest and admit that some guests, who have been in our home on previous occasions, jokingly sigh when the chocolates appear. They realize that another happy event is drawing to a close!

On occasions when guests drop in unexpectedly, never am I in the awkward situation of not having something to serve. There is certain to be a supply of homemade chocolates in our refrigerator.

Making chocolates is much more than "therapeutic" for me; it is a treat! Most of my recipes are extremely simple, absolutely "fail proof" and can be prepared in minutes. Many include dried fruit, nuts and ginger. They come in a variety of sizes, shapes and flavours — but all are unique and "scrumptious"! Of course, hostess gifts are not an issue. I present the host/hostess with a dozen or more (never 13!!) of my homemade chocolates.

Separately, in this section, there are other "Finishing Touches". All are a combination of fruit and chocolate. "My Fruit and Chocolate Duets" are certain to offer a few final surprises as this book draws to a close.

Note: 🐰 designates a "No Time, No Talent" recipe.

Toasted Almond and Currant Clusters (page 194); Dark Chocolate Toffee Dominoes (page 194)

FINISHING TOUCHES

CRANBERRY NUT CLUSTERS

Makes 18 chocolate clusters

Could this be one of the greatest chocolate recipes you will ever taste? If you are a fan of cranberries and/or white chocolate, it might be! The combination of flavours, textures and colours are original and exciting. Every ingredient plays its unique and special role in contributing to all those qualities; omitting one will make a difference! You must try this quick and easy chocolate recipe for yourself! With the dried cranberries, I proudly claim it as my "Canadian" chocolate.

FLASH: *This recipe* **won "Recipe of the Year — Published"** *in the Cordon d'Or — Gold Ribbon Annual International Cookbook and Culinary Arts Awards. So, you see, I was not exaggerating!*

3¹/₂ oz (100 g) white chocolate, chopped
¹/₂ cup (125 mL) dried cranberries
¹/₃ cup (80 mL) chopped roasted pecans
2 tbsp (30 mL) desiccated coconut

1 Line a baking sheet with wax paper.

2 Partially melt chocolate over barely simmering water in a double boiler (or soften in a microwave oven at **medium-low** heat*). Remove from heat; stir until chocolate is very smooth. (**Note:** White chocolate may not always appear to have completely melted.)

3 Add all other remaining ingredients and combine.

4 Drop clusters of chocolate mixture (about 2 tsp or 10 mL portions) onto wax paper-lined tray.

5 Refrigerate until firm.

6 Transfer chocolates to an airtight plastic container and store refrigerated for up to several months.

* **My Technique:** Put chocolate in a heavy earthenware soup bowl (microwave proof); place in a microwave oven at medium-low heat until softened but not melted (about 2¹/₂ to 3 minutes). **Note: *The bowl should never become hot.***

> **TIP (FOR STEP 1):** Secure the wax paper to the baking sheet with a couple of dabs of soft butter or margarine.

GINGER CHOCOLATE COINS

Makes about 20 chocolates

For those who adore ginger and dark chocolate, this recipe will prove addictive! It is simple, quick and a perfect marriage of 2 widely appreciated flavours.

3¹/₂ oz (100 g) semisweet* chocolate, coarsely chopped
2¹/₂ tbsp (38 mL) chopped ginger in syrup (drained)

1 Partially melt chocolate over barely simmering water in a double boiler (or soften in a microwave oven at **medium-low** heat). Remove from heat; carefully stir until chocolate is completely melted and smooth. (Avoid having chocolate too soft or fluid.)

2 Add ginger; stir to incorporate.

3 Drop 1 tsp (5 mL) of chocolate mixture into shallow round moulds of chocolate mould trays; tap trays gently on surface of counter to spread chocolate evenly in moulds. Refrigerate until firm.

4 Invert chocolate trays and tap gently to release chocolates from moulds.

5 Place chocolates in a wax paper-lined airtight plastic container, separating layers of chocolates with wax paper. Store refrigerated for up to several months.

* **Option:** Substitute a portion (e.g., 1 oz or 30 g) with bittersweet chocolate.

> **CONVENIENCE TIP:** If chocolate mould trays are not available, spread soft chocolate mixture evenly and very thinly on a wax paper-lined tray and refrigerate. When firm, break/crack chocolate slab into pieces as desired.

Dark Chocolate Toffee Dominoes/Coins/Butterflies

Makes about 18 chocolates

*I personally believe that these chocolates should be made as flat "wafers" rather than thicker chocolates. Biting through thin chocolate with the fun of crunching on dispersed bits of crisp toffee is certainly part of the recipe's appeal. (**Note:** A photo appears on page 191.)*

3¹/₂ oz (100 g) semisweet* chocolate,
   coarsely chopped
2¹/₂ tbsp (38 mL) coarsely chopped hard toffee bits
²/₃ oz (20 g) white chocolate (optional), melted

1 Partially melt semisweet chocolate over barely simmering water in a double boiler (or soften in a microwave oven at **medium-low** heat). Remove from heat; carefully stir until chocolate is completely melted and smooth. Add toffee bits and stir to incorporate.

2 Spoon soft chocolate mixture into shallow** plastic chocolate mould trays (e.g., dominoes, coins, butterflies). Gently tap trays on counter so that chocolate mixture spreads evenly. Refrigerate until firm.

3 Invert chocolate mould trays and tap gently to remove chocolates from moulds.

4 Decorate top surface of chocolates with dots or drizzles of melted white chocolate; refrigerate to set.

5 Store chocolates refrigerated for up to several months in a wax paper-lined airtight plastic container, separating layers with wax paper.

* **Option:** Substitute a portion with bittersweet chocolate.
** Depth: ¹/₅ inch or 0.5 cm (**Note:** Chocolate moulds are usually available at cake decorating stores and some craft shops.)

> **CONVENIENCE TIP:** If chocolate mould trays are not available, spread soft chocolate mixture thinly and evenly on a wax paper-lined tray and refrigerate. When firm, break/crack chocolate slab into pieces.

Toasted Almond and Currant Clusters

Makes about 20 chocolates

*Regardless of your culinary skill or the time available, you can produce your own fantastic chocolates with three common ingredients. Quick to make, these chic black and white chocolates have it all — crunch, chewiness and a rich flavour of fruit, nut and chocolate! (**Note:** A photo appears on page 191 with the Dark Chocolate Toffee Dominoes/Coins.)*

3¹/₂ oz (100 g) white chocolate, chopped
¹/₃ cup (80 mL) currants
¹/₃ cup (80 mL) toasted slivered almonds

1 Partially melt chocolate over barely simmering water in a double boiler (or soften in a microwave oven at **medium-low** heat). Remove from heat; carefully stir until chocolate is completely melted and smooth.

2 Add currants and almonds; combine carefully. Drop clusters of chocolate mixture (about 2 tsp or 10 mL portions) onto a wax paper-lined tray. Refrigerate until firm.

3 Transfer chocolates to an airtight plastic container and store refrigerated for up to several months.

MACADAMIA NUT CLUSTERS/PEARLS

Makes 10 clusters or 30 pearls

*As I say, "less is more"! Macadamia nuts temptingly coated in bittersweet chocolate is a taste combination provoking the illusion of decadence. Make the chocolates either as refined individual "pearls" or as more hearty "clusters"; there is a difference! (**Note:** A photo appears on page 187 with the Taster Dessert Plates.)*

2¹/₂ oz (75 g) semisweet* chocolate, coarsely chopped
30 macadamia nuts (shelled), whole

1 Partially melt chocolate over barely simmering water in a double boiler (or soften in a microwave oven at **medium-low** heat). Remove from heat; carefully stir until chocolate is completely melted and smooth.

2 Drop nuts, a few at a time, into melted chocolate and coat thoroughly.

3 Using a coffee spoon and allowing excess chocolate to drip off, transfer chocolate-coated nuts (one at a time) to a wax paper-lined tray. (A toothpick is helpful in pushing chocolate-coated nuts off spoon.) Arrange in a triangular cluster of 3 attached chocolate-coated nuts, or individually to form pearls. Refrigerate until firm.

4 Transfer chocolates to a wax paper-lined airtight plastic container, separating layers of chocolates with wax paper. Store refrigerated for up to several months.

* **Option:** Substitute a portion (i.e., ¹/₃) with bittersweet chocolate.

MAPLE MARZIPAN PEARLS

Makes 15 chocolates

*The title leaves little to one's imagination! The recipe is indeed a "jewel" in itself where the delicate flavours of maple and marzipan are sealed in a seductive film of white chocolate. Those who are usually not tempted by "marzipan" will love these pearls! (**Note:** A photo appears on page 187 with the Taster Dessert Plates.)*

¹/₄ cup (60 mL) marzipan paste
¹/₂ tsp (3 mL) maple extract
2 oz (60 g) white chocolate

1 Place marzipan on a flat plate. Drizzle with maple extract; knead or use a fork to combine thoroughly.

2 Roll ³/₄ tsp (4 mL) size portions (not larger) between palms of hands. Arrange small balls on a parchment paper-lined tray; refrigerate. Five minutes before dipping, remove marzipan balls from refrigerator.

3 Partially melt chocolate over barely simmering water in a double boiler* (or soften in a microwave oven at **medium-low** heat). Remove from heat; stir carefully until chocolate is completely melted and smooth.

4 Using a small spoon, roll marzipan balls, one at a time, in melted chocolate until thoroughly coated. Transfer chocolate-coated marzipan balls to a wax paper-lined tray and refrigerate until firm.

5 If desired, trim bases of chocolates with a small sharp knife so that chocolates resemble pearls.

6 Place Maple Marzipan Pearls in a wax paper-lined airtight plastic container, separating layers with wax paper. Store refrigerated for up to several months.

* Instead of using a double boiler, use a heat-proof bowl placed over a saucepan of barely simmering water.

SAUCY CHOCOLATE BLUEBERRY SPOONS

Makes 16 taster spoons

Sometimes I like to make my blueberries "saucy" to give them a bit of pizzazz! In this recipe, oriental spoons carry plump blueberries suspended in pools of Decadent White Chocolate Sauce and dusted with a fine illusive film of powdered sugar. The contrast of sweet and sour, dark blue and white, playful and elegant is dramatic! The delicious and rather "classy" spoons (just one gracious mouthful in size) make a fascinating fruit "taster" dessert —
perfect for a drinks, tea, coffee, cocktail or garden party.
Of course, they can be included on Taster Dessert Plates or a fruit station.

16 oriental porcelain spoons
1/4 cup (60 mL) Decadent White Chocolate Sauce
   (page 215)
1 cup (250 mL) fresh blueberries
1 tsp (5 mL) orange-flavoured liqueur
1/2 tsp (3 mL) icing sugar
1/2 tsp (3 mL) superfine sugar

GARNISH (optional or as desired)
sprigs of fresh mint
edible flowers (e.g., purple Johnny Jump-Ups)

1 Arrange oriental porcelain spoons (or larger teaspoons) individually on a tray. Spread 3/4 tsp (4 mL) Decadent White Chocolate Sauce over bottom of each spoon.

2 Toss blueberries with orange-flavoured liqueur. Drop 1 tbsp (15 mL) of blueberries over sauce in each spoon, pressing down gently to secure blueberries in position.

3 Combine icing sugar and superfine sugar in a tiny bowl.*

4 Just before serving, using a small fine mesh sieve, lightly dust surfaces of blueberries and bowls of spoons with sugar mixture.

5 Transfer spoons to a serving tray. If desired, garnish individual spoons and/or tray with fresh mint and/or edible flowers. Place an oversized cognac glass (or suitable container) on serving tray to catch empty spoons.

* This combination is important. The superfine sugar and the "dusty" nature of the icing sugar work well together, clinging to surfaces and remaining as a white powder.

CONVENIENCE TIP (FOR STEP 1): I arrange my spoons in 2 rows (with bowls of spoons facing in and handles facing out) on long narrow styrofoam utility trays. (**Note:** I ask for these at the meat counter of our local grocery store. They are always a "gift".)

MAKE-AHEAD TIP: The Saucy Chocolate Blueberry Spoons may be prepared, covered loosely with plastic wrap and refrigerated for up to a couple of hours before being served. (**Note:** Dust them with icing sugar just before serving.)

CHOCOLATE-DIPPED CHERRIES

Makes 24 Chocolate-Dipped Cherries

Dark plump cherries dipped in rich chocolate are an easy way to add a touch of pizzaz to any event. Curiously, as simple as they may be, not everyone has tasted Chocolate-Dipped Cherries, never mind made them. Added to individual dessert plates, even a single cherry can become an effective garnish.

24 fresh cherries (dark and plump), with stems attached
2 oz (60 g) semisweet chocolate,* coarsely chopped

1 Wash cherries and dry very well, keeping stems attached; set aside.

2 Partially melt chocolate over barely simmering water in a double boiler (or soften in microwave oven at **medium-low** heat). Remove from heat; stir carefully until chocolate is completely melted and smooth.

3 Picking up cherries one at a time by their stems, dip bottom halves of cherries into melted chocolate; allow excess chocolate to drip off before transferring to a wax paper-lined tray, resting cherries on their bottoms (with stems in a vertical position). Refrigerate until chocolate is firm and until ready to serve.

4 If serving later, refrigerate covered very loosely with plastic wrap for 12 hours or longer.

* **Option:** Substitute a small portion with bittersweet chocolate, if desired.

SERVING TIP: When serving the Chocolate-Dipped Cherries, if necessary, include a **small dish to catch the discarded stems and pits**.

Minted (or Toffee) Chocolate-Dipped Strawberries

Makes 12 dipped strawberries

Did you know that there are options to the traditional chocolate-dipped strawberry? Chocolate mint "anything" is wonderful, as is a chocolate and toffee combination! With a little imagination, I came up with this recipe. It also solves the problem of "being left holding" a strawberry stem!

12 large strawberries, washed and dried
2¹/₂ oz (75 g) semisweet chocolate, coarsely chopped
¹/₃ cup (80 mL) Peppermint Coconut* or toffee bits**

1 Cut stems and leaves off strawberries with a horizontal cut. Put strawberries, cut edge down, on a paper towel for a few minutes.

2 Partially melt chocolate over barely simmering water in a double boiler (or soften in a microwave oven at **medium-low** heat). Remove from heat; stir carefully until chocolate is completely melted and smooth.

3 Picking up strawberries one at a time, dip cut end into melted chocolate; allow excess chocolate to drip off before pressing into Peppermint Coconut (or toffee bits). Transfer to a wax paper-lined tray, resting strawberries on their sides. (Keep dipped berries well separated.) Refrigerate until chocolate is firm and until ready to serve. (**Note:** Serve within 6 hours.)

* To make Peppermint Coconut, in a 1 cup (250 mL) airtight plastic container, mix together ¹/₂ tsp (3 mL) of water and ¹/₄ tsp (1 mL) of both peppermint extract and green food colouring. Add ¹/₂ cup (125 mL) of unsweetened desiccated coconut, secure lid and shake until coconut is uniformly coloured. (Makes ¹/₂ cup or 125 mL.) Store refrigerated for months.
** **Note:** The "toffee bits" come as a packaged commercial product. They are **hard and crunchy** and should not be confused with the softer "butterscotch chips".

Pecan Chocolate-Dipped Pears

Makes about 20 pieces

Asian pears have a "leathery" skin which many people prefer to remove before eating. However, I have discovered, the leathery skin effectively lends itself to being dipped into melted chocolate. Lusciously coated with chocolate and studded with roasted pecans, everyone eats the skin of the pear in this recipe!

1 Korean/Asian pear, whole and unpeeled
   (weight: 10 oz or 280 g)
2 oz (60 g) semisweet chocolate, coarsely chopped
¹/₂ cup (125 mL) roasted chopped pecans

1 Remove stem and cut pear vertically into long wedges (width: 1 inch or 2.5 cm). Cut away and discard stem fibers and core. Working from skin side toward interior, cut each wedge into pieces (length: 1 inch or 2.5 cm).

2 Partially melt chocolate over barely simmering water in a double boiler (or soften in a microwave oven at **medium-low** heat). Remove from heat; stir carefully until chocolate is completely melted and smooth.

3 Picking up pieces of pear one at a time, dip skin side into melted chocolate; allow excess chocolate to drip off before pressing chocolate-coated area into roasted pecans.

4 Transfer to a wax paper-lined tray, placing pieces on their sides. (Keep dipped pieces well separated.) Refrigerate until chocolate is firm and until ready to serve. (**Note:** Serve within 6 hours.)

A recipe is not complete until I have plated it and added the final garnish or decorative touch. As much as anything, a plate is given its own special "identity" — one that can please and entice guests/family to savour what is before them. It is a fact that well-garnished food tastes better! So, I encourage you to take the extra few minutes and include a dash of decorative pizzazz! Why not try my "Signature Drizzle" of sauce or flavoured mayonnaise, a "dot" of wasabi paste or threads of fried vermicelli noodles? Indeed, these decorative details add more than pizzazz. In reality, my garnishes and final touches are designed to give extra flavour, texture, colour and character to a plate. Of course, these final additions can also be an indication of the warm hospitality being extended by the host/hostess. Guests appreciate personal effort and the attention to detail.

My favourite decorative ideas for food and plates include the use of fresh herbs, colourful salad leaves and edible flowers. Among my "playful" techniques are "dusting" (with chopped herbs, icing sugar, cocoa or instant coffee powder), "frosting" (with sugar or dry tinted gelatin dessert powder), painting or writing with chocolate as well as drizzling with whatever!

Although many of my decorative ideas appear throughout this book, I have selected a few to describe more fully on the following pages.

Note: 🐰 designates a "No Time, No Talent" recipe.

DECORATIVE DETAILS

CHOCOLATE CURL STICKS

Makes 12 Chocolate Curl Sticks

This is my little secret! How does one create perfectly curled chocolate spirals? Seek "assistance"! I start with spirals of dried ramen noodles!

1 package ramen noodles (dry)
As required vegetable oil for deep frying
4 oz (115 g) semisweet chocolate*, coarsely chopped

1 Using tip of a paring knife for assistance, carefully separate dry ramen noodles (taken directly from package) into individual curly noodle sticks.

(**Note:** Many of the ramen noodles break. Be patient. Retrieve at least 12 of the longest and/or most attractive "thin curl" sticks.)

2 Using a deep fat fryer (with basket), fry noodle sticks in hot oil (350°F or 180°C) until golden (about 30 seconds). Allow fried noodle sticks to drain well (over the oil) before transferring to a paper towel-lined tray. Let cool.

3 Partially melt chocolate over barely simmering water in a double boiler (or soften in a microwave oven at **medium-low** heat). Remove from heat; stir carefully until chocolate is completely melted and smooth.

4 Dip fried noodle sticks (one stick at a time) into melted chocolate; allow excess chocolate to drip off sticks before transferring to a rimmed wax paper-lined baking sheet. (**Note:** Rest top of chocolate curl sticks on rim of tray thus allowing minimum contact with tray.) Refrigerate until chocolate sets.

5 If necessary, cover any "bare" areas with touches of extra melted chocolate and refrigerate curl sticks briefly until firm.

6 Transfer Chocolate Curl Sticks to a wax paper-lined airtight container, separating layers with wax paper. Store refrigerated for up to a couple of months.

* **Option:** Substitute a portion with bittersweet chocolate.

> **MAKE-AHEAD TIP (FOR STEPS 1 & 2):**
> The fried noodle sticks may be prepared in advance (to be dipped in chocolate later). Place them in a paper towel-lined container, cover loosely and store in a dry cool place for up to a few weeks.

DRIED APPLE WAFERS

Makes about a dozen apple wafers

*I find that Dried Apple Wafers can add very appropriate decorative detail to a plate or a glass. Presented in a vertical, horizontal, intertwined or stacked position, they readily elevate "simple" to "spectacular"! The trick is to slice the apple as thinly as possible and avoid making this recipe on a humid day. (**Note:** A photo appears on page 122 with the Apple Brandy Trou Normand.)*

1 small whole Empire or McIntosh apple
　(weight: 3 oz or 85 g)
2 tbsp (30 mL) lemon juice
1 tbsp (15 mL) water

1　Twist stem off apple.

2　Slice apple crosswise into paper-thin, even, translucent slices using a sharp straight-edged knife (or mandolin).

3　Combine lemon juice and water in a small bowl; dip apple slices. Allow apple slices to rest for a few minutes between paper towels before arranging slices in a single layer on a parchment-lined baking sheet.

4　Place in a 225°F (110°C) preheated oven for 12 minutes. Transfer to a wire rack (or place directly on oven rack) and reduce temperature to "warm" (e.g., 150°F or 73°C). Turning occasionally, bake apple wafers until dry (about another 30 minutes or longer). (**Note of Caution: Avoid overbaking**, as the apple wafers tend to darken quickly.)

5　Transfer Apple Wafers to a wire cooling rack and allow to cool.

6　If not using promptly, arrange Dried Apple Wafers in a wax paper-lined airtight container and store in a cool dry place for up to several weeks.

FRIED VERMICELLI NOODLE STRAW

Makes about 5 cups (1.25 litres) of Fried Vermicelli (Bean) Noodle Straw

*Fried vermicelli noodles offer the playful experience of crunching on inflated strings of air! It is a decorative trick/garnish that can add creativity and fun to many recipes from hors d'oeuvres to dessert. (**Note:** A photo appears on page 76 with the Sweet-and-Sour Salmon in Zucchini Cups.)*

1 oz (30 g) vermicelli bean* noodles, uncooked
As required oil for deep frying
As required salt (optional)

1　Using a deep fat fryer, heat oil to 350°F (180°C). **Place noodles in small quantities (i.e., 4 or 5 batches)** in frying basket.** Carefully lower basket into hot oil and fry noodles for about 30 seconds, turning once with a fork.

2　Drain noodle "straw" well (over oil) before transferring to a paper towel-lined tray; salt if desired.

3　If not using fried noodle straw immediately, place in a paper towel-lined plastic container, cover loosely with a paper towel and store in a cool dry place for up to several weeks.

* Bean vermicelli noodles produce a "puffy" white straw. If a golden coloured, fine and more delicate straw is preferred, use rice vermicelli noodles. (**Note:** The volume will be slightly less.)
** **Be cautious as the noodles will immediately inflate into a voluminous mass (particularly the bean vermicelli).**

Petit "Plate" Bouquets
(of Fresh Shoots/Enoki Mushrooms/Small Edible Flowers/Salad Leaves/Herbs)
Makes 12 or more petit bouquets

*As the perfect garnish for almost any savoury plate/tray (cheese trays included), I suggest making these delicate bouquets. (**Note:** A photo appears on page 91 with Smoked Salmon Crispy Stack and on page 171 with the Ice Cream Meringue Nest.)*

3¹/₂ oz (100 g) fresh shoots (e.g., asparagus, young snow peas, sunflower)*
12 fresh chive stems, thin

1 For each petit bouquet, gather about 15 to 20 fresh shoots together into a sheaf.

2 Take one thin chive stem and tie shoots together at centre of sheaf. (If desired, tie stem ends of chive into a bow.)

3 Trim chive stem ends and bottom of sheaf/bouquet.

4 Continue to make more petit bouquets of fresh shoots.

* These are available at specialty fruit and vegetable stores as well as some supermarkets. (**Note:** As an alternative, use stems of enoki mushrooms, small edible flowers, salad leaves or fresh herbs such as dill, chervil and chives.)

Sugar Stencil Art

*I am truly passionate about devising clever and attractive presentations in order to bring an extra dimension of excitement to my recipes. Often for dessert plates, playful or unique stencils are "called into service"! (**Note:** A photo appears on page 24 with the Alfresco Lunch theme.)*

Equipment and Ingredients
plastic stencil (available in craft stores)
scotch tape
egg white
small artist's paint brush
granular sugar

1 Place stencil on plate in desired position, verifying that stencil is flat against surface of plate. (*Note:* To assist in holding stencil in position, temporarily tape it to plate in a few strategic places.)

2 Using an artist's small paint brush and working with limited areas at a time, dab egg white onto plate in cut-out portions of stencil; immediately, sprinkle sugar lightly onto egg white. (Avoid adding sugar beyond cut-out areas.) Continue this process until pattern is completed.

3 Carefully remove tape. Cautiously lift and remove stencil from plate, holding it in a stable horizontal position and transporting excess sugar away from plate on stencil. Set plate aside to dry.

4 Clean and dry plastic stencil thoroughly (both sides) before continuing to decorate next plate.

5 Once plates are dry, with a quick movement turn plates upside down to allow excess sugar to fall from "stenciled" areas. If necessary, use a clean dry artist's paint brush to remove undesirable sugar crystals and to sharpen details of stenciled pattern.

6 Store sugar-stenciled plates in a cool dry place until ready to use (for up to several weeks).

> **Colour Tip:** To introduce colours, I simply **use dry gelatin dessert powder** (i.e., directly from the package).

I absolutely could not survive without my "Basic Recipes"! They keep me organized and relaxed! It is also amazing how many people have adopted this technique and admit to having become so much more efficient and confident in the kitchen, indeed comfortable about entertaining.

As mentioned in the opening chapters of this book, these are indispensable recipes which may be prepared in small pockets of time. Most may be kept on hand for weeks or months, appropriately stored in the refrigerator, freezer or a cool dry cupboard. My "Basic Recipes" include both "savoury" and "sweet" recipes plus mayonnaises, vinaigrettes, dressings and sauces. They may be used independently or in a variety of other recipes.

One of my greatest culinary secrets is the repeated inclusion of "Basic Recipes" within principle recipes in order to simplify preparation and to easily add a memorable depth of flavour and a distinct professional touch. Indeed, my "Basic Recipes" often make my "Signature Recipes" multifaceted without being unduly fanciful. **For many of my "Basic Recipes", a commercial product exists (readily available at a local supermarket or deli) or readers may have their own faithful version of the recipe.** In general, homemade recipes seem to be infinitely better than purchased items; however, there are some excellent products to be found/discovered on store shelves.

Note: 🐇 designates a "No Time, No Talent" recipe.

BASIC RECIPES

SAVOURY

BALSAMIC VINEGAR SYRUP

Makes 2/3 cup or 170 mL

Having Balsamic Vinegar Syrup in my refrigerator is most inspiring. I find myself adding drops of this sweet-tart "agent" to many of my recipes and presentations from hors d'oeuvres to desserts!

1 cup (250 mL) balsamic vinegar
1/2 cup (125 mL) granulated sugar

1 Place balsamic vinegar and sugar in a small uncovered saucepan over medium heat; stir to dissolve sugar. Bring mixture to a boil; reduce heat to a gentle simmer. (**Note of Caution:** Simmer "gently" **to avoid scorching of the syrup.**)
2 Stirring occasionally, allow volume to reduce by half (i.e., about 2/3 cup or 170 mL). Remove from heat.
3 If not using until later, store refrigerated in a well-sealed airtight glass jar for up to several months.

"WOW" FLAVOUR TIP: Mix Balsamic Vinegar Syrup with an equal volume of sesame oil to make an absolutely fantastic drizzle/sauce. It is nothing short of "extraordinary" when drizzled over breaded scallops, grilled quail, chicken, duck or tuna, as well as crisp salad leaves. (**Note:** The sauce will naturally separate; just stir before using.)

BUCKWHEAT CRÊPE BATTER/CRÊPES

Makes about 3 2/3 cups or almost 1 litre of batter (about 5 dozen small crêpes with a 4 1/2 inch or 11 cm diameter)

In my recipe, a touch of molasses gives the crêpes a distinct flavour which successfully counterbalances the "grittier" nature of buckwheat flour. Buckwheat crêpes are an indisputable treat when served in combination with more delicately flavoured ingredients (e.g., sour cream, cottage cheese, crème fraîche and avocado). I always have buckwheat crêpe batter on hand in the freezer. Never do I specifically prepare crêpes for freezing; only "left over" crêpes are frozen for family dining. (Note: A photo appears on page 66 with Avocado Crêpe Rolls.)

3/4 cup (180 mL) all-purpose flour
3/4 cup (180 mL) buckwheat flour
1/2 tsp (3 mL) salt
1/2 tsp (3 mL) ground ginger
2 cups (500 mL)* milk
1 1/2 tbsp (23 mL) white vinegar
3 large eggs
3 egg yolks
3 tbsp (45 mL) molasses
3 tbsp (45 mL) butter or margarine, melted

1 In a large bowl, sift together flours, salt and ginger.
2 In a medium bowl, combine milk and vinegar; set aside for about 10 minutes. Add eggs, egg yolks and molasses to milk mixture. Using an electric mixer, beat ingredients together.
3 Make a well in centre of dry ingredients and pour in milk mixture; beat to form a smooth batter. Beat in melted butter (**Note:** If batter is not completely smooth, pass it through a sieve.) Allow batter to rest refrigerated for at least 30 minutes.
4 To make crêpes, stir crêpe batter thoroughly and spoon/pour batter (as desired) into a preheated nonstick skillet over medium-low heat (or onto a preheated nonstick griddle). To spread batter thinly and evenly, quickly tilt pan in a circular fashion or, using underside of a spoon, spread batter from centre in a circular fashion. Cook until bubbles on surface burst and batter just sets (i.e., no longer moist).
5 Using a pancake flipper, carefully peel crêpe from skillet and turn over; cook second side briefly. Stack cooked crêpes on a plate, cover with wax paper and place in an airtight plastic bag until ready to use. (Refrigerate if not using until later.)

* **Option:** Use slightly less milk if a thicker crêpe batter is desired.

MAKE-AHEAD TIP (STEPS 1 TO 3): The batter can be prepared, placed in airtight plastic containers and stored refrigerated for up to 2 days or frozen for several months. (**Note:** After thawing previously frozen batter, whisk it thoroughly before using.).

TIP: For a small crêpe (diameter: 4 1/2 inches or 11 cm), use 1 tbsp (15 mL) of batter. For a 7 inch (17 cm) diameter crêpe, use 1/4 cup (60 mL) of batter.

CRÈME FRAÎCHE (WITH GOAT'S CHEESE)

Makes 1 cup (250 mL)

Simple to prepare, I often make Crème Fraîche with the last remaining portions of heavy cream on hand. In our home, we use it like others might use sour cream or whipped cream. It is fabulous with muffins. (Hold the butter!)

1 cup (250 mL) heavy cream (35% fat)
2 tsp (10 mL) sour cream
3 tbsp (45 mL) goat's cheese (soft, unripened)

1 In a small bowl, mix together heavy cream and sour cream; whisk in goat's cheese. Pass several times through a fine sieve until smooth.
2 Pour into a glass jar, cover loosely with plastic wrap and allow to rest in a warm place (e.g., in a warm summer kitchen, at back of stove, near a radiator) for about 6 to 9 hours* until thick (i.e., "yogurt-like" consistency). **Note:** If desired, Crème Fraîche may be flavoured once it has thickened.**
3 Refrigerate until firm and until ready to use. Pour off any liquid which may separate from the Crème Fraîche and do not stir before using.
4 Serve directly from refrigerator with smoked salmon, tuna carpaccio, muffins, pancakes, waffles, scones, fruit, coffee cake, etc.

* The length of time will vary with the season, temperature of room and/or location. The longer the mixture remains at room temperature, the thicker and sharper it becomes.

** I: **Maple Crème Fraîche:** Stir 2 tbsp (30 mL) of maple syrup and about 1 tsp (5 mL) of maple extract into 1 cup (250 mL) of Crème Fraîche. Serve chilled.

II: **Coffee Crème Fraîche:** Stir up to 3/4 tsp (4 mL) of Coffee Paste (page 208) and 2 tbsp (30 mL) of maple syrup into 1 cup (250 mL) of Crème Fraîche. Serve chilled.

III: **Wasabi Crème Fraîche:** Stir 3/4 tsp (4 mL) of wasabi paste into 1 cup (250 mL) of Crème Fraîche. Serve chilled.

MAKE-AHEAD TIP: Crème Fraîche retains its quality for about 2 weeks or longer.

"WOW"! ALTERNATIVE RECIPE TIP: My **"flavoured" versions**** of crème fraîche are devastatingly delicious!

CRÊPE BATTER/CRÊPES

Makes about 2²/₃ cups (675 mL) of batter or 10 regular size crêpes (i.e., diameter: 7 inch or 17 cm)*

As an important part of my culinary repertoire, crêpes are incorporated into recipes for break-fast, hors d'oeuvres, appetizers, main course dishes and desserts. I only make crêpe batter in large quantities (i.e., 3 times the recipe below) and freeze it in 1 or 2 cup (250 or 500 mL) portions. The majority of my crêpes are made with previously frozen batter. A stack of freshly cooked crêpes only takes a few minutes to prepare, especially if one uses several skillets at a time. (Note: As mentioned, I never specifically prepare crêpes for freezing; only "left over" crêpes are frozen for family dining.)

1 cup (250 mL) all-purpose flour
1¹/₂ tsp (8 mL) granulated sugar
1/8 tsp (Pinch) ground ginger
2 eggs
2 egg yolks
1¹/₂ cups (375 mL) milk, divided
1/4 cup (60 mL) unsalted butter or margarine, melted

1 In a medium-size bowl, sift together flour, sugar and ground ginger.
2 In another medium-size bowl, using an electric mixer, beat together eggs, yolks and 3/4 cup (about 180 mL) milk.

3 Continuing to beat constantly, gradually add 1/2 cup (125 mL) of flour mixture, then remaining milk (3/4 cup or 180 mL) and remaining flour mixture (1/2 cup or 125 mL). Beat to form a smooth batter.
4 Beat in melted butter. (**Note:** If batter is not perfectly smooth, pass it through a coarse mesh sieve.)
5 Allow batter to rest refrigerated for at least 30 minutes before using.
6 Whisk batter thoroughly before using. For each regular size* crêpe (i.e., diameter: 7 inch or 17 cm), pour 1/4 cup (60 mL) of batter into centre of a large preheated nonstick skillet over medium-low heat. Quickly tilt and rotate skillet to form a thin, even crêpe. Cook until edges begin to turn golden and top surface is set.
7 Using a pancake flipper, carefully peel crêpe from skillet, turn and cook second side briefly (a matter of seconds).
8 Transfer crêpes to a plate and pile in a stack. If not using immediately, cover with wax paper, place in an airtight plastic bag and refrigerate.

* A. **Small Crêpes (diameter: 4 inches or 10 cm):** Prepare each small crêpe by dropping 1 tbsp (15 mL) of crêpe batter onto a preheated nonstick skillet/crêpe pan and by quickly spreading the batter in a circular manner using the underside of the spoon. (Work from the centre toward the outer circumference of the enlarging crêpe.) One cup (250 mL) of batter makes 16 small crêpes.

B. **Mini Hors d'Oeuvre Pancakes (diameter: 2 inches or 5 cm):** To make thicker and firmer "mini hors d'oeuvre pancakes", whisk 1¹/₂ tbsp (23 mL) of all-purpose flour into 1 cup (250 mL) of crêpe batter. Slowly and carefully (in a steady stream), pour 1 tsp (5 mL) of batter at a time onto a perfectly level preheated nonstick skillet, allowing the batter to spread into a tiny pancake. One cup (250 mL) of batter makes about 48 mini hors d'oeuvre pancakes.

MAKE-AHEAD TIP (STEPS 1 TO 5): Crêpe batter may be prepared and stored refrigerated in an airtight plastic container for up to 2 days or frozen for months.

TIP: Crêpes are best used the day they are cooked. However, if using previously stored crêpes (refrigerated or frozen), **warm them briefly** in their plastic storage bag in a microwave oven to restore much of their original quality.

TIP: Whenever I have extra egg yolks and a ten minute "pocket" of time, making crêpe batter becomes my task of choice!

HERB CREAM CHEESE

Makes 1 cup or 250 mL

Little effort is required to transform ordinary cream cheese into an exquisite product with appealing fresh herb flavour. Use my Herb Cream Cheese on its own as a versatile spread or as a component in hors d'oeuvres, appetizers or sandwiches. It freezes well, so you will always find it on hand in our freezer.

1 cup (250 mL) cream cheese*
(regular or low-calorie)
2 tsp (10 mL) mayonnaise
1¹/₂ tsp (8 mL) finely chopped fresh** dill weed
1/2 to 3/4 tsp (3 to 4 mL) finely chopped fresh garlic

1 Using a fork and working on a flat plate, combine ingredients thoroughly to form a smooth mixture. (**Note:** Add garlic according to taste.)
2 Place in an airtight plastic container and store refrigerated for up to a week or frozen for months.

* I use the wrapped block type of cream cheese, not the "spreadable" type.

** **Option:** 1 tsp (5 mL) crushed dried dill weed

HERB GARLIC BUTTER

Makes 1 cup or 250 mL

The untraditional addition of dill weed provides my garlic butter with yet another discreet dimension of flavour. Use Herb Garlic Butter for sautéeing, preparing garlic bread, adding to freshly cooked vegetables, pasta, rice and so much more.

1 cup (250 mL) soft butter
1 tsp (5 mL) finely chopped
fresh garlic
1 tsp (5 mL) finely chopped
fresh* dill weed
1¹/2 tbsp (23 mL) finely chopped
fresh parsley

1 Cream together butter, garlic and dill weed.
2 Add parsley and combine thoroughly.
3 Place in an airtight plastic container and store refrigerated for up to a few weeks or frozen for months.

* **Option:** ¹/2 tsp (3 mL) of dried dill weed

CASUAL-GIFT TIP: A container of "Herb Garlic Butter" often makes a much appreciated treat for close friends and relatives who do not prepare their own.

LIGHTLY SPICED FLOUR

Makes ¹/2 cup or 125 mL

The particular mixture of herbs and spices in my Lightly Spiced Flour allows me to use it on virtually anything from chicken to fish.

¹/2 cup (125 mL) flour
³/4 tsp (4 mL) curry powder
¹/2 tsp (3 mL) salt
¹/2 tsp (3 mL) crushed dried
tarragon leaves
¹/4 tsp (1 mL) crushed
black peppercorns
¹/4 tsp (1 mL) garlic powder
¹/4 tsp (1 mL) ground nutmeg
¹/4 tsp (1 mL) powdered mustard

1 Combine the ingredients together thoroughly.
2 Dust desired product with Lightly Spiced Flour mixture, shaking off and discarding any excess.

MAKE-AHEAD TIP: To save another step during meal preparation, I keep seasoned flour on hand in the freezer. Every few months, I prepare a large batch and place ¹/3 cup (80 mL) portions in individual resealable plastic bags (medium size), ready to "dust" items when required!

PESTO

Makes 1 cup or 250 mL

Pesto has to be one of the "greatest" culinary creations! It elevates simple cooked pasta to gourmet fare; it adds remarkable flavour when drizzled over certain vegetables, meats and bread. There are many types of Pesto; this is my traditional basil variety.

1 cup (250 mL) firmly packed fresh
basil leaves
¹/4 cup (60 mL) toasted pine nuts
¹/4 cup (60 mL) grated
Parmesan cheese
1 to 2 tbsp (15 to 30 mL) grated Asiago
cheese (optional)
¹/2 to ³/4 tsp (3 to 4 mL) finely
chopped fresh garlic
¹/2 cup (125 mL)* olive oil, divided

1 Place basil, pine nuts, cheeses, garlic and ¹/4 cup (or 60 mL) of oil in a blender; process to combine ingredients.
2 While blender is operating, gradually add remaining oil in a thin thread*; blend well but avoid overprocessing.
3 Transfer pesto to a well-sealed jar or airtight plastic container. Store refrigerated for up to a week or frozen for months.

* If desired, add more oil to create a thinner/more fluid pesto.

SAVOURY KASHA

Makes more than 3 cups or 750 mL
(4 to 6 servings)

*A love for tasty kasha is fondly rooted in my Ukranian farm background. Serve it hot or cold as the basis for kasha pilafs or as a component for salads, appetizers or stuffings. Kasha marries well with a broad range of items including spices (e.g., nutmeg), sun-dried tomato and nuts. This is a basic recipe for cooking savoury kasha. (**Note:** A photo appears on page 84 with Smoked Salmon Kasha/Wild Rice Martinis.)*

1¹/2 tbsp (23 mL) crushed beef
bouillon cubes (or powder)
2 cups (500 mL) boiling water
2 tbsp (30 mL) butter
¹/2 tsp (3 mL) finely chopped
fresh garlic
¹/8 tsp (Pinch) crushed
black peppercorns
1 cup (250 mL) kasha (i.e., roasted
whole buckwheat groats*)
To taste salt (optional)

1 Dissolve crushed bouillon cubes in boiling water. Add butter, garlic and crushed black peppercorns; stir until butter melts; set aside.
2 Heat a large nonstick (or heavy) skillet over medium-high heat. Add kasha and stir constantly for 2 to 3 minutes until kernels are hot and slightly further roasted. Reduce heat to low immediately; remove skillet of roasted kasha from heat.
3 Carefully add bouillon mixture to hot roasted kasha (beware of splattering) and stir; cover skillet tightly and return to heat.
4 Simmer over low heat until kernels are tender and liquid is basically absorbed (about 8 to 9 minutes). (Avoid removing lid during cooking.)
5 Remove lid and set heat at medium. (**Note:** Kasha will be very damp/slightly wet.) Turn kasha in skillet gently with a fork, "cooking off" extra liquid and drying kasha slightly (about 3 minutes). (**Note:** Exterior of kasha kernels seems quite soft, however interior should be tender but firm.)
6 Immediately transfer cooked kasha to 2 large plates. Turn hot kasha gently with a fork to stop cooking process, to separate kernels and to allow excess moisture to escape. Adjust seasoning if necessary (e.g., add salt to taste). Allow kasha to cool thoroughly (at least 30 minutes) on plates. (**Note:** *The kasha definitely becomes* **"drier"/ less sticky and firmer/not "mushy" as it is allowed to cool and rest on the plates.** *I definitely prefer this "drier" and firmer product.*)
7 Use kasha at temperature desired/ required. If not using until later, refrigerate cooked kasha in an airtight plastic container.

* **Note:** These are whole roasted kernels (i.e., whole granulation) versus cracked roasted groats (e.g., medium or fine granulation). Kasha is available in health food stores and some supermarkets.

MAKE-AHEAD TIP: Kasha may be refrigerated for up to 3 days and may also be frozen. **Note:** The kernels of previously frozen kasha will not be quite as firm as the original product. Before using, spread thawed kasha on a parchment-lined baking tray and place in a 350°F (180°C) oven until heated through (about 5 minutes). Transfer hot kasha to a plate; allow to cool and rest for at least 15 minutes before using or serving.

SECRET TIP: I have found that the secret to making great kasha is to add deep-flavoured beef bouillon (along with butter, garlic and crushed black peppercorns) to hot roasted buckwheat kernels. My cooking technique ensures that the final product is splendidly rich in flavour and colour and not overcooked.

SUSHI RICE

Makes about 3 cups (750 mL)
cooked rice*

I have found my sushi rice to be a surprisingly useful product suitable for making many more recipes beyond the traditional Japanese sushi. With its slightly sweet vinegar flavour and its sticky consistency, this sushi rice can be combined with smoked oysters, beef carpaccio, fruit and other tasty ingredients to create truly outstanding hors d'oeuvres, appetizers, main course accompaniments and even desserts.

1¼ cups (300 mL) sushi rice
1⅓ cups (325 mL) cold water
2 tbsp (30 mL) rice vinegar
1½ tbsp (23 mL) granulated sugar
1½ tbsp (23 mL) rice wine (mirin)**
¾ tsp (4 mL) salt

1 Rinse rice several times and drain well.
2 In a medium size (preferably nonstick) heavy saucepan, combine rice and water. Cover and bring to a boil over medium-high heat, stirring from time to time. Allow rice to boil for two minutes, stirring occasionally. Reduce heat to simmer. Cook for 15 minutes.
3 Remove rice from heat. (Don't remove lid.) Allow to stand, covered, for another 15 minutes.
4 Meanwhile, make a rice wine syrup. Put vinegar, sugar, rice wine and salt in a small saucepan. Bring to a boil over medium heat, stirring until sugar dissolves. Set aside.
5 Transfer cooked rice to a large flat glass baking dish (or platter); quickly drizzle ½ of rice wine syrup evenly over rice and toss to combine. Drizzle remaining rice wine syrup over rice; toss well.
6 If not using until later, cool rice, place in airtight plastic containers and store refrigerated for up to 3 days or frozen for months. **Note:** To restore original quality, just before using, reheat (thawed) rice briefly (only until hot) in a loosely covered microwave-proof bowl in a microwave oven.

* This is sufficient to cover 4 standard sheets of nori (seaweed) when making sushi rolls.

** Available in Asian food stores and most supermarkets.

TIP: Unlike "Perfect Rice" (page 168), cooked sushi rice does freeze fairly well and I usually have a supply of it in my freezer. Although I use only freshly cooked sushi rice when making sushi rolls, I have no problem using previously frozen sushi rice in many of my other recipes (e.g., hors d'oeuvres). (See "note" in **Step 6**.)

TASTY WILD RICE

Makes 2½ cups or 625 ml
(4 to 5 servings)

Perception can be extremely effective! Let's face it, with wild rice as an accompaniment, main course is easily perceived to be gourmet! This is my basic (but absolutely fabulous)

recipe for cooking basic wild rice. It works with almost anything (e.g., chicken, meat, game, poultry, fish and seafood). Because wild rice takes a reasonably long time to cook, I almost exclusively prepare it in advance (i.e., earlier in the day for dinner parties, or when required to replenish my "freezer" supplies). Yes, you are certain to find containers of cooked wild rice in our freezer. I use it in every part of the menu from hors d'oeuvre to main course recipes. But remember, I am Canadian and wild rice is one of Canada's internationally renowned products!

1 cup (250 mL) wild rice
¾ cup (180 mL) cold water
½ tsp (3 mL) finely chopped fresh garlic, optional
2 tsp (10 mL) crushed dark beef bouillon cubes (or powder)
1½ tsp (8 mL) herb garlic butter (e.g., page 205) or butter, optional
To taste salt, optional

1 Rinse wild rice thoroughly. Place rice, water and garlic in a small saucepan over high heat; bring to a boil. Cover saucepan tightly and reduce heat to low.
2 Cook until grains are tender (about 40 minutes for very long grain, top quality wild rice), stirring in crushed bouillon cubes during the final stage of cooking.* (**Note:** Grains burst partially open, showing a reasonable amount of white interior. Avoid overcooking rice.)
3 Remove from heat and drain off any excess water. Return wild rice to saucepan, stir in garlic butter and season with salt if necessary.

* It may be necessary to add a few extra drops of water during cooking.

MAKE-AHEAD TIP: Place cooled wild rice in an airtight plastic container and store it refrigerated for up to 3 days or frozen for several weeks. **Note:** When reheating the wild rice, avoid overcooking it. Just before serving, place wild rice and a few drops of water in a nonstick skillet over medium heat. Cover and heat only until the rice is hot. Remove from heat, stir in an additional touch of garlic butter (about 2 tsp or 10 mL) and serve promptly.

"WOW" SECRET TIP: My secret to making wild rice succulent in flavour and colour is to **add crushed beef bouillon cubes or powder** to the rice during the last minutes of cooking.

SWEET

BASIC SUGAR SYRUP

Makes 3 cups or 750 mL thin syrup

I keep Basic Sugar Syrup on hand to brush on freshly baked cakes or to sweeten cold fruit soups, homemade flavoured liqueurs, iced tea and coffee. Brushing sugar syrup on un-iced cakes not only makes them moister, but also adds an unidentifiable depth of flavour and richness. I find my Basic Sugar Syrup to be a practical product to have on hand.

**2 cups (500 mL) granulated sugar
2 cups (500 mL) water**

1 Place sugar and water in a medium saucepan over medium-high heat; stir constantly until sugar dissolves.
2 Bring syrup to a boil; reduce heat and allow mixture to boil for a few minutes. Remove from heat.
3 When cool, pour syrup into sterilized well-sealed glass jars and store refrigerated for up to a few weeks or frozen for months.

COFFEE PASTE

Makes 3 tbsp (45 mL)

Who doesn't like coffee or coffee-flavoured "whatever"? Coffee Paste is great to have on hand to add an enchanting coffee flavour to icings, fillings, ice creams, yogurt, crème fraîche, sweet sauces and desserts! Personally, I always make it with decaffeinated coffee.

**1/2 cup (125 mL) instant
coffee* powder
2 tbsp (30 mL) boiling water**

1 Press instant coffee through a sieve.
2 Pour boiling water into a small bowl and add sieved instant coffee. Stir thoroughly to dissolve coffee as well as possible.
3 Pass Coffee Paste through a fine sieve.
4 Place in a well-sealed small jar and store-refrigerated for months.

* Options: Regular or decaffeinated

DELICATELY TENDER PASTRY

Makes one pie crust 9 inches or 23 cm in diameter (or about a dozen dessert tart shells or up to 3 dozen mini tart shells)

This pastry is indeed very tender and flaky with a discreet butter flavour. Everyone can make successful pastry; just follow the recipe. And don't be "afraid" of your pastry! If it happens to crack during rolling, patch it!

**1 cup (250 mL) pastry flour
(freezer chilled)
1 tsp (5 mL) granulated sugar (optional)
1/4 tsp (1 mL) salt
1/3 cup (80 mL) unsalted butter (cold)
2 1/2 tbsp (38 mL) shortening (cold)
3 to 3 1/2 tbsp (45 to 53 mL) ice water**

1 Sift flour, sugar and salt together in a chilled large bowl.
2 Using a grater (i.e., side with largest holes), grate butter into flour mixture, drawing in flour mixture constantly during grating process in order to keep butter flakes separated. Similarly, grate in shortening.
3 With fingertips, break apart larger clumps of fat so that mixture resembles coarse crumbs.
4 Sprinkle ice water, 1 tbsp (15 mL) at a time, over flour-fat mixture and toss lightly with a fork until dough begins to form a mass.
5 Using fingertips, gather dough together and press into a ball.
6 Flatten dough into a disk (diameter: 4 inches or 10 cm); wrap disk in plastic wrap and refrigerate for at least 30 minutes (or overnight).
7 Lightly flour counter (or preferably a cool marble slab) and rolling pin (preferably

fitted with a stockinette). Place disk of chilled dough on floured surface and roll out dough evenly, always starting at centre and rolling towards edge with light, quick movements and lifting rolling pin at edge of pastry to ensure even thickness (i.e., no thin edges). Constantly pick up and rotate pastry, dragging rolled pastry through a light dusting of flour. (Throughout process, keep rolling pin lightly dusted with flour and reshape circle of dough so that edges are not cracked.) Roll pastry into a thinner and larger circle of desired thickness (e.g., about 1/8 inch/ 0.3 cm or less).
8 Cut pastry and arrange in pie plate/pan or as required for recipe (e.g., pie*, tarts**).
9 Refrigerate, allowing dough to rest another 30 minutes (to avoid shrinkage). Bake in a pre-heated oven at 425°F (220°C) until golden brown.

* For a single crust pie, roll pastry out to form a circle 3 inches (8 cm) larger than top diameter of pie plate. Fold the pastry circle in half; lift over pie plate. Place folded straight edge of pastry evenly across centre of pie plate and unfold to cover/hide entire plate. Working from centre, gently press dough against bottom and sides of plate to prevent formation of air pockets. (Avoid stretching dough.) Using scissors, cut "overhanging" pastry to 3/4 inch (2 cm) beyond rim. Fold "overhanging" pastry under pastry edge to create a double layer of pastry on rim of pie plate. Flute edge with finger and thumbs. Chill for 20 minutes before baking.

To make a pre-baked pie shell, "blind bake" the pastry in the pie plate. To do this, prick the bottom and sides of the chilled pastry shell in many places to prevent puffing during baking. Line the shell with aluminum foil (shiny side facing "down") and completely fill it with dried beans or pie weights. Bake the shell on the bottom rack of a preheated 425°F (220°C) oven for 14 minutes. Remove it from the oven; quickly remove the foil and beans/weights; cover the edges with 2 inch (5 cm) wide strips of aluminum foil (shiny side out); return the pie shell to the oven until the pastry is baked and golden in colour (about another 7 to 10 minutes). (If necessary, remove the foil during the last stages of baking to ensure even browning.) Cool the crust (in the pie plate) on a wire cooling rack.

** The amount of pastry is sufficient for about 12 to 14 dessert tart shells with a diameter of 2 1/2 inches or 6 cm (using circles of dough with a 4 inch or 10 cm diameter) or for about 32 to 36 mini-tart shells with a diameter of 1¹/₂ inches or 3.5 cm (using circles of dough with a 2¹/₂ inch or 6 cm diameter). To make pre-baked shells (dessert or mini cocktail size), prick the interior bottom of the shells very well once the pastry has been cut out and arranged in the tart pans; chill. Bake in middle of a preheated oven until tart shells begin to turn golden (about 8 to 10 minutes for the dessert tart shells and about 7 to 8 minutes for the mini tart shells).

TIP: Try to **keep ingredients cool** and **avoid handling the pastry** too much. I find that grating the butter and shortening into the flour is my preferred technique for incorporating the "fat".

TIP: If desired, for pies that are filled and then baked, preheat unglazed tiles or a pizza stone on the bottom rack of a 425°F (220°C) oven for 30 minutes. Bake the filled pie (in its pan) on the preheated tiles/stone. This technique helps to ensure that the bottom crust is baked.

DELUXE CHOCOLATE CUPS

Makes 4 chocolate cups

Although chocolate cups are available commercially, you would be surprised how quick and easy they are to make — particularly when using the following technique. It is my discreet addition of hard toffee bits to the melted chocolate that sets these chocolate cups apart from others! To prepare simple chocolate cups, use only 4 oz or 115 g of chocolate and initially line each paper muffin cup with about 1¹/₃ tbsp or 20 mL of melted chocolate. (Note: A photo appears on page 178 with Caramel Mousse Chocolate Cups.)

5 oz (150 g) semisweet chocolate,*
coarsely chopped
1 tbsp (15 mL) hard toffee bits
8 paper muffin cups**

1 Partially melt chocolate over barely simmering water in a double boiler (or soften in a microwave oven at **medium-low** heat.) Remove from heat; stir carefully

until chocolate is completely melted and smooth. (Avoid having "melted" chocolate too soft. It should be thick and not fluid.)
2 Stir in coarsely chopped hard toffee bits.
3 Work with 2 paper muffin cups fitted together at a time. Pour 1¹/₂ tbsp (23 mL) of chocolate mixture into "double thickness" muffin cup. With a spoon, spread chocolate mixture evenly (i.e., to same thickness) over interior surface of cup. (**FLASH: Don't worry about how "pretty" the interior surface is.** The cup will be filled!)
4 Invert cup on a wax paper-lined tray.
5 Repeat process to make 3 more chocolate cups.
6 Refrigerate until firm (about 15 minutes).
7 Remove from refrigerator; place chocolate cups in an upright position. Add another 1¹/₂ tsp (8 mL) of melted chocolate mixture to each chocolate cup, paying particular attention to reinforcing rims and any thin areas. (**Note of Caution: Avoid using too much or too little chocolate.** Chocolate cups must be strong but not impossible to break safely with a fork and spoon.)
8 Invert cups on the wax paper-lined tray and refrigerate until firm.
9 Carefully and patiently peel away paper and/or foil muffin cups from chocolate cups. (**Note:** If necessary, repair any cracks or breaks with extra melted chocolate.)
10 Cautiously place chocolate cups (in an inverted position) in a wax paper-lined airtight plastic container. Store refrigerated until ready to use or for up to several months.

* **Option:** Substitute a portion with bittersweet chocolate if desired.

** These cups are 2¹/₂ inches or 6 cm in diameter and about ¹/₃ cup (80 mL) in volume. However, chocolate cups of any desired size may be prepared using this technique.

TIP: "Double thickness" paper muffin cups offer greater stability. Actually, I like to use a foil muffin cup with a paper liner.

TIP: Chocolate cups are wonderful to have on hand for a quick "assembly" dessert. They never cease to generate great excitement and appreciation. Remember to secure the filled cups on the dessert

plates with an edible "glue" (e.g., hazelnut chocolate spread or caramel sauce). This holds them in position when being taken to the table and when being consumed.

KATAIFI STRAW DISKS

Makes 8 disks with a diameter of 3¹/₂ inches or 9 cm

*The intriguing, thread-like nature of Kataifi appeals to the playful side of my character, urging me to come up with yet another way of using this Arabic pastry dough. My Kataifi Straw Disks are quick and simple to prepare; however, **be careful when working with hot oil and hot equipment! Do a "dry run", practicing the technique without the use of hot oil. Follow instructions carefully and with recommended equipment. FLASH: a "compromised" version of Kataifi Straw Disks may be prepared using an "oven bake" technique (see * below).** (Note: A photo appears on page 91 with Smoked Salmon Crispy Stacks and on page 47 with Berries and Cream Exotic Straw Sandwiches.)*

4 oz (115 g) kataifi pastry**
As required oil for deep frying

SPECIAL EQUIPMENT REQUIRED
metal ring/cookie cutter
(diameter: 4 inches or 10 cm;
height: 1 inch or 2.5 cm)

1 Heat oil in a deep fat fryer to 350°F or 180°C.
2 To loosen kataifi strands, gently pull apart kataifi dough with two hands.
3 Divide into 8 equal portions (i.e., just less than ¹/₂ oz or about 15 g each); set aside; cover well with plastic wrap and then a damp tea towel.
4 With fryer basket set on a large dinner plate, place metal ring in basket and evenly distribute one portion of kataifi pastry within ring.
5 Carefully, while gradually submerging basket into hot oil, use a large metal slotted spoon to press kataifi down, keeping it within ring and submerged until barely golden in colour (about 30 seconds).

(**Note of Caution:** The hot kataifi will continue to cook when removed from oil. **Avoid overcooking.**)

6 Allow excess oil to drain off (over the oil) before transferring basket with contents back to dinner plate. With tongs, remove metal ring and place on a second dry plate. Using a pancake turner, transfer Kataifi Straw Disk to a paper towel-lined tray. With tongs, return metal ring to basket and repeat the process to make remaining disks. (**Note of Caution:** *Be careful — everything is hot! Make good use of the tongs, slotted spoon and pancake turner. The fryer basket is also hot and remains hot!*)

7 If not using until later, arrange cooled Kataifi Straw Disks in a single layer in a large paper towel-lined box (e.g., large metal rectangular cookie box) and store in a cool dry place for up to a few weeks.

* Separate kataifi strands thoroughly, divide them into 8 equal portions and keep covered as outlined in recipe. Working with 1 portion at a time, toss gently and completely with 1 tsp (5 mL) of melted unsalted butter. Arrange lightly and evenly inside individual metal rings (diameter: 4 inches or 10 cm) set on parchment paper-lined baking sheets. (**Note:** Alternatively arrange the portions of buttered kataifi strands in tart pans with broad shallow cups similar in diameter to proposed metal rings.) Bake in a preheated 375°F (190°C) oven until golden in colour (about 5 to 6 minutes). Immediately and carefully transfer kataifi disks to wire cooling racks.

** This Arabic thread-like pastry is available fresh at some Arabic bakeries or frozen in packages at many Arabic or specialty food stores. (**Note:** There are various ways of spelling and pronouncing "kataifi".)

"WOW" TIP: These kataifi disks are most inspiring. As single disks, they become fascinating bases for dessert or appetizers; double disks naturally lend themselves to "sandwich"-type presentations and enticing stacks.

Velvety Lemon Curd

Makes about 1¹/₄ cups or 300 mL

Velvety Lemon Curd is a "must" as a basic "sweet" recipe to be used in making a variety of desserts. It only takes minutes to prepare,

can be refrigerated for a week or longer, and may even be frozen. Lemon curd, however, can be "tricky" to make and may be too aggressive in flavour. I have developed a technique which is easy and fail-proof; and by using equal portions of lemon and orange juice along with a touch of grated lemon zest, the resulting lemon curd charms the palate.

2 eggs*
2 egg yolks*
¹/₄ cup (60 mL) fresh lemon juice, strained
¹/₄ cup (60 mL) orange juice, strained
¹/₂ cup (125 mL) granulated sugar
1 tsp (5 mL) grated lemon zest
1 tbsp (15 mL) butter (unsalted), soft

1 In a medium-size bowl, whisk together eggs and egg yolks until smooth.

2 In a small saucepan over medium-high heat, combine lemon and orange juices, sugar and lemon zest. Stir until sugar is dissolved and mixture comes to a boil.

3 Gradually and in a steady stream whisk hot juice mixture into beaten egg mixture. Pour combined mixture into saucepan.

4 Place saucepan over medium-low heat, add butter and whisk constantly until mixture is thick and **bubbling** (about 4 to 5 minutes).

5 Remove lemon curd from heat and **immediately** transfer to a bowl (to avoid overcooking).

6 If not using until later, place cooled lemon curd in an airtight plastic container and store refrigerated for up to a week.

* **Note:** If a slightly thicker lemon curd is desired, use 3 eggs and 1 yolk; however, the final product is less "velvety".

Cooking Tip: I prefer to stir the mixture with a heat-proof rubber spatula during the final minutes of cooking. (i.e., The lemon curd may be moved more effectively away from the sides and bottom of the saucepan. As well, I can more accurately judge the thickness of the mixture and avoid overcooking.)

TIP: I often freeze "leftover" portions. (Previously frozen lemon curd may not be as firm as the original product; therefore if necessary, reheat it over medium-low heat,

stirring constantly, until it becomes thick. Transfer it immediately to a bowl to avoid overcooking.)

Alternative-Use Tip: Frequently, I combine my Velvety Lemon Curd with whipped cream, sour cream or cream cheese to make **tasty fillings and sauces**. Or, I use small amounts on its own to give a more dramatic burst of flavour!

Whisky Whipped Cream

Makes 2 cups or 500 mL

For a full-flavoured whipped cream, add a touch of whisky! It does make a noticeable and much "appreciated" difference!

1 cup (250 mL) heavy cream (35% fat), chilled
2¹/₂ tbsp (38 mL) icing sugar
1¹/₃ tbsp (20 mL) whisky

1 Place heavy cream in a chilled medium-size bowl and beat with chilled beaters at high speed.

2 When cream begins to thicken, reduce speed and gradually add sugar.

3 Continue to beat at high speed, adding whisky when soft peaks form. Beat until whisky is incorporated and peaks are definitely firm.

4 Store Whisky Whipped Cream refrigerated until ready to serve.

Make-Ahead Tip: Whisky Whipped Cream may be prepared hours before serving and stored refrigerated in its mixing bowl. Should the whipped cream lose any degree of stability, re-beat it briefly with chilled beaters just before serving/using.

Secret Tip: The secret to whipping cream successfully is to **have everything cold** (i.e., bowl, beaters and cream). This allows the cream to be whipped to a definite "firm" stage and to remain stable.

MAYONNAISES/ VINAIGRETTES

HONEY MUSTARD MAYONNAISE

Makes about 1²/₃ cups or 400 mL

To make a sweetly mellow mayonnaise with a tantalizing edge, try this recipe. Being one of my three most frequently used flavoured mayonnaises, I keep it on hand in the refrigerator in both a handy plastic squeeze bottle and a glass jar. Honey Mustard Mayonnaise marries well with a myriad of ingredients including chicken, turkey, ham, scallops, fish, crêpes, cold pasta, kasha, regular and sushi rice to mention a few.

1¹/₂ cups (375 mL) mayonnaise*
2 tbsp (30 mL) Dijon mustard
2¹/₂ to 3 tbsp (38 to 45 mL) honey (liquid)
¹/₈ tsp (Pinch) crushed black peppercorns

1 Place mayonnaise in a small bowl. Whisk Dijon mustard into mayonnaise, and then honey according to taste; combine thoroughly.
2 Add crushed peppercorns to taste.
3 Place Honey Mustard Mayonnaise in well-sealed glass jars or airtight plastic containers and refrigerate for up to several weeks.

* **Option:** Regular or low calorie

MUSTARD HERB VINAIGRETTE

Makes 1¹/₂ cups or 375 mL

Because of its sweetly mellow (verus sharp) full-bodied flavour, my Mustard Herb Vinaigrette is outstandingly popular. Its uses are limitless. For that reason, I whisk the recipe up by the litre.

³/₄ cup (180 mL) salad oil
¹/₄ cup (60 mL) olive oil
¹/₄ cup (60 mL) vinegar
2 tbsp (30 mL) lemon juice
1¹/₃ tbsp (20 mL) granulated sugar
1 tbsp (15 mL) chopped fresh dill weed
1 tbsp (15 mL) chopped fresh parsley
1¹/₂ tsp (8 mL) powdered mustard
1¹/₂ tsp (8 mL) finely chopped fresh garlic
1¹/₂ tsp (8 mL) salt
1 tsp (5 mL) crushed black peppercorns

1 In a medium-size bowl, whisk ingredients together well.
2 Pour vinaigrette into well-sealed glass jars and store refrigerated for up to several weeks.
3 Stir well before using.

ALTERNATIVE-USE TIP: Besides salads of all kinds, drizzle this vinaigrette over beef/tuna carpaccio, cooked cold vegetables, vegetable purées, cold seafood — the list is ongoing!

ORANGE PEEL DRESSING/SAUCE

Makes 1 cup or 250 mL

Orange juice simmered together with orange marmalade, lemon juice, mustard and ginger, then thickened with enticing slivers of blanched orange zest results in a phenomenally unique sauce! With its flexibility and popular appeal, I include it in recipes from hors d'oeuvres to desserts! Try it drizzled lightly over cooked vegetables (e.g., asparagus and beets), sliced fresh fruit (e.g., pears, plums, strawberries), grilled or roasted chicken, duck, game, couscous, rice . . . It freezes well, so I recommend you make it in quantity.

¹/₄ cup (60 mL) finely slivered fresh orange zest*
1 cup (250 mL) hot water
¹/₂ cup (125 mL) frozen concentrated orange juice, thawed (but not diluted)
¹/₄ cup (60 mL) orange marmalade
¹/₄ cup (60 mL) water
2 tbsp (30 mL) lemon juice

2 tsp (10 mL) prepared mustard (sandwich type)
1 tsp (5 mL) peeled and grated fresh gingerroot

1 Place slivered orange zest in a saucepan with hot water. Bring to a boil and cook for 2 or 3 minutes. Drain and set aside. (Discard liquid.)
2 Combine remaining ingredients in saucepan over medium heat. Bring to a boil; reduce heat and simmer for 10 minutes uncovered.
3 Remove from heat; stir in cooked orange zest and allow to cool.
4 Pour dressing into a well-sealed glass jar and store refrigerated for up to a couple of weeks or frozen for months.
5 Stir well before using. Serve sauce warm, cold or at room temperature. (**Note:** I generally use it directly from the refrigerator.)

* Use only the outer orange part of the rind (i.e., no white pulp).

ORANGE ZEST MAYONNAISE/SAUCE

Makes 1 cup or 250 mL

It thrills me to discover a superb and simple compliment for recipes. Blanched orange zest and concentrated orange juice resurrect common mayonnaise, transforming it into a stunning orange-scented sauce. The grated fresh gingerroot provides a strategic "zip". I urge you to try this Orange Zest Mayonnaise/ Sauce particularly with seafood, fish and poultry (grilled, poached or oven baked). It also makes an enticing dip.

1 tbsp (15 mL) finely grated fresh orange zest
1 cup (250 mL) mayonnaise*
1 tbsp (15 mL) frozen concentrated orange juice, thawed (but not diluted)
2¹/₃ tsp (12 mL) peeled and grated fresh gingerroot
2 tsp (10 mL) granulated sugar

1 Simmer orange zest in a small saucepan with 1 cup (250 mL) of water for one or two minutes. Drain well through a fine sieve, squeezing out extra water.

2 In a small bowl, whisk "blanched" orange zest together with all remaining ingredients.
3 Place Orange Zest Mayonnaise/Sauce in a well-sealed glass jar/airtight plastic container and/or a handy plastic squeeze bottle. Store refrigerated for up to several weeks.

* Option: regular or low-calorie

CAUTION TIP: Do not freeze or heat the Orange Zest Mayonnaise/Sauce.

TIP: Cold chicken and turkey salads and sandwiches are "awesome" with a touch of this popular orange and ginger mayonnaise/sauce.

ZESTY GINGER MAYONNAISE/SAUCE

Makes 1¹/2 cups or 375 mL

It might be difficult to appreciate how discreet quantities of wasabi and sugar along with a "healthy" dose of grated fresh gingerroot can assist in redefining virtually any type of mayonnaise as a "culinary essential"! Zesty Ginger Mayonnaise/Sauce is another product which occupies a permanently designated place on our refrigerator door! You will find yourself using it much like regular mayonnaise except more often! It is excellent with grilled or deep-fried foods, salads, savoury crêpes, pastry dishes, in sandwiches or as a dip.

1¹/2 cups (375 mL) mayonnaise*
2 tbsp (30 mL) peeled and grated fresh gingerroot
2 tsp (10 mL) granulated sugar
¹/4 tsp (1 mL) wasabi paste (optional)**

1 In a small bowl, whisk ingredients thoroughly together.
2 Place Zesty Ginger Mayonnaise/Sauce in a well-sealed glass jar/airtight plastic container and/or a handy plastic squeeze bottle. Store refrigerated for up to several weeks.

* **Option:** Regular or low-calorie

** Available in oriental and specialty food stores as well as some supermarkets

CAUTION TIP: Do not freeze or heat the Zesty Ginger Mayonnaise/Sauce.

SAVOURY SAUCES

(ARMAGNAC) CREAMY STEAK SAUCE

Makes about 2¹/2 cups or 625 mL

In this recipe, additions of cream, parsley, garlic and crushed black peppercorns rapidly transform a bouillon base into a deliciously popular and convenient sauce! Sometimes I add a splash of Armagnac! This sauce is always on hand in our freezer. With sautéed mushrooms and baked potatoes, the sauce elevates a quick steak dinner into a feast! It's also wonderful with veal and pork.

1²/3 tbsp (25 mL) crushed dark beef bouillon cubes (or powder)
2 cups (500 mL) hot water
¹/4 cup (60 mL) butter
3¹/2 tbsp (53 mL) all-purpose flour
¹/2 to ²/3 cup (125 to 170 mL) heavy cream (35% fat)
3 tbsp (45 mL) chopped fresh parsley leaves
¹/2 tsp (3 mL) finely chopped fresh garlic
2 tbsp (30 mL) Armagnac liqueur (optional)
To taste crushed black peppercorns and salt (optional)

1 Dissolve bouillon cubes in hot water; set aside.
2 Melt butter in a medium-size saucepan over medium heat. Reduce heat to medium-low, blend in flour and cook for a minute.
3 Add bouillon, whisking constantly to form a smooth sauce; bring to a boil.
4 Whisk in cream according to taste; bring sauce to a gentle simmer.
5 Stir in parsley, garlic and if desired, Armagnac. Add crushed black peppercorns and if necessary salt to taste. (**Note:** Or instead of salt, stir in additional very finely crushed beef bouillon cubes/powder.)

---

6 Remove sauce from heat, cover and let rest for 5 to 10 minutes, allowing flavours to develop.

MAKE-AHEAD TIP: Place cooled sauce in airtight plastic containers and store it refrigerated for up to 2 days or frozen for months. (**Note:** I make the sauce in large quantities. For convenience, I freeze it in muffin tins. The frozen "muffin size" portions are then transferred to a plastic bag to be used in the amounts required.)

FLAVOUR TIP: Crushed bouillon cubes or powder (beef or chicken) are the secret to many of my sauces and soups. They can be conveniently and "tastefully" combined with other key ingredients to produce amazing results. (**Note:** When using beef bouillon cubes, I try to use the "dark coloured" variety which tends to be more flavourful and generally less salty than the lighter option.)

ASIAN CASHEW SAUCE/DRESSING

Makes 1²/3 cups or 425 mL

This splendid cashew sauce/dressing adds a gentle Asian flavour to noodles, salads, chicken, pork, kebabs and rice. The myriad of flavours come together to make this recipe a fabulous alternative to peanut sauce.

¹/2 cup (125 mL) cashew butter* (creamy)
¹/3 cup (80 mL) sesame oil
¹/3 cup (80 mL) vegetable oil
1¹/2 tbsp (23 mL) honey (liquid)
¹/4 cup (60 mL) rice wine (mirin)
2 tbsp (30 mL) rice vinegar
2 tbsp (30 mL) soya sauce
¹/2 to 1 tsp (3 to 5 mL) finely chopped fresh garlic

1 In a medium-size bowl, stir together cashew butter, oils and honey until smooth.
2 In a small bowl, whisk together rice wine, vinegar and soya sauce.
3 Whisking constantly, pour rice wine mixture in a thin thread into cashew butter mixture. Add garlic to taste; whisk to form a smooth dressing.

4 Pour dressing into well-sealed glass jars and refrigerate.

5 Whisk/stir well before using.

* Cashew butter is available at health food stores. (**Note:** As an option, use peanut butter.)

MAKE-AHEAD TIP: The sauce may be stored refrigerated for up to several weeks.

BALSAMIC RED WINE DRIZZLE/SAUCE

Makes ⁴/₅ cup or 200 mL

I wanted to develop a fabulous reduction suitable for drizzling over pâté, beef, game, pork, lamb, veal and poultry. A combination of beef bouillon, red wine, honey and balsamic vinegar did the trick! My family and guests rave about this Balsamic Red Wine Drizzle/Sauce. It truly makes any seared pâté quite "exquisite"!

1 tbsp (15 mL) crushed beef bouillon cubes (or powder)
1¹/₂ cups (375 mL) hot water
2 cups (500 mL) red wine
¹/₂ cup (125 mL) honey
¹/₂ cup (125 mL) balsamic vinegar
1 tbsp (15 mL) cornstarch
1 tbsp (15 mL) cold water

1 Dissolve bouillon cubes in hot water; set aside.

2 In a medium-size saucepan over medium heat, combine wine and honey, stirring until honey is dissolved.

3 Add balsamic vinegar; bring to a boil. Stirring occasionally, allow mixture to boil gently (uncovered) and reduce to 1 cup (250 mL).

4 Add bouillon mixture and bring to a boil. Stirring occasionally, allow mixture to boil uncovered and reduce to about ⁴/₅ cup (200 mL).

5 In a small bowl, combine cornstarch and cold water to form a smooth mixture. Add a couple of tablespoons (30 mL) of hot balsamic sauce to cornstarch mixture, stirring constantly until well blended.

6 Whisking constantly, add cornstarch balsamic mixture to saucepan. Bring sauce back to a boil and cook until slightly thickened.

7 Remove sauce from heat and allow to cool.

8 If not using sauce immediately, store cooled sauce refrigerated in a well-sealed glass jar and/or in a handy plastic squeeze bottle for up to several weeks.

TIMING TIP: Plan to make this recipe when you are doing other tasks in the kitchen. The reduction process takes about 1¹/₂ hours. Watch the volumes closely for accuracy and stir occasionally to avoid scorching.

TIP: I use the sauce directly from the refrigerator when its consistency is the thickest. Sometimes I combine it with sesame oil, usually in a 1 to 1 ratio, to create another very seductive drizzle/sauce.

(COGNAC) WHITE WINE CREAM SAUCE

Makes 2 cups or about 500 mL

When I have heavy cream in the refrigerator and a few extra minutes, I whisk together this sauce — by the quart/litre! Having it on hand saves me hours of decision-making and time in the kitchen. It is lovely with chicken, veal, pasta, sweetbreads, fish and seafood.

1¹/₃ tbsp (20 mL) crushed chicken bouillon cubes (or powder)
2 tsp (10 mL) prepared mustard (sandwich type)
1¹/₂ cups (375 mL) hot water
2 tsp (10 mL) finely chopped fresh garlic
¹/₂ tsp (3 mL) peeled and grated fresh gingerroot
2 tbsp (30 mL) butter
3 tbsp (45 mL) all-purpose flour
¹/₄ cup (60 mL) white wine
¹/₂ cup (125 mL) heavy cream (35% fat)
1 tbsp (15 mL) cognac (optional)

1 Dissolve bouillon cubes and mustard in hot water.

2 In a medium-size saucepan, sauté garlic and ginger in melted butter over medium heat for about 1 minute; blend in flour and cook for another minute.

3 Remove saucepan from heat; whisking constantly, add bouillon mixture and wine; whisk until smooth.

4 Return saucepan to heat; whisking constantly, bring to a boil.

5 Reduce heat to medium-low; continuing to whisk constantly, add cream and bring sauce to a simmer.

6 Allow sauce to simmer gently for a couple of minutes; remove from heat; stir in cognac.

7 Cover and let sauce rest for at least 5 to 10 minutes, allowing flavours to develop.

8 If serving later, cool sauce, transfer to airtight plastic containers and refrigerate.

9 Serve sauce hot or warm.

MAKE-AHEAD TIP: The sauce may be stored refrigerated for up to 3 days or frozen for months.

MUSTARD MINT SAUCE/DRIZZLE

Makes 1 cup or 250 mL

Ordinary mint jelly can be elevated to the level of a "serious" sauce with the subtle assistance of Dijon mustard, white wine vinegar and crushed dried mint! My Mustard Mint Sauce is a "must" when lamb is served in our home. For a beautiful final presentation, drizzle plates with this sauce.

1 cup (250 mL) mint jelly (commercial)
1¹/₃ tbsp (20 mL) Dijon mustard
2 tsp (10 mL) white wine vinegar
1 tsp (5 mL) crushed dried mint

1 Heat jelly in a small saucepan over low heat; stir regularly until jelly melts.

2 Whisk in mustard and vinegar to form a smooth sauce; remove from heat.

3 Stir in mint. Continue to stir sauce occasionally as it cools to incorporate mint.

4 Serve sauce warm, cold or at room temperature. (**Note:** I tend to serve it directly from the refrigerator.)

5 Store refrigerated in a well-sealed glass jar and/or a handy plastic squeeze bottle for up to several months.

ROASTED RED PEPPER CREAM SAUCE

Makes 1¹/2 cups or 375 mL

Bouillon, garlic and hot chili paste discreetly contribute to the full roasted red pepper flavour of this mellow cream sauce. Served with Roasted Red Pepper Cream Sauce, virtually anything and everything (from chicken and seafood to pasta and savoury crêpes) becomes a tantalizing treat.

**4 large whole red bell peppers
(total weight:1 lb or 450 g)***
2 tsp (10 mL) olive oil
1 tbsp (15 mL) crushed chicken bouillon cubes (or powder)
1 tsp (5 mL) finely chopped fresh garlic
¹/2 cup (125 mL) heavy cream (35% fat)
¹/4 tsp (1 mL) (Indonesian) hot chili paste (optional)

1 Rub whole red bell peppers with olive oil and arrange on a parchment paper-lined baking tray.
2 Place in a preheated 400°F (200°C) oven; turn every 5 minutes, until skins blister and are lightly charred.
3 Remove roasted peppers from oven; place in a pot and cover securely; allow peppers to cool.
4 Remove and discard stem areas, skins, seeds and membranes.
5 Place red pepper flesh (and any juice) into a blender jar; purée well.
6 Place red pepper purée in a loosely covered small saucepan over medium-low heat. (Beware of splattering.) Add crushed bouillon cubes, garlic, cream and if desired, hot chili paste; bring to a boil. Reduce heat immediately. Stirring frequently, allow sauce to simmer for a few minutes until thick.
7 Serve sauce hot or warm.

* This will give about 12 oz or 340 g cooked flesh (stems, skin, seeds and membranes removed).
Note: I frequently make this sauce with roasted red pepper flesh which is on hand in my freezer.

TIP: For a thicker sauce, mix a touch of cornstarch into 1 or 2 tsp (5 to 10 mL) of cold water and whisk it into the sauce. (This may be particularly true when using previously frozen roasted red pepper flesh.)

MAKE-AHEAD TIP: Place cooled sauce in an airtight container and store refrigerated for up to 3 days or frozen for months.

SESAME HONEY MUSTARD COGNAC SAUCE/DRIZZLE

Makes almost ¹/2 cup (125 mL)

Taste buds are happily stimulated by the pairing of honey and mustard. Add sesame oil, cognac and crushed black peppercorns and one comes up with a cleverly unique sauce/drizzle with flavour hints of "East Meets West". I combine this slightly sweet and spicy sauce with chicken, beef, cooked bean noodles and sushi rice to devise unusual recipes which appeal to children and adults alike.

3 tbsp (45 mL) Dijon mustard
3 tbsp (45 mL) sesame oil
2¹/2 tbsp (38 mL) honey, preferably buckwheat*
1 tbsp (15 mL) cognac
¹/3 tsp (2 mL) crushed black peppercorns

1 In a small bowl, whisk all ingredients together until smooth.
2 Pour sauce into a well-sealed jar and store refrigerated for up to several weeks. Stir/shake well before using.

* Buckwheat honey definitely works best with the cognac and the nutty flavour of the sesame oil.

MAKE-AHEAD TIP: The **sauce can be prepared in just a matter of minutes** and kept on hand refrigerated for weeks.

SWEET-AND-SOUR HOT SAUCE

Makes 2 cups or 500 mL

The ingredient list may be a tad long but preparation certainly is effortless! The melange of sweet, salt, spicy and sour is exceptional. Try this Sweet-and-Sour Hot Sauce drizzled into Vietnamese salad rolls, over cold cooked vermicelli noodles, oven roasted and barbecued chicken, or as an oriental dipping sauce.

*(**Note:** Reduce this recipe to one half or one third of the quantity if you do not intend to keep it on hand for frequent use.)*

1¹/2 cups (375 mL) granulated sugar
¹/4 cup (60 mL) rice vinegar
¹/4 cup (60 mL) lemon juice
¹/4 cup (60 mL) soya sauce
¹/4 cup (60 mL) fish sauce
¹/4 cup (60 mL)* (Indonesian) hot chili paste
¹/4 cup (60 mL)* finely chopped fresh garlic
³/4 tsp (4 mL) * crushed black peppercorns
¹/4 cup (60 mL) chopped fresh coriander leaves (optional)

1 In a medium-size bowl, whisk all ingredients together (except coriander).
2 Pour sauce into well-sealed glass jars and store refrigerated for months. Stir well before serving, adding coriander if desired.
3 Serve chilled or at room temperature.

* **Option:** If necessary, adjust quantities according to taste.

ALTERNATIVE-USE TIP: For a change, drizzle a touch of this **Sweet-and-Sour Hot Sauce along with a herb vinaigrette over your salad.** It adds an appealing oriental dimension.

SWEET SAUCES

CREAMY BUTTERSCOTCH DESSERT SAUCE

Makes about 2¹/4 cups or 550 mL

With absolutely no exceptions, those who taste my Creamy Butterscotch Dessert Sauce vow that they have gone to heaven! Our Dickenson Blackberry Butterscotch Fondue owes its stellar reputation to this sauce! I keep the creamy butterscotch sauce on hand in the refrigerator and freezer ready to play its paramount role in my signature "fondue" or to be used in tempting dessert, pancake or waffle presentations.

1/3 cup (80 mL) unsalted butter
1¹/2 cups (375 mL) heavy cream
(35% fat), divided
1¹/2 cups (375 mL) (packed) light
brown sugar

1 In a medium-size saucepan, melt butter over medium heat. Stir in ³/4 cup (180 mL) of heavy cream and bring to a boil.
2 Add remaining cream and brown sugar; stir constantly until sugar dissolves and mixture comes to a boil.
3 Reduce heat and allow sauce to boil fairly vigorously over low heat (uncovered) for 8 minutes without stirring. Remove from heat. Whisk well.
4 With a clean damp cloth, thoroughly wipe interior (exposed) surfaces of saucepan (above sauce) to remove any lingering sugar crystals. (**Note:** This assists in preventing crystallization during storage.)
5 Set aside until cool.
6 Stir sauce extremely well and transfer to airtight plastic containers. (Avoid scraping "clean" inside surfaces of saucepan as sugar crystals may be present.)
7 Refrigerate to thicken and until ready to use.
8 Serve this Creamy Butterscotch Dessert Sauce chilled from the refrigerator, at room temperature or warm. Stir well before serving.

MAKE-AHEAD TIP: The sauce may be stored refrigerated for up to several weeks or frozen for months. (**Note:** If sugar crystals should happen to form during storage, place the sauce in a saucepan over medium-low heat and bring it to a boil, stirring constantly until sugar crystals dissolve. If desired, add a touch of heavy cream.)

TIP: The desired consistency of the sauce should determine at what temperature the sauce is served. I usually serve "refrigerated" sauce, allowing it to rest briefly (i.e., 5 minutes) at room temperature so that the sauce is creamy, thick and fluid. (Warm sauce is more liquid in nature.)

DECADENT WHITE CHOCOLATE SAUCE

Makes ³/4 cup or 180 mL

My delicate white chocolate sauce, subtly enhanced with a drop of almond extract, brings the ultimate touch of "finesse" to poached fruit, certain fresh fruits, strudels, pies, cakes and puddings. Indeed, its uses are limitless when it comes to the preparation of sweets. Be creative!

**4 oz (115 g) white chocolate,
finely chopped
¹/2 cup* (125 mL) heavy cream
(35% fat)
¹/8 tsp (2 drops) almond extract**
(optional)**

1 Partially melt chocolate over barely simmering water in a double boiler (or soften in a microwave oven at **medium-low** heat). Remove from heat; stir until chocolate is completely melted and smooth.
2 Meanwhile, heat cream in a small saucepan over low heat until hot. (Do not boil.)
3 Stirring constantly, gradually add hot cream to melted chocolate forming a smooth mixture. (Sieve if traces of chocolate remain.)
4 Transfer sauce to an airtight plastic container or well sealed glass jar. Refrigerate for several hours (or overnight) to allow sauce to thicken and until ready to use.
5 Stir in almond extract if desired.
6 Serve sauce cold (if a thick sauce is desired) or at room temperature.

* **Option:** For a thicker sauce, use less cream.

** **Option:** ¹/8 teaspoon or 2 drops of coconut extract

"PRACTICAL" MAKE-AHEAD TIP: My practical nature sees me preparing this "N/N" (No Time, No Talent)" dessert sauce whenever there are bits of heavy cream to use up! Store it refrigerated for up to a week (or longer) or frozen for months.

EASY CARAMEL SAUCE

Makes 1 cup (250 mL)

Caramel Sauce must be included in everyone's repertoire of recipes. It is simply "too delicious" to be omitted. This is my basic recipe which is quick, easy and retains its quality for months.

**1 cup (250 mL) granulated sugar
3 tbsp (45 mL) cold water
2/3 cup (170 mL) heavy cream (35% fat)**

1 Place sugar and water in a medium saucepan over medium heat. Stirring constantly, bring mixture to boil. With a pastry brush dipped in cold water, brush down any sugar crystals on inside of saucepan. Without stirring, cook until syrup just turns a golden amber colour (about 5 to 7 minutes). Immediately remove from heat. (**Note of Caution:** *Watch carefully so that the syrup does not burn. It will continue to cook when removed from heat.*)
2 Promptly but very carefully, add heavy cream. (Mixture will bubble dramatically.) Whisk until sauce is very smooth. If necessary, return saucepan **to low heat** and stir mixture until absolutely all sugar crystals have dissolved*. (**Note:** If some sugar crystals still remain, pour the sauce through a fine mesh sieve into a second saucepan over low heat. Stir constantly for 1 minute.)
3 Allow sauce to cool. Pour into an airtight plastic container; refrigerate to thicken and until ready to use.**
4 Use sauce at temperature desired (chilled, at room temperature or warm) or according to consistency required. (**Note:** The sauce is thickest when used directly from the refrigerator. As it warms, it becomes softer and more fluid.)

* This prevents the formation of sugar crystals during storage.

** If the sauce becomes too thick, reheat it in a small saucepan over low heat and whisk in a touch of heavy cream.

MAKE-AHEAD TIP: The sauce may be stored refrigerated for up to several weeks or frozen for months.

SETTING A TABLE
(See theme photos, pages 22 to 33)

Having the table attractively set when guests arrive automatically creates the perception that the event is under control! Setting a perfect table is not difficult because regardless of the occasion, simple basic guidelines exist.

Either **PLACE MATS** or a **TABLECLOTH** may be used. (Some prefer a tablecloth for dinner; however, this is not the case in our home.)

Place **FORKS** on the left-hand side of a place setting. Arrange them in the order in which they are to be used, starting from the extreme left of the place setting and working toward the plate.

Place **KNIVES** and **SPOONS** on the right-hand side of a place setting. Arrange them in the order in which they are to be used, starting at the extreme right of the place setting and working towards the plate. The blades of the knives should face the centre of the place setting. The butter knife is often set on the bread and butter plate (at the top) with the handle pointing to the right and the blade facing the centre of the bread and butter plate.

Place **DESSERT CUTLERY** (spoon or spoon and fork) together in a horizontal position at the top centre of the place setting, above the plate. The handle of the fork always points to the left and that of the spoon to the right. At dessert time, the cutlery is frequently repositioned to the left and right of the plate respectively.

Arrange **WINE/CHAMPAGNE GLASSES** in the order in which they are to be used, starting directly above the cutlery on the right (i.e., knives and spoons) and working toward the centre of the place setting. Place the **WATER GLASS** beyond these, closer to the top centre of the place setting. When several glasses are used, it is more pleasing to the eye when some glasses are arranged behind others in a slightly irregular fashion. (**Note:** Normally, the water and/or Champagne glasses take that position.) This technique makes the positioning of the glasses easier if space on the table is limited.

If using **BREAD AND BUTTER PLATES**, set them directly above the forks or slightly to the left of the forks.

NAPKINS may be folded in many different ways and placed at individual place settings in a variety of positions (e.g., on chargers, on bread and butter plates, in glasses). Most frequently, napkins are placed on the extreme left hand side of the place setting, beyond the forks. (**Note:** Never place napkins to the right.) If folded in the traditional rectangular manner, the long folded edge of the napkin should be in a parallel position beside the "outside" fork, with the open corner at the bottom left. This allows the napkin to be picked up at that corner and opened easily before placing it on one's lap.

If **SALT AND PEPPER SHAKERS** are placed on the table, ideally there is one pair for every two individuals. This avoids reaching and/or passing as well as adds a touch of pizzazz. (**Note:** Small ones may be purchased inexpensively.)

If there are **PLACE CARDS**, stand them in a central position at the top of the place settings and above the dessert cutlery. Place cards indicate the seating position of each person at the table. It is best to inscribe the name of the person on both sides of the card (especially if guests do not know each other) so that the place card can be read from both sides of the table.

Remember, a **CENTREPIECE** should be no more than 12 inches (30 cm) high to avoid blocking the sight line of those at the table.

Put **CANDLES** on the table only at night. If candles are on a table, they should be lit.

CHARGERS are oversized plates (often made of metal) that are placed at each individual place setting before the meal begins and usually stay on the table until the meal is completed. Place plates/bowls directly on top of the chargers. Chargers add a touch of elegance to a table. Occasionally, chargers are removed during the meal when the plates for a particular course do not fit comfortably on the chargers. (This may be due to shape or size.) Chargers may be returned to the table if they are appropriate for the next course(s). (**Note:** "Show Plates" are frequently confused with chargers. Show plates are often seen on tables in chic restaurants or clubs but they are removed before the actual meal is served.)

Place Coutreau Bars on the table to function as knife rests. (**Note:** Many chopstick bars are suitable for this purpose.)

Tips on Seating Plans and Service of Food and Beverages

Basic guidelines also exist for seating plans, as well as the service of food and beverages. They are not complicated.

SEATING PLANS: Generally, the host and hostess sit at opposite ends of a traditional rectangular table or opposite one another at the centre of such a table. The female guest deemed "most important" for whatever reason (e.g., guest of honor, her professional position/rank or that of her spouse) sits to the right of the host, the second most important female guest to the host's left. Similarly, the most important and second most important male guests sit to the right and left of the hostess respectively. People are seated at the table in a "boy, girl, boy, girl" arrangement. (**Note:** This is not possible when 8, 12, 16 or any multiple of "4" are at the table.) The placement of guests at the table ("to the right" and "to the left") continues according to the order of descending priority. Therefore, if the host and hostess sit at the ends of the table, the guests of lower profile will be at the centre. Conversely, if the host and hostess sit across from one another at the centre of the table, the guests of lower profile will be at the ends of the table.

FLASH: For a lunch/dinner in which one wishes to discuss business with the most senior guests, consider having the host and hostess sit across from one another at the centre of the table.

SERVICE OF FOOD and BEVERAGES: At the table, food and drinks are served to women first in order of priority with the hostess being served last. Then men are served in a similar fashion with the host being served last. Dishes are removed in the same manner.

Food served on trays is presented from the left of the individual seated at the table. All empty dishes are removed from the right except for the bread and butter plate. Empty plates or plated food may be placed in front of those at the table from either the left or right depending on the style of service used. (**Note:** On this latter point, the important factor is to be consistent.)

Drinks are always served from the right.

Dishes are removed from the table only when everyone has completed that particular course.

HELPFUL TIPS ON TABLE ETIQUETTE

1 When to Begin to Eat: Those seated at the table may begin to eat each course only when everyone has been served and when the host and hostess have begun (unless the host and/or hostess suggest otherwise). (**Note:** With the host and hostess taking the lead on each course, the guests are able to confirm what cutlery to use and how to consume certain dishes.)

2 How to Arrange the Cutlery when One is Finished Eating: When an individual has finished each course, the fork (tines up) and knife (blade facing down or towards the centre of the plate) are arranged parallel together on the plate at the 4 o'clock position with the handles on the rim of the plate. The soup spoon is removed from a soup cup or deep bowl and placed on the liner under the bowl at the 4 o'clock position. With a flat bowl or soup dish, it remains in the bowl with the handle on the rim at the 4 o'clock position. (**Note:** The host/hostess should be the last to finish individual courses.)

FLASH: Used flatware should never touch the table (or the charger). If a piece of flatware falls on the floor, you should request a replacement.

3 Eating Food and Bread: Cut pieces of food as you eat them. Break a piece off a roll, butter it and eat it before breaking off another piece.

4 Napkin Etiquette: Once a napkin is opened, it is never refolded. If a napkin falls on the floor, pick it up. If you have to excuse yourself from the table during a meal, leave your napkin on your chair, or place it loose to the left of your plate as you would do at the end of the meal.

5 Salt and Pepper Etiquette: To avoid awkward reaching, ask for items which are beyond your place setting to be passed to you. When someone asks for the salt, pick up both the salt and pepper together; place them on the table next to the person seated beside you. He/she will then pass them on in a similar manner until they reach the person who requested the salt. (**Note:** Avoid passing the salt and pepper in a "hand to hand" manner.) Others seated at the table may want to use the salt and pepper shakers while "en route"; however, the person who requested it/them should use it/them first unless he/she insists that others help themselves along the way.

6 Clearing the Table Before Dessert: Salt and pepper shakers, couteau bars, bread and butter plates and all other such items (e.g., sauce bowls, bread) are removed from the table before dessert is served.

Crumbs may be brushed from the table (using a napkin or crumb brush) onto a small tray before dessert is served.

If smoking is allowed by the host/hostess, ashtrays could be placed on the table immediately before dessert (i.e., never before this time). Even if ashtrays are placed on the table, it is only polite to ask those around you for their approval if you wish to smoke at the table.

7 Toasts: Traditionally, two toasts are generally given by the host during a meal. At the beginning of the meal, the host makes a simple toast to welcome everyone. (This is also a signal that those at the table may begin their drinks.) Usually, at the beginning of the dessert course, the host gives another toast focusing on the guest(s) of honour or the occasion. If a person is being toasted, he raises his glass but does not drink to himself. He could return the toast, by making some brief remarks to thank the host and hostess and by asking his fellow guests to raise their glasses to them.

8 Elbows, Cell Phones/Hand-Held Devices: Wrists may rest on the table (but not elbows). Cell phones/hand-held devices should be turned off and/or not taken to the table.

9 Service of Coffee/Tea: Coffee/tea may be served either at the table (after or with dessert) or in another location (e.g., living room, patio). It is sometimes preferable to serve coffee/tea at the table to avoid any break in conversation. Conversely, if you wish to provide an occasion for alternative conversational groups, leaving the table can facilitate this.

10 Accepting Compliments and Apologizing: A hostess and host should accept compliments graciously. And, there is rarely a need for them to apologize for any real or perceived "shortcomings" during an event. Often those issues would otherwise go completely unnoticed!

INDEX

Margaret Dickenson's books and products include:
(1) *Margaret's Table: Easy Cooking and Inspiring Entertaining*
(2) The international award-winning cookbook *From the Ambassador's Table: Blueprints for Creative Entertaining*
(3) The international award-winning TV series *Margaret's Sense of Occasion*
(some episodes are available on video and/or DVD)

For more information on ordering the above items, please contact:
Margaret's Sense of Occasion
Fax (613) 730-0604, or
www.margaretssenseofoccasion.com, or
2 Seneca Street,
Ottawa, Ontario,
Canada K1S 4W5